The Philosophical Animal

The Philosophical Animal
On Zoopoetics and Interspecies Cosmopolitanism

EDUARDO MENDIETA

Published by State University of New York Press, Albany

A digital version of this book is freely available in an open access edition thanks to TOME (Toward an Open Monograph Ecosystem)—a collaboration of the Association of American Universities, the Association of University Presses, and the Association of Research Libraries—and the generous support of the Pennsylvania State University. Learn more at the TOME website, available at: openmonographs.org.

© 2024 State University of New York

All rights reserved

Printed in the United States of America

No part of this book may be used or reproduced in any manner whatsoever without written permission. No part of this book may be stored in a retrieval system or transmitted in any form or by any means including electronic, electrostatic, magnetic tape, mechanical, photocopying, recording, or otherwise without the prior permission in writing of the publisher.

For information, contact State University of New York Press, Albany, NY
www.sunypress.edu

Library of Congress Cataloging-in-Publication Data

Name: Mendieta, Eduardo, author.
Title: The philosophical animal : on zoopoetics and interspecies cosmopolitanism / Eduardo Mendieta.
Description: Albany : State University of New York Press, [2024] | Includes bibliographical references and index.
Identifiers: ISBN 9781438498096 (hardcover : alk. paper) | ISBN 9781438498102 (ebook) | ISBN 9781438498119 (pbk. : alk. paper)
Further information is available at the Library of Congress.

10 9 8 7 6 5 4 3 2 1

Contents

Preface   vii

Acknowledgments   ix

Introduction: The Poetic Species   1

I. Ceasing to Be Animal

Chapter 1 Zoopoetics: Coetzee's Animals and Philosophy   25

Chapter 2 Political Bestiary: On the Uses of Violence   49

Chapter 3 Heidegger's Bestiary: The Speechless and
           Unhistorical Animal   67

II. Not Yet Human

Chapter 4 Habermas on Human Cloning: The Debate on the
           Future of the Species   93

Chapter 5 Communicative Freedom and Genetic Engineering   115

Chapter 6 We Have Never Been Human, or How We Lost
           Our Humanity: From Habermas and Derrida to
           Midgley and Haraway by Way of Agamben   131

III. Toward a Companion Species Ethics

Chapter 7 Animal Is to Kantianism As Jew Is to Fascism:
          Adorno's Bestiary   159

Chapter 8 Interspecies Cosmopolitanism   175

Chapter 9 Bestiaries of Extinction: Anthropodicy or
          Anthropohippology   193

Notes   211

Index   241

Preface

This book was essentially finished some years ago. However, I moved from Stony Brook University to Penn State University, and then we had the pandemic. Additional obstacles came in the way, which should not be mentioned. The upside of the delay is that I had a chance to reconsider its contents. I was also able to revise many of the chapters to bring it up to my own current thinking and revise some of my own arguments to make them more legible and persuasive. The book was instigated by a long-term philosophical concern of mine: namely on the relationship between war and philosophy. More specifically, what I have been thinking was on how war shaped the history of philosophy, how philosophy sanctioned war, and how the figure of the philosopher, both metaphorically and factually, has been deeply impacted by wars. As I thought about wars, their ferocity, destructiveness, and genocides, I came to realize that human wars require what I call in this book animalization, bestialization, and verminization. To turn another human into an animal, a beast, a vermin, means you are already sanctioning the "genocide imperative," the will to exterminate who is seen as a pest. Thus, this book had to come first. The book is threaded by the trope of *bestiary*. I return to this genre and tradition throughout the book. I aimed not to be repetitive, but to approach this important tradition through different angles and perspectives: literary, political, philosophical, and so on. Above all, I return to the bestiary because it played and continues to play such an important role in the education of our moral, political, and philosophical imaginaries. As I try to show, philosophy itself is a kind of bestiary, especially when it tells us that we are not like those other animals. This book, nonetheless, does not seek to answer the question "what is an animal?" Instead, it is concerned with how we humans avow or disavow our own animality by means of our complex, convoluted, moral, poetic, and philosophical animal inventions.

Acknowledgments

Books are written alone, but not in loneliness. In fact, they are full of disapproving gazes from the shelves of an author's several libraries: her home, her office, her summer home, and the boxes that travel back and forth as chapters and research notes are written. Yet, they are full of a cacophony of approving or questioning voices, those of philosophical friends. You write for an audience, for your colleagues, but also for your friends who have endured and sustained you in your efforts. This book is the product of much philosophical companionship along decades. I have to single out philosophical animals who have been long-term friends: Linda Alcoff, Amy Allen, Stuart Elden, Matthias Fritsch, John Lysaker, Amos Nascimento, Noelle McAffee, Peter Niesen, Kelly Oliver, Max Pensky, John Stuhr, Cynthia Willett, and Martin Woessner. Our long conversations, and unfortunately emails, about the "animal question" have been a philosophical nest. Of course, I am alone responsible for what came out of conversations, papers, emails, letters, postcards, and dinners across the world. I also benefited from conversations along the way with: David Allison, Nandita Batra, Samir Amin, Matthew Calarco, Edward Casey, Santiago Castro-Gómez, Maeve Cooke, Megan Craig, Robert Crease, Gerard Delanty, Oscar Guardioala-Rivera, Tomaž Grušovnik, Don Ihde, Baruk Kesgin, Eva Kittay, Michael Naas, Anne O'Byrne, Maria Pia Lara, John Sanbonmatsu, Lenart Škof, Wendy Weissman, and Mario Wenning, The ideas for this book came out of a couple of decisive encounters. First, I spent a year in Santa Cruz, where I had an opportunity to interact, philosophize, and "chat"—an euphemism, evidently—with Donna Haraway and Angela Y. Davis. These conversations and lunches were more than a dog's bowl, obviously. Second, I spent a joyous winter in Durham, England, close to where Mary Midgley lived and retired, where I had the chance to meet her in person and have some dinners and tea with her. There is not enough discussion of her pioneering work in this book. As it is clear, this is a book about corporeal vulnerability, gender, and animality. The book is in very obvious ways about women philosophical beasts, which include Kelly Oliver and Cindy Willett. Third, in the early 2000s, I was fortunate to spend time with Jürgen Habermas when he was a visiting professor at Stony Brook, right after the 9/11. At the time he showed me manuscripts of what became his book on "cloning" and "the future of the human species." I wrote Habermas a couple of long letters explaining why I thought he was wrong. He was gracious to acknowledge my reservations about his approach. This is how the middle section of the book was born: from letters to Habermas. Finally, there was a fascinating moment at a conference in Prague when I was giving a twenty-minute version of the chapter on interspecies cosmopolitanism, and Rainer Forst asked me something to the effect of "whether we should prevent lions from predating on other animals." The question was about the limits of interspecies cosmopolitanism. At the time, I answered that we have species protection laws and animal-suffering regulations. I am a caged animal, in my gilded holding pen of anthropocentric supremacy and hubris. I can't thank enough my research assistants, Adam Israel and Tianqui Kuo, who had to get through all my revisions, additions, etc. I also must thank the institutional spaces that allowed me to pursue, present, argue, and refine some of the ideas in this book: the Society for Phenomenological Research, the American Philosophical Association, the American Philosophies Forum, and the Prague summer conference on "Philosophy and the Social Sciences." Finally, I can't thank enough my editors at SUNY Press, with whom I have worked over decades, Michael Rinella and James Peltz. Special thanks to Susan Geraghty for seeing the manuscript so masterfully through production. Thank you to the whole team at SUNY Press, and to Judi Gibbs for the work on the index.

Eduardo Mendieta
State College, Pennsylvania

I also need to acknowledge the following publishers for permission to use materials from earlier versions of the following chapters:

- "Jew Is to Nazism as Animal Is to Kantianism: On Adorno's Animals," *Critical Theory and Animal Liberation*, John Sanbonmatsu, ed., Lanham, MD: Rowman & Littlefield. All Rights Reserved.

- "Interspecies Cosmopolitanism," *Handbook of Cosmopolitanism Studies* 2 edition—Gerard Delanty | Edn. 2 | Hardback | Origin UK

Introduction

The Poetic Species

> For beyond the vocabularies useful for prediction and control—the vocabulary of natural science—there are the vocabularies of our moral and our political life and of the arts, of all those human activities which are not aimed at prediction and control but rather in giving us self-images which are worthy of our species. Such images are not true to the nature of species or false to it, for what is really distinctive about us is that we can rise above questions of truth or falsity. We are the poetic species, the one which can change itself by changing its behavior—and especially its linguistic behavior, the words it uses. The ability is not to be explained by discovering more about the nature of something called "the mind" any more than by discovering more about the nature of something called "God." Such attempts to "ground" our ability to recreate ourselves by seeking its ineffable source are, in Sartre's sense, self-deceptive. They are attempts to find a vocabulary, a way of speaking, which will be more than just a way of speaking. To say, with nominalism, that language is ubiquitous and to deny, with verificationism, that there are intuitions to which our language must conform, is just to assert that we need nothing more than confidence in our own poetic power.
>
> —Richard Rorty, "Contemporary Philosophy of Mind"[1]

The title of this book is deliberately ambiguous. It should be read as having many valences. Humans are philosophical animals, that is, we are animals that philosophize, that is, that ask questions about their nature, their being, their finitude, their very animality.[2] We are the animal that is despondent at its animality. To be human is to wonder at our very existence and how much our humanity is or is not an extension of our animality. As Anat Pick put it: "Being human is grappling with what is inhuman in us."[3] Here the "inhuman" is the shadow of the animal, but the animal is also shadowed by the human. Derrida's "the question of the animal," is always the "question of the human." The two have always been inextricably tied. In this sense any and every attempt at an ontological analysis of the being of the human is inescapably entwined with the question of the being of the animal. Every existential ontology of the human—if this is not an oxymoron—is thus a "zoontology"—to use that felicitous expression of Cary Wolfe.[4] Indeed, this was one of Derrida's main points in his now indispensable *The Animal That Therefore I Am*.[5] Humans, however, philosophize about their humanity and their animality by conjuring up philosophical animals. Our books of philosophy are veritable zoos of philosophical animals: from Plato's dogs and Aristotle's elephants, to Heidegger's beetles and Nagel's bats, to Haraway's own menagerie. Our philosophical texts are populated by animals that philosophize, and of course, it could be said that this is philosophical ventriloquism, but even then, we are philosophizing with animals. Philosophy is a conversation of humanity with itself across time, as Gadamer taught us to recognize, but that conversation has been conducted by the means of these figures I call "philosophical animals." In fact, humanity's entire literary and poetic bequest is full of such animals, as Coetzee's Elizabeth Costello teaches us in her lectures, "The Lives of Animals." Let us imagine a *Gedankenexperiment*, following Arturo Danto. Take pages from Genesis, from Hesiod, from Aristotle's *History of Animals*, from Plato's *Republic*, Plutarch's *Moralia*, Aquinas's *Summa Theologica*, Cervantes's *The Dialogue of Dogs*, part 4 of Jonathan Swift's *Gulliver's Travels*, Montaigne's *Essays*, Descartes's *The Passions of the Soul*, Kant's *Lectures on Ethics*, Heidegger's lectures from the 1930s, Kafka's parables—in fact, let us simply use Élisabeth de Fontenay's monumental and indispensable *Le silence des bêtes*[6] as well as Paul Waldau and Kimberly Patton's ecumenical anthology *A Communion of Subjects: Animals in Religion, Science, and Ethics*[7] as our indexes and guides in this thought experiment in which we are selecting pages from these different texts and we are then putting them in a lottery wheel barrel, which then we spin, and as if picking winning numbers for the lotto, we take out a page and then ask: do we know whether this is a page from a "philosophy" book, or a novel, a comedy, a satire, a parable, a myth? It is not clear that we could, nor desirable that we should, be able to say: this is philosophy and this is fiction. For we are the animal that becomes human by philosophizing with and through "philosophical animals." Our human exceptionality is traced and caged by imagining animals that display what they lack that we have or have too much of what we imagine ourselves no longer to have. Armelle Le Bras-Chopard put it eloquently: "The meaning of humanity is nourished from the non-meaning of animality. The zoo only exists because it is full of vacuum, and the greater this vacuum, that is to say, the more extensive is animality, until it comes to affect group of humans . . . the more pure and perfect is humanity."[8] Le Bras-Chopard's book, where the sentence I translated is to be found, is titled *The Zoo of the Philosophers: From Bestialization to Exclusion*. I want to claim that philosophy as a genre, as a discipline, as a form of intellectual domestication has been producing zoos, some with insurmountable fences and abysmal moats, some with broken fences, some with ever shifting boundaries.

In the epigraph I selected to open this introduction, Rorty writes about the "poetic species" for which it is more important to give itself "self-images which are worthy of our species" than getting things right. One of the claims of this book is that it is more important for us as the poetic species that when we philosophize as the philosophical animal that our philosophical animals be to the stature of our animality. In his beautiful book, *Biophilia: The Human Bond with Other Species*, Edward O. Wilson, wrote this provocative sentence, a very Rortyian one it should be added, "Scientist's do not discover in order to know, they know in order to discover."[9] I like to riff on that sentence and claim that "philosophers don't poeticize in order to philosophize, but philosophize in order to poeticize," that is, create, conjure up, dream up, invite us to imaginary dialogues, better, more humane, more empathic, more compassionate, more dignified images of our animal nature and bond with other animals. Then, one of the central claims of this book is that we are the poetic species that creates and recreates itself, and in so doing, creates and recreates its world and the world of other animals, through its poetic inventions.

Philosophy, like literature and poetry, broadly construed, are exemplars of what I called in the subtitle of the book zoopoetics. Philosophy is an instance of zoopoetics, but one that must continuously produce its *animalia*, to be corralled into its imaginary or real zoos, including the human animal. In this sense, I am totally in agreement with what Matthew Calarco suggested with the title of his uncircumventable book *Zoographies: The Question of the Animal from Heidegger to Derrida*,[10] namely that we are animals that leave traces, and the trace of our humanity/animality is precisely this writing about animals. I take it that Calarco's "zoography" is a paean to Derrida's work in general and more specifically a reference to the conference at Cerisy-La-Salle in 1997 devoted to Derrida's work, "L'Animal autobiographique," which resulted in the eponymously titled book that included the essay that went on to become *The Animal That Therefore I Am*.[11] I like to argue that before we have zoontologies, we must have zoographies, but before we can have zoographies, which turn out to be but autobiographies, as Derrida and Coetzee show, we must have zoopoetics. Philosophy, since its birth, has been creating zoos that include and exclude by creating a zone of exception that is predicated on sundering humanity from its animality. Zoos, however, have their dark counterparts in the abattoirs and slaughterhouses that feed humans and other animals. What must be included in a zoo is most likely not going to the slaughterhouse, but what goes to the slaughterhouse at some point made it there through the zoo. Le Bras-Chopard's book *The Zoo of the Philosophers* is instructively divided in three sections: the first is titled "What Is an Animal? A Non-Human," the second, "What Animals to Put in the Zoo?," and the third, "What Human Species Should be Sent to the Zoo?" This structuring of the book argues that the transit in and out of the zoo, on the way to the slaughterhouse, is also a transit humans have traversed with other animals. Zoos are counterparts of bestiaries—they are two sides of the same practice. This is why I devote a chapter to bestiaries, although I return to the trope throughout. Thus, another claim of this book is that insofar as philosophy produces its zoo, with its special cages and zones of exception, it is thus also always already projecting a bestiary.

Zoos are reprieves and preserves, anterooms of killing and extermination whether deliberate and machinated or inadvertent and thoughtless. I read, but don't remember anymore where, that when the Allies bombed Berlin toward the end of the war, the Berlin zoo turned into a slaughterhouse, and some of the animals there were used to feed the starving Berliners. Zoontologies, zoographies, and zoopoetics are implicated in the transit that takes place between the zoo and the slaughterhouse—in this sense every zoopoetics is always already an exercise in ethics. As Rorty notes in the passage I quoted above, the aim of our poeticizing is precisely to transform the moral and political languages through which we humanize ourselves. *This book is about what bestiaries our philosophical zoopoetics produces and thus what ethics of coexistence or non-coexistence it calls for and demands.*

The book is divided in three parts. In the first I am concerned with how we have imagined ourselves to have ceased to be animals, how through our zoopoetics and philosophical animals we have imagined ourselves to have become non-animal. I begin, however, with an analysis of Coetzee's work through the lens of two intimately connected tropes in his work: women and animals. Cora Diamond captured beautifully the link between these two tropes when she wrote on *Elizabeth Costello*:

> She [Elizabeth Costello] describes herself as an animal exhibiting but not exhibiting, to a gathering of scholars, a wound which her clothes cover up, but which is touched on in every word she speaks. So the life of this speaking animal and wounded and clothed animal is one of the "lives of animals" that the story is about; it is true that we generally remain unaware of the lives of other animals, it is also true that, as readers of this story, we may remain unaware, as her audience does, of the life of the speaking animal at its center.[12]

I argue there that the pivot on which these two tropes gyrate is the philosopheme of corporeal vulnerability. Horkheimer and Adorno wrote in one of their "Notes and Sketches," titled "Man and Beast," for their *Dialectic of Enlightenment*: "For the being endowed with reason, however, concern for the unreasoning animal is idle. Western civilization has left that to women. They have no autonomous share in the capabilities which gave rise to this civilization."[13] Horkheimer and Adorno also analyzed the imbrication of bestialization with embodiment, that is, how when in Western culture we are urging the human to ascend to the exceptional pedestal of rationality, the human body has to be animalized in order to be domesticated, and in the process, women are put as an intermediary between corporeal animality and disembodied autarchic rationality. Domesticating our passions in order to be fully impassioned Cartesian subjects is a process of both domesticating our bodies, qua unruly beasts, and ceasing to be like women, at the mercy of their bodies. Coetzee's work, in my analysis offers us a zoopoetics that explicitly sets out to unsettle this trajectory and ascend up the marble steps of rational, dispassionate, and disembodied autonomy. Chapter 1, thus, also sets the tone for the rest of the volume, and that tone has to do with being attentive to the corporeal suffering of humans and animals, a suffering that is co-inflicted. What Coetzee's philosophical animals do is to invite us to be attentive to our "being-with" and "becoming-with" through our corporeal vulnerability so that we can also be attuned to what Ralph Acampora has called "corporeal compassion."[14]

In the next two chapters I explore the theme of how zoopoetics produces bestiaries; some that like those found in Coetzee's work are pedagogies of the "good animal," to use that provocative expression from Adorno, as I show later in the book. In chapter 2, I offer an eagle's eye perspective of the role of animals in philosophy, but more specifically, about their role as figures of the political. If every zoopoetics is an ethics, it is also a politics. Every zoopoetics is thus also a prelude to a zoopolitics with its implied zoopolis.[15] Since Aristotle, we speak of the human as the *zoon politikon* (ζῷον πολιτικόν), as the animal that in order to flourish must dwell in a political community, a community of friends, of companions who are his equal. But, we are friends not simply with other humans. In a wonderful book edited by Ivano Dionigi, titled *Animalia*,[16] one can find two excellent chapters about the question of the animal and the political. One is by Massimo Cacciari, and carries the title of "L'animale politico" (with all its dual references), and the other is by Ivano Dionigi himself, with the title "*Res publica naturalis:* animali politici." Both create the bridge I am trying to make in this first part of the book, namely the bridge of our being a political animal, whose republic is carved out of nature and is populated by all kind of political animals—both human and nonhuman. If the zoo is the sanctuary of the animal, the polis is the abode proper to the human; but the zoo is a polis and the polis is a zoo, as is already implied in the derogatory formulation "political animal"—I will unfold this argument later in this introduction.

In these two chapters I trace the trope of the founding of the political through the use and abuse of animals, their exclusion from the polis. The polis is precisely founded on the exclusion of the animal, the beast, the beastly—a philosopheme already present in Homer and Hesiod, and carried through in the political philosophy of the Sophists. In Homer, we find it announced in book 9 of the Odyssey, "In the One-Eyed Giant's Cave," about which I will say more later in this introduction. In Hesiod, it appears in his *Theogony* and *Works and Days*, specifically when he discussed the myths of Prometheus and Epimetheus, and what they both give to humans. These myths, and what they have to say about animality and the founding of the city, are taken up by Plato in his *Protagoras*, when he has Protagoras discuss the myths vis-à-vis the quest for justice.[17] In Plato's *Republic*, the healthy, beautiful, Kallipolis is predicated on the exclusion of the Sophists, who are portrayed as beastly, as beasts that threaten to destroy the city. Philosophizing, however, may also make one appear beastly, unhinged, and rabid, like a violent wolf, as Plato says in the *Sophist*. In these two chapters, however, I am interested in the critical task of demonstrating the ways in which the political is dependent on the definition of the animal versus the human. We have asked, along with Le Bras-Chopard, who should be in the zoo? We should also ask: who can be in the polis and who should be excluded? The transit in and out of the zoo is also the transit in and out the polis, where polis is a metonym for the sheltering dwelling of normativity, of the sheltering dwelling of the community of those worthy of moral considerability, and protection.

In chapter 3, "Heidegger's Bestiary," I set out to expand on the work of Matthew Calarco, Stuart Elden, and William McNeill on Heidegger's phenomenology of animality by analyzing the intense and instructive shifts that take place in this work from the mid-1920s through the late 1930s. I look at this decade of work through the lens of the relationship of his phenomenology of Dasein, which grounds his metaphysical anthropocentrism, to his political ontology. I show that Heidegger's work epitomizes the grounding of the political in the exclusion of the animal, with its inevitable logics of exclusion and extermination. Heidegger's work also illustrates in chillingly precise images and philosophemes (especially in the lecture courses from the years when he was closest to the Nazis) the ways in which the traversal from the zoo to the slaughterhouse is one in which human and nonhuman animals commingle.

The second section is the staging of an exchange that never took place between two philosophers who have shaped the trails of this book, Derrida and Habermas, who are the two philosophical animals—should we say philosophical beasts?—I have tracked most assiduously. The question that brings together these chapters and engagements is: should we outlaw human cloning, human genetic engineering, and genetic therapy? Evidently, in the background is the specter of posthumanism and transhumanism, and inevitably, antihumanism.[18] As I argue in these chapters, how Derrida and Habermas answer the questions about the "integrity and dignity" of the human species is dependent on their implicit dependence on what I called "negative philosophical anthropology." We know that Habermas's philosophical project began as a philosophical anthropology, inasmuch as he aimed to ground a theory of knowledge interests in the capabilities of the human species.[19] In his 1965 Goethe University inaugural lecture, "Knowledge and Human Interests," Habermas formulated five theses, which guided his work leading him to his magnum opus, the two-volume *Theory of Communicative Action*. The first thesis reads: "*The achievements of the transcendental subject have their basis in the natural history of the human species.*"[20] I like to underscore "the natural history of the human species," because I take it that Habermas as a historical materialist is informed by the post-Darwinian notion that we are animals that evolved the supreme evolutionary adaptation, namely language, and with it, culture. The third thesis reads: "*Knowledge-constitutive interests take form in the medium of work, language, and power*" (313). Here work, language, and power are the media through which we apprehend reality, by providing the following: *knowledge* that allows us to cope with and enhance our control of our natural environment; *interpretations* that enable and facilitate interactions with others and cultural traditions; and analyses and *self-reflection* that liberate consciousness from "hypostatized powers." The fourth thesis reads: "*In the power of self-reflection, knowledge and interest are one*" (314). This is so, because: "Reason also means the will to reason. In self-reflection knowledge for the knowledge attains congruence with the interest in autonomy and responsibility" (314). Knowledge is thus immanently self-transcending because of what Habermas calls the emancipatory knowledge interest. The fifth and final thesis proclaims: "*The unity of knowledge and interest proves itself in a dialectic that takes the historical traces of suppressed dialogue and reconstructs what has been suppressed*" (315). Self-reflection, according to Habermas, is thus also the reconstruction and redemption of past repression.

Through my analysis, I aim to show that what informs Habermas's natural history of the human species is what I identified as the tradition of negative philosophical anthropology, which I think Derrida also subscribes to, albeit in more explicit and avowed ways, as I show in the third chapter of this section. I would like readers of these chapters to note how I used Habermas against Habermas to make Habermasian points, and how I am flanked by Derrida in making points that both would agree on, namely that we are the symbolic animal, the poetic species, that is continuously refashioning itself through its use of language. I draw attention, specifically, to Habermas's commitment to an unsustainable form of scientism and above all speciesism that is based on "genetic determinism." Habermas takes recourse to a conception of the human that is based on the notion of humanity's genetic identity, genetic sovereignty, and ipseity, one that is both simultaneously secured and threatened by biotechnology. I argue that just as there is no gene for human freedom, there is no gene for what is proper to the human. As Haraway has pointed out, we are made up of a soup of shared genomic material. If we follow Humberto Maturana and Francisco Varela in talking about "co-ontogenies,"[21] we ought to think with Haraway that genetic sovereignty is both impossible and undesirable.

The stronger point of this section, however, is that the task of humanizing ourselves is the task of producing normativity ex nihilo, but also only through languaging, poeticizing in the broadest possible sense. I play with the Latourian trope of "never having been," and I talk about "never having been human," but not because there is a humanity to be discovered, but because our humanity is a task. "We are not yet human" is an injunction and not an invective. Here then emerges another key theme of the entire book.

As the "mangled" and "incomplete" animal, to use Nietzsche's language, part of our task as animals is to accomplish our humanity. But, we don't accomplish it alone or against other animals. The "natural history of the human species" is the natural history of our being-with, dwelling with, worlding with other animals. This is something both Marx and Engels already acknowledged in their early writings, but this is a theme that is inchoate in all historical materialism. Donna Haraway, that other philosophical animal I have tracked most assiduously, coined the beautiful expression: "companion species." The becoming human of the human animal could not have taken place without our fellow companion creatures with which we have "become with." Haraway wrote in her 2012 essay "Species Matters, Humane Advocacy: In the Promising Grip of Earthly Oxymorons": "Companion species, the term and the fleshy knots, are relentlessly about 'becoming with,' and to focus on companion species is for me one way to refuse human exceptionalism without invoking posthumanism."[22] This "becoming with" that is implied by historical materialism leads me to also be reticent to speak of posthumanism in an unequivocal sense. Attending to animal welfare, our embodied compassion and co-vulnerability, does not mean that we must reject our own humanity. Rejecting metaphysical anthropocentrism should not lead us to embrace a form of posthumanism that may also mean disavowing what we owe to our companion species. I think an ethics commensurate with our corporeal vulnerability, as I argue in later chapters, is one that is already attentive to our webs of relationships with animals. If we are always already implicated in what Acampora calls "somatic sociability," then animals don't require a ne plus ultra, or a transcendental jump that uproots out from our alleged zone of human exceptionality.[23] They are already within our moral universe. They are already worthy and deserving of our moral considerability.

Learning to coexist with other animals cannot mean that we cease to be human, for we became human with other animals—in many ways, they humanized us through their interaction with us, and their many lessons, whether real or spoken through philosophical ventriloquism, have been central in the story of "how animals made us human." Thus posthumanism is acceptable to me, or my arguments in this book, but only as a philosophical position that advocates the overcoming of a certain conception of the human, one that could be characterized as "positive philosophical anthropology," which sets out to delineate for us what the human as such is, should be, and is not. Staunched humanism, the kind we may attribute to Thomists and Christian theologians, as well as metaphysical anthropocentrists, such as that of Heidegger, is the frontal face of an equally suspect posthumanism that is bent on rejecting the former. Acknowledging that we are not yet human is also a way to invite us to create new worlds in which we can begin to recognize our "becoming with" in the midst of earthly entanglements and communities of interspecies "intersomatic" vulnerability—to appropriate some language from Acampora.[24]

The third part of the book is made up of two chapters that take on a positive key with the themes of being with, becoming with, being corporally vulnerable, and the demand and possibility of zoophilic polis. Chapter 8, "Interspecies Cosmopolitanism," written at my countersuggestion for a handbook on cosmopolitanism, is an attempt to articulate a non-metaphysical grounding of animal rights. I think some colleagues are right to suspect that the discourse of rights is so entrenched in "metaphysical chauvinism" and above all "metaphysical anthropocentrism," that pursuing the "rights" approach is a liability, a way to get into the lion's mouth, so to say. As well intentioned as this reserve is, it is also misguided and self-defeating—fighting against the animal rights theory may lead at best to a pyrrhic victory, and at worst, to the obsolesce of our philosophical work and its having no political efficacy. Philosophy as a form of poesis is about changing the world, by changing how we conceive ourselves. But this change in self-images and self-conceptions has to have claws, jaws, hooves, tusks, toes, and fingers, so that it can change the way we make worlds.

Law, as Habermas has so aptly put it, is Janus-faced. One face is instrumental and administrative—it gets things done, it allow us to get things done, together, and it imposes on us a force of sanction that means that when we fail to respect it and fulfill it, we are liable and can be punished. The other face is moral-ethical. I deliberately use the dash because law (*Recht*) is where the post-Hegelian distinction between morality and ethics, i.e., *Moralität* and *Sittlichkeit*, come together into the menagerie of the polis. What I mean is that in law is where particular ethical insights, projects, practices gain traction when they met the scrutiny of morality. In the process of juridifying, of codifying into law, our ethical insights and intuitions are tested against the procedural and normative demands of morality. Evidently, the more ethics pushes the legal envelope, the more we have a better insight into the horizon of normativity of morality. Law is the one mechanism through which universality become historically effective, as human rights have shown. De Fontenay's observation on rights is correct: "Rights cannot be inferred on the basis of scientific facts: either they are consecrated and proclaimed by the state on the basis of a metaphysical, transcendental-immanent conception of natural law, or else they are to be invented, declared, and proclaimed, proceeding the history of men."[25] The discourse ethics approach to law allows us to do the latter without taking recourse to the former. As Habermas has argued in recent texts, the history of rights is the history of our acknowledgment of violations to human dignity and, evidently, the dark and sobering history of human genocide. Implicit, however, in this history of human rights, and animal rights as well, is the "inventing and reinventing universality"[26]—to put it as de Fontenay does. It is thus easy to see, I hope, why we simply can't abandon the animal rights theory, to use the language of Donaldson and Kymlicka. If our philosophical speculation about what we owe to animals is to have any traction, we thus must also be committed to transforming the ways in which we generate and produce those tools that coordinate our interactions. I thus agree with what Ian Hacking said with respect to Peter Singer's advocacy for animal rights: "The place of Singer's reasons may be more forensic than moral. We need codes and precedents to regulate civil society. Singer and his fellows are forging the laws of tomorrow. Laws have moral stature not only because they create legal duties and obligations but also because they are bench marks from which to move on."[27]

Now, this chapter is my contribution to the Frankfurt School theory of Critical Theory, in a positive and constructive way. I was a student of Karl-Otto Apel and Jürgen Habermas, and I consider myself a critical theorist, for the simple reason that I am also a historical materialist and a de-colonial Marxist. But in this chapter I begin with the argument that Habermas, along with his students and colleagues, have produced a mighty and very impressive discourse on law and democracy, which more than adequately makes up for the "state and law" theory deficit of Marx, but which above all is uniquely and powerfully endowed to give us the tools that we animal rights advocates need. The argument is that we need to give teeth to those powerful intuitions that Adorno and Horkheimer had in their work. I am arguing that we post-Habermasian critical theorists don't forget the historical materialist sensibility to the becoming together with other animals, and above all to strive to co-dwell in the zoophilic polis by Adorno's other version of the categorical imperative: "to have lived as though we had been good animals"—to anticipate the focus of my chapter on Adorno in the last section.

With the last chapter, I wanted to bring us full circle to the first chapter, namely zoopoetics. In this chapter, however, instead of focusing on literary or written texts, I wanted to focus on some artists who have been doing in their installations, performances, and creations what Coetzee did for us in his fiction, namely bring us to the food bowl of corporal compassion. However, this chapter would have entailed spending months acquiring permissions, high-quality reproductions, and so on. The chapter is now in a book that is easily accessible.[28] Instead, this new last chapter is about my animal autobiography, that is, how I grew up around and with animals, how they sheltered me, fed me, gave me companionship, and how they touched me, physically and figuratively. I return to the theme of the bestiary, but now from another angle, what I call the bestiaries of extinction. I focus on horses for three reasons: because they were essential to our humanization; because they were pervasive in our existences until cars took over the streets of cities, and the highways their hooves had carved into the soil and mountains; and because notwithstanding their emotional and physical prowess, they have become "relic species." In this last chapter I turn to another one of my teachers: Reinhart Koselleck, the major German intellectual historian. Koselleck, who had been a soldier in the Eastern Front during World War II, argued that human history can be divided in terms of our relationship to the horse: prehorse, horse, and posthorse epochs. Horses, like few animals, have inspired our imaginations, ability to project affect, and to develop what I call forms of interspecies cosmopolitanism.

Rorty argued for the greater efficacy of literature, over philosophy, in our moral pedagogy. I think he is right. But fiction can't do the work it does, without translations, without interpretation, without vociferous and irreverent engagement. By the same token, without art, we cannot learn and unlearn how to be human and how not to become a certain type of hideous human animal. Adorno wrote in his *Aesthetic Theory* that great artists produce "works" that we don't know what they are, but which educate us to understand them. In the chapter I would have included, but which I did not, I argue that we have to learn to become a different kind of animal, and that the work of Patricia Piccinini, Jane Alexander, and Guillermo Gomez-Peña, along with Koselleck's reflections on the horse and human history, challenges us to understand our corporal vulnerability and "somatic sociability" in ways that we can translate into learning to be a good animal.

The book, thus, is structured according to the logic of both discourse ethics and deconstruction ethics. In her book, *Without Offending Humans: A Critique of Animal Rights*, de Fontenay writes: "I will be distinguishing among three levels of deconstruction that are, even as they interpenetrate one another, testimony to the radicalization and shift of argument: a strategy *through* the animal, exposition *to* an animal or *to this* animal, and compassion *toward* animals."[29] I was electrified when I read that passage, because I then realized that this is what I was also trying to do as a critical theorist. First, we must work through how we conjure up and corral our philosophical animals. Then, I have sought to focus our attention on specific animals, our companion species, and as it is evident throughout the chapters, I have been a fortunate beneficiary of both animal love and animal interpellation (should I say with Rainer Forst, demand to justify myself, give an account of myself?). Third, this is a book about what we owe to animals, not because it is something extra, but because it also something we owe each other. For in the end, we circle around each other like dogs smelling butts, and walk together like elephants holding up each other, and howl and wail when we lose each other.

Animal Philosophy

On the stairway of the Tower of Victory there has lived since the beginning of time a being sensitive to the many shades of the human soul and known as the A Bao A Qu. It lies dormant, for the most part on the first step, until at the approach of a person some secret life is touched off in it, and deep within the creature an inner light begins to glow. At the same time, its body and almost translucent skin begin to stir. But only when someone starts up the spiraling stairs is the A Bao A Qu brought to consciousness, and then it sticks close to the visitor's heels, keeping to the outside of the turning steps, where they are most worn by the generation of pilgrims. At each level the creature's color becomes more intense, its shape approaches perfection, and the bluish light it gives off is more brilliant. But it achieves its ultimate form only at the topmost step, when the climber is a person who has attained Nirvana and whose acts cast no shadows. Otherwise, the A Bao A Qu hangs back before reaching the top, as if paralyzed, its body incomplete, its blue growing paler, and its glow hesitant. The creature suffers when it cannot come to completion, and its moan is a barely audible sound, something like the rustling of silk. Its span of life is brief, since as soon as the traveler climbs down, the A Bao A Qu wheels and tumbles to the first steps, where, worn out and almost shapeless, it waits for the next visitor. People say that its tentacles are visible only when it reaches the middle of the staircase. It is also said that it can see with its whole body and that to the touch it is like skin of peach. In the course of centuries, the A Bao A Qu has reached the terrace only once.

—Jorge Luis Borges, *The Book of Imaginary Beings*[30]

I argue in this book that philosophy has been complicit with the project of exiling animals from the world of moral considerability as well as from the polis. Additionally, philosophy is that which alone a certain type of animal does, and thus philosophy is property of the human, or the humanity of the human is defined in terms of its ability to philosophize. The definition of philosophy is therefore implicated in the definition of the human—this is what I also intend to draw our attention to with the title of the book: the philosophical animal. Derrida's extensive analysis of the phrase that the human is the *zōon logon echo* (ζῷον λόγον ἔχον) allows us to recognize that inasmuch as nonhuman animals are deprived of language, they are also deprived of philosophy. Philosophy after all is only possible in and through language. The point I want to make, however, is that when we triangulate philosophy, humanity, and the "animal" we can see that the question of the animal, which is the question of the *humanitas* of humanity, which is the question of what is and who does philosophy, we can come to the realization that the animal question in philosophy is a metaphilosophical question, that is, that it is a question about what philosophy itself is and should be for those to whom it is allowed, granted, gifted, or claimed in the name of. In what remains of this introduction, I want to undertake a metaphilosophical reflection about how the question of the animal is at the heart of the birth of philosophy itself, and how we have to begin to poeticize different philosophies. I will do so by revisiting two key mythemes that are foundational for the development of critical theory. I am referring to Odysseus's encounter with Polyphemus, the Cyclops, and the story of the Sirens. But, I will revisit Polyphemus's cave after having come out of Plato's cave in book 7 of the *Republic*. I want to weave a trace between Homer's Odysseus, Plato's alpinist of caves, the philosopher par excellence, and Horkheimer and Adorno's dialectics of the enlightenment qua critique of the myth of enlightenment.

Book 9 of the *Odyssey* narrates the story of Odysseus's cunning escape from the one-eyed giant's cave. The story however is also Homer's reflection on what constitutes the humanity of the human and the animality of the animal. The Cyclops dwell in caves, they don't toil the lands, for their island is plentiful and provides for all their needs. They don't have merchant or war ships, and thus they neither wage war nor engage in commerce. They are, as Homer puts it: "lawless brutes, who trust so to the everlasting god they never plant with their own hands or plow the soil. . . . They have no meeting place for council, no laws either, no, up on the mountain peaks they live in arching caverns—each a law to himself, ruling his wives and children, not a care in the world for any neighbor."³¹(9.120–27) They are brutes, or as classist Ulrich von Wilamowitz-Moellendorff put it, the Cyclops were "really animals."³²

The story is well known, and I will return to it in chapter 1. The Cyclops "inadvertently" captures Odysseus and his men, when he returns from pasturing his flock of sheep. Odysseus had entered the cave intent on stealing food from it but is imprisoned when the Cyclops closes the exit with a boulder that neither Odysseus nor his men can lift. If Odysseus kills the Cyclops as he sleeps, then they are doomed, as they cannot exit the cave. Odysseus thus comes up with a stratagem to have the Cyclops lift the boulder that closes the cave. The plot entails getting him drunk, and then Odysseus and his men slipping out of the cave, under the bellies of the sheep, when the Cyclops has to pasture his flock. To do this, Odysseus has to wound but not kill Polyphemus, and he has also to partly ingratiate himself to him, so as to get him drunk. In order to do this, he has to identify himself and thus name himself. This is where Horkheimer and Adorno find traction for their own unpacking of the dialectic of the Enlightenment. In order to save himself, Odysseus has to refuse his name. He identifies himself as "Nobody (*Udeis*)" (9.409–10). The path to subjectivity is that of the rejection of identity. To use some Freudian language, the inner space of subjectivity is an empty castle won at the expense of rejection of one's somatic vulnerability. Horkheimer and Adorno put it this way: "In reality, Odysseus, the subject, denies his own identity, which makes him a subject, and preserves life by mimicking the amorphous realm. He calls himself nobody because Polyphemus is not a self, and confusion of the name with the thing prevents the duped barbarian from escaping the trap" (53).

We cannot leave unmentioned that the staging of this drama, for the sake of exhibiting Odysseus's cunning, is really a debacle instigated by his curiosity and above all his narcissism and need to win admirers and the gifts of strangers.[33] On the other hand, we ought not to neglect the juxtaposition between Polyphemus's anthropophagy and his gentle tending to his herd. Here is Polyphemus addressing his ram, which Odysseus will later sacrifice: "Dear old ram, why last of the flock to quit the cave? In the old good old days you'd never lag behind the rest—you with your long marching strides, first by far of the flock to graze the fresh young grasses, first by far to reach the rippling streams, first to turn back home, keen for your fold when night comes on—but now you're last of all. And why? Sick at heart for your master's eye that coward gouged out with his wicked crew? Only after he'd stunned my wits with wine—that, that Nobody." (9.498–508).

The second mytheme is that of the Sirens, which appear in book 12 of the *Odyssey*. In order to descend to Hades and consult Tiresias, Odysseus must pass by the island where these enchantresses dwell. The Sirens "spellbind any man alive" with their voices. "The high, thrilling song of the Sirens will transfix him, lolling there in their meadow, round them heaps of corpses, rotting away, rags of skin shriveling on their bones" (12.50–53). Following Circe's instructions, Odysseus plugs up the ears of his men, who must row, and has himself bound to the mast of the ship. He alone can hear the Sirens' transfixing voices, while his men are deprived of their beautiful singing. For Horkheimer and Adorno, Odysseus binding himself in order to hear the voice of the Sirens is a defiance of the gods and a rejection of fate. Odysseus's "cunning" is "defiance made rational" (12.46). This cunning thwarting of mythic power and divine predetermination is achieved at the price of the self's sacrifice. Both subjectivity and civilization are based on the "introversion of sacrifice—in other words, the history of renunciation" (12.43). Odysseus must sacrifice himself in order to survive. He must give himself to the gods, precisely in order to cunningly defeat them at their game. Odysseus is the sacrificial victim that demands the abolition of sacrifice. For Horkheimer and Adorno, then, already in Homer's retelling of the archaic myths of the Greeks there is a critique of myth. Homer's mythology as anti-myth is proleptic of the Enlightenment. Myth is already a form of the critique of myth, at least as it is poeticized by Homer.

At play in Homer's texts, from the *Iliad* to the *Odyssey*, is also a critique of reason as that which must subdue and domesticate nature and the animal. The *Iliad* may be the first and last great hymn to war, but it is also an exacting document of the fury and destruction human war unleashes on nature and other animals. The misery, destruction, anguish unleashed by the fury of men with his death-dealing weapons of war is depicted with equal gore whether it cuts down men or animals. One may even speak of animal compassion in Homer. As Gary Steiner notes in his *Anthropocentrism and Its Discontents*, Homer's work is guided by identification of humans with animals and animals with humans. "Homer's view of the relationship between human beings and animals is not . . . a conception of the fundamental superiority of human over animals. Like the *Iliad*, the *Odyssey* gives prominence to a sense of continuity."[34] It is this sense of continuity that allows Homer to recognize how important and irreplaceable our "companion species" are to us. It is important to note that one of the most foundational stories of Western culture also contains one of the most moving stories about human and animal companionship. When Odysseus finally returns to his beloved island, no one recognizes him except his faithful dog Argos. "Infested with ticks, half-dead from neglect, here lay the hound, old Argos, But the moment he sensed Odysseus standing by he thumped his tail, nuzzling low, and his ears dropped, though he had no strength to drag himself an inch toward his master. Odysseus glanced to the side and flicked away a tear, hiding it from Eumaeus" (17.328–34). Again Steiner: "The encounter between Odysseus and Argus [sic] bespeaks an intimate sense of kinship and community that puts to shame Odysseus's relationship with other human beings."[35] To become himself, he must deny his name and identity before an animal, the Cyclops, but to return to himself and be recognized as himself, he is acknowledged as himself by another animal, Argos. In Homer, thus, we can discern another philosopheme that resounds between two names: Argos and Bobby (Levinas's dog). "Perhaps the dog that recognized Ulysses beneath his disguise on his return from the Odyssey was a forebear of our own. But, no, no! There, they were in Ithaca and the Fatherland. Here, we were nowhere. This dog was the last Kantian in Nazi Germany, without the brain needed to universalize maxims and drives. He was a descendant of the dogs of Egypt. And his friendly growling, his animal faith, was born from the silence of his forefathers on the banks of the Nile."[36]

If Homer's mythopoesis unleashes the dialectics of enlightenment, Plato's own mythopoesis instigates its own form of reason as myth. Commenting on Rachel Bespaloff's reflections on Homer's and Plato's mythogenesis in her *On the Iliad*, Hermann Broch writes: "Philosophy is a constant fight against the remnants of mythical thinking and a constant struggle to achieve mythical structure in a new form, a fight against the metaphysical convention and a struggle to build a new metaphysics; for metaphysics, itself bounded by myth, bounds philosophy, without which these boundaries would have no existence at all."[37]

There is no place where this reversion of reason into myth, and the creation of myth to bind philosophy, is executed more exemplarily than in Plato's *Republic*. Plato's relation to the founders of the Greek intellectual tradition is a fertile territory, but at the very least, one can claim that Plato works are rewritings of Homer and Hesiod, or very original and generative rereadings of those two founding fathers. As David K. O'Connor put it: "We are never closer to Plato as writer than when we are reading Plato reading."[38] As O'Connor argues, we should read Plato's characters and dramatization of the *Republic* as Plato's skillful readings and rewriting of key moments in both Homer and Hesiod. Thus, the *Republic*'s repeated language of descent and ascent are modeled on Homer and Hesiod's mythemes of both descent and ascent from Hades, the escape of the gods from the underworld of the earth, the fashioning of humans from the earth, and so on. The transit between the underworld, the earth, and the heavens allows us to talk about a mythological geography or topography. In parallel, Plato's *Republic* is also configured around a topography of reason. The *Republic* begins with Socrates descending to Piraeus, the port of Athens, where he had gone to offer a prayer and see the celebration of the new rite to the goddess Bendis. It culminates with the retelling of the myth of Er, which is about metempsychosis or the ascent of souls. Socrates says to Glaucon: "But if we are persuaded by me, we will believe that the soul is immortal and able to endure every evil and also every good, and always hold to the upward path, practicing justice with wisdom every way we can, so that we will be friends to ourselves and to the gods" (621c). Socrates departs the Piraeus as he departs the cave. If the former stands for the mundane of politics, the latter stands for the quotidian existence of the masses in ignorance. The trope of ascent also determines how Plato conceives of politics. Descending and ascending from the Piraeus is an allegory of the leave-taking of the world of politics, which is also the world of shadows. Piraeus is the *pars pro toto* of the metonymic "city of pigs" (372d), which is juxtaposed to the "true city," Kallipolis.

We can thus speak, along with Luce Irigaray, of a Platonic topology or topography of reason that involves the ascent from the cave of shadows and doxa, of subjection and delusion, to the blinding light of reason and liberation from ignorance, and the immortality of the gods.[39] This topography of reason is determined by the vector of escape and ascent from the cave of subjugating ignorance. Philosophy as a praxis is this escaping from caves. Philosophy is a *Höhlenausgänge*, to use that wonderful expression by Hans Blumemberg.[40] Plato's topography of reason, with its geography of escape from ignorance and ascent to wisdom, is succinctly and poetically captured in the "Allegory of the Cave." In fact, this allegory becomes the *locus classicus*, the point of condensation, for Plato's own metaphilosophy. In as much as the allegory of the cave is a rejection of doxa and the role that Sophists play in contributing to our subjection to the world of shadows, and the injunction to engage in the pursuit of the true love of wisdom, it is the summary articulation of Plato's own philosophy of philosophy. The allegory of the cave is the synecdoche for Plato's topography of reason. It is also, as Irigaray notes, the "silent prescription for Western metaphysics but also, more explicitly, proclaims (itself as) everything designated as metaphysics, its fulfillment, and its interpretation."[41] The allegory of the cave, then, is the ur-metaphor that conditions all of Western thinking.

"The famous 'Allegory of the Cave' is many things. But prominent among them, it is a rewriting of Homer. Socrates has guided Glaucon to a new mythic identity, from an ambitious Achilles to a chastened Odysseus. But this rewriting has complicated and elaborated Socrates's own mythic projection onto the triumphant hero."[42] In this passage O'Connor has captured exactly the ways in which the cave is key to Plato's appropriation and rewriting of both Homer and Hesiod, for at the pivot of Plato's own turning is the ambivalent casting of Socrates as Odysseus. "Plato's myth [of the ascent from the cave] refuses us the satisfaction of Homer's *Odyssey*, since we cannot say whether the main character found his way through many labors at last to home, or remained stranded in that dead-world of politics and ambition, saving others though he could not save himself. It is hard to see an accident in an ambiguity so subtly composed."[43]

Odysseus and Socrates must escape caves. In order to do so, they must blind. In one case, Polyphemus must be blinded, so he can still remove the bolder that closes his cave. In the other, Socrates, or the philosophers, must submit to a temporary blindness of eternal truth, the light of reason. We should thus speak with Irigaray of a hysterical philosophical optics.[44] Polyphemus and the Sirens are animals, and Socrates, who is sometimes referred to as an ox, a gadfly, and is compared by Alcibiades to Silenus and the satyr Marsyas (*Symposium*, 215b), is too not entirely human. All are mixed creatures, embodying the animal in man and the human in animals. Satyrs, which should remind us of Jonathan Swift's Yahoos, "had the sexual appetites and manners of wild beasts and were usually portrayed with large erections. Sometimes they had horses' tails or ears, sometimes the traits of goats."[45] Socrates is thus also an animal, a long distant cousin of Polyphemus.[46] Between Homer and Plato, then, the project of ascent to our rational autonomy is a project of the blinding and muting of our nature, the blinding and silencing of our animality. Philosophy, in Plato's topography of reason, is this blinding of animal nature qua blinding of the animal philosopher, the departure from the city of pigs to the city of philosopher-kings. To become a philosopher means to cease to see and hear like an animal, to cease to live like one, to be blind and deaf to the color and sound of nature.

Franz Kafka has many animal parables, but among them there is one that is particularly chilling and edifying. It is titled "The Silence of the Sirens." There he writes:

> Now the Sirens have a more fatal weapon than their song, namely their silence. And though admittedly such a thing never happened, still it is conceivable that someone might possibly have escaped their singing; but from their silence certainly never. Against the feeling of having triumphed over them by one's own strength, and the consequent exaltation that bears down everything before it, no earthly powers could have remained intact . . . Ulysses, it is said, was so full of guile, was such a fox, that not even the goddess of fate could pierce his armor. Perhaps he had really noticed, although here the human understanding is beyond its depths, that the Sirens were silent, and opposed the afore-mentioned pretense to them and the gods merely a sort of shield. These are the seductive voices of the night; the Sirens, too, sang that way. It would be doing them an injustice to think that they wanted to seduce; they knew they had claws and sterile wombs, and they lamented this aloud. They could not help it if their laments sounded so beautiful.[47]

I began this section with an extensive quote from one of my favorite books of Borges, *The Book of Imaginary Beings*. Borges first wrote this book in the 1950s and continued to expand it and revise it, until its English edition, which was done with the cooperation of di Giovanni, his translator. The original 1957 edition was titled *Manual de zoología fantástica* (*Handbook of Fantastic Zoology*). It is unfortunate that this original title was dropped. I argue in this book that we think of philosophy, among the many things it is, as the writing, gathering, imagining of a fantastic zoology. Some of the fantastic animals that populate the philosopher's zoo have domesticated us to growl and screech at the sight or mere thought of animals, to demean the animal in us as our inhumanity; others have husbanded us into docile animals that are happy to curl up with a dog or two, a cat or two, in bed. Borges surely did not by accident open his book with the A Bao A Qu, nor was his pen forced by the logic of alphabetic ordering. I take it that for Borges the A Bao A Qu is the perfect allegory for the human-animal, animal-human relation. So are Kafka's lamenting and barren Sirens. We can't ascend to our enlightenment without our companion species; their well-being is our well-being. Their silence or their lament is the silence and lament of our own nature.[48] We need animal philosophy that is to the height of this ascent, in which we neither blind nor silence those with whom we have to accomplish our humanity.

I
Ceasing to Be Animal

Chapter 1

Zoopoetics

Coetzee's Animals and Philosophy

> Let me add, *entirely* parenthetically, that I, as a person, as a personality, am overwhelmed, that my thinking is thrown into confusion and helplessness, by the fact of suffering in the world, and not only human suffering. These fictional constructions of mine are paltry, ludicrous defenses against that being-overwhelmed, and, to me, transparently so.
>
> —J. M. Coetzee, *Doubling the Point: Essays and Interviews*[1]

> The eyes of an animal when they consider a man are attentive and wary. The same animal may well look at other species in the same way. He does not reserve a special look for man. But by no other species except man will the animal's look be recognized as familiar. Other animals are held by the look. *Man becomes aware of himself returning the look.*
>
> —John Berger, *About Looking*[2]

Zoopoetics: The Philosophical Animal

There are suffering animals everywhere in J. M. Coetzee's works; more generally, in fact, there are suffering bodies everywhere in his corpus.[3] As a whole, Coetzee's novels have been the stage on which the torture of human and animal bodies has been dramatized and exhibited. His novels are the staging of a "theater of execution, disembowelment, flaying, quartering"—to use a sentence from an essay he wrote two years before his famous Tanner lectures.[4] Coetzee's oeuvre has received the attention it merits, not only because in 2003 he was awarded the Nobel Prize in Literature, but also because throughout the 1980s his work was the target of a censoring criticism from both the liberal and right wings sectors of South African society. Yet, aside from such deserved and undeserved attention, his work merits our attention because of the way it has registered the power of fiction to challenge our most fundamental assumptions about ethics, the power of literature in society, and what we take to be the boundaries that separate society from nature. Coetzee's work has already received sustained critical analysis, and literary critics have waged debates about how to categorize his work. Some have forcefully argued that it is an instance of postcolonial fiction that converges with and make use of postmodern techniques. Some have argued that his work is primarily a form of postmodern fiction. Others yet, specifically Derek Attridge, have argued that what we find in Coetzee's work is a form of neomodernism, a type of modernism that holds on to some of the techniques and insights of Robert Musil, Samuel Beckett, Thomas Mann, Fyodor Dostoevsky, and Franz Kafka, to mention the most prominent.[5] Postcolonial theorists cannot quite claim him, notwithstanding Coetzee's clear and unflinching political stance. His work is too self-reflexive, too cerebral, too equivocal, mercurial, elusive, and inconclusive, to be directly useful in postcolonial political struggles. On the other hand, if we understand postcolonialism as a conceptual, theoretical, even *Weltanschaung*, stance that departs from the crisis of all forms of consciousness, a crisis that is deeply implicated and freighted with the inheritances of colonialism, then Coetzee's work is unambiguously postcolonial. Yet, it is also more than that. Postcoloniality is not a supplement, but it also does not exhaust it.

Nonetheless, it is not as important that we define conclusively whether Coetzee's work is postmodern, postcolonial, or neomodernist, as it is that we discern that all of his work has always been marked by a relentless, almost unbearable, self-reflexivity. There is no work by him that is not at the same time a reflection on the act of writing. From his earliest book, *Dusklands* (1974), to *Slow Man* (2005), we encounter in each one of his works an engagement with the impossible innocence of literature. Literature, like positivism, invites us to revel in a guilty naïveté. Coetzee takes great pains to disabuse us of this inertia in complacency, in abandon and surrender to the tutelage of an authorial voice that will create for us a world that is hermetically sealed, a world unto itself, a self-enclosed reality that is preserved from doubt, questions, suspicions. If our mundane reality is one that is always melting away behind the myriad of perspectives, then the novel will restore for us a world that is solid, univocal, and stable, even in its very blatant fictionality. Coetzee withdraws this comforting fiction from his readers. The novel, all fiction, is always an act of selection, a gathering of narratives, of perspective, choices, exclusions, and occlusions. Literature, in Coetzee's performance, is always the scene of an ethical struggle. It is the trace of an ethical malaise and doubt. Coetzee, it is my contention, has offered us a hermeneutical key that allows us to unlock its ethical urgency, an ethical urgency and hyper-consciousness furthermore that is directly related to the "animal question." In an essay from 1986, entitled "Into the Dark Chamber: The Writer and the South African State,"[6] Coetzee glosses on a passage from Nadine Gordimer's novel *Burger's Daughter*, a passage that echoes an analogous passage in Dostoevsky's *Crime and Punishment*. The passage in Gordimer's novel reads: "The infliction of pain broken away from the will that creates it; broken loose, a force existing of itself, ravishment without the ravisher, torture without the torturer, rampage, pure cruelty gone beyond the control of the humans who have spent thousands of years devising it. The entire ingenuity from thumbscrew and rack to electric shock, the infinite variety and gradation of suffering, by lash, by fear, by hunger, by solitary confinement—the camps, concentration, labor, resettlement, the Siberias of snow or sun, the lives of Mandela, Sisulu, Mbeki, Kathrada, Kgosana, gullpicked on the Island."[7] Coetzee comments: "It is important not to read the episode in a narrowly symbolic way. The driver and the donkey do not stand respectively for torturer and tortured. "Torture without torturer" is the key phrase. Forever and ever, in Rosa's memory, the blows will rain down and the beast shudder in pain. The spectacle comes from the inner reaches of Dante's hell, beyond the scope of morality. For morality is human, whereas the two figures locked to the cart belong to the dammed, dehumanized world."[8]

Rosa Burger, Gordimer's character, leaves South Africa because she finds impossible to live in a country that is the horizon for such scenes of damnation. We know that Coetzee himself left South African for similar reasons. It would not be entirely inappropriate to suggest that Rosa is Coetzee's alter ego. He finds it also unbearable to live in a country where one is confronted with such impossible decisions: to stop the torture, to ignore it, to let one's conscience became inured to such suffering, frustration, deep hate, and rage. Toward the end of this essay, Coetzee returns to Rosa, when he writes:

> What Rosa suffers and waits for is a time when humanity will be restored across the face of society, and therefore, when all human acts, including the flogging of an animal, will be returned to the ambit of moral judgment. In such a society it will once again be *meaningful* for the gaze of the author, the gaze of authority and authoritative judgment, to be turned upon the scenes of torture. When the choice is no longer limited to *either* looking in horrified fascination as the blows fall *or* turning one's eyes away, then the novel can once again take as its province the whole of life, and even the torture chamber can be accorded a place in the design.[9]

These passages are extremely important because in them Coetzee is directly talking about the ethical challenge and responsibility of the author to return to the "ambit of moral judgment," not just the flogging and torturing of animals, but also of the torturing of humans in the torture chamber.

There are suffering, tortured, bestialized, raped, killed, brutally disfigured humans, but also maimed, flogged, flayed, incinerated, euthanized, animals in Coetzee's work. While both forms of suffering are not equated in Coetzee fiction, although he does use the language of analogy and comparison, it is clear that both forms of suffering are implicated in each other. Neither form of suffering is supplemental to the other, yet they are irreducibly held together. It is possible that Coetzee presupposes at some level something like Donna Haraway's notion of "animal companionship." (I will return to this toward the end). For Coetzee, like for Kant and Haraway, we are partly humanized through our treatment or mistreatment of animals. When we refuse to acknowledge the humanity of other humans, we generally do so by bestializing them, by treating them as animals. So, dehumanization is directly related to our relationship to animals. Yet, it is also true that when we bestialize and seek to exterminate others from whom we withdraw the designation of human, we do so bypassing the animal in them. There are some forms of torture and suffering that we are not even willing to inflict on animals. We would never do *that* to our pets and cattle! For this reason, we may say that bestiality and bestialization is an excess outside the economy of mutuality between the human and the animal.[10] On the other hand, as Kant pointed out in his *Lectures on Ethics*, cruel treatment of animals is a precursor to the maltreatment of other humans. The maltreatment of animals is a sure way to inaugurate the mistreatment of other humans, and for this reason Kant proscribed it.

Coetzee's fiction is unmistakably about this animal pedagogy. More precisely, however, animals in Coetzee's work form part of a literary menagerie that is not like the modern zoo, where animals are to be seen, but where they cannot look back, as John Berger so eloquently put it in his seminal essay "Why Look at Animals," from which the second epigraph to this chapter is extracted.[11] Animals in Coetzee's fiction are our "fellow" companions, who incite us to moral questioning.

In the following I will offer an analysis of the ways in which Coetzee's menagerie, or bestiary, is the setting for an animal pedagogy that is performed through a zoopoetics, or animal poesies, which incites us to formulate the question of the animal in the human and the human in the animal in ways that allow us to bring back into the "moral ambit" the question of their suffering, which is in many ways, always our suffering. A question arises, inevitably and predictably: in what ways is the philosophical and ethical dimension of Coetzee's animal moral pedagogy not supplemental, that is, something to be properly pursued by philosophy and only subsequently to be smuggled, perhaps surreptitiously, into fiction? This is the question of the status of the philosophical in Coetzee's work. I already noted that his fiction and entire literary work is marked by an unwavering and unmitigated self-consciousness. This overbearing self-reflexivity, in fact, is but the expression of the fact that Coetzee's literary productions are instances of what we have called "philosophical novels." His novels are indeed philosophical novels of the highest order, but they are also philosophical in a unique way, one that challenges the boundaries between fiction and philosophy, in a mutually advantageous way.

There are two very clearly recognizable forms of the philosophical novel, at the very least. There is the philosophical novel in which philosophy is quoted. Let us call this the "philosophy as quotation" novel. These are novels in which characters may quote philosophical texts, and may make reference to philosophical problems, currents, traditions, personalities, but in which what is quoted remains extrinsic and supplemental. The characters in these novels could just as easily be talking about soccer, baseball, the stock market, or mathematical equations (Saul Bellow's novels are a perfect example of this type of quotational novel). Another form of the philosophical novel is what we can call the "philosophical personification novel"; that is to say, these are novels in which characters and persons are not necessarily talking or quoting philosophy, but their characters or protagonists unmistakably stand for philosophical ideas. Characters personify a philosophical idea, problem, or stance.

Clear examples of personifications of philosophy novels are the works by Voltaire, Diderot, Mann, Musil, Sartre, and DeLillo. It is possible to mix both genres, and in fact there are cases where characters personifying a philosophical problem or quandary do quote philosophers, whether consciously or unconsciously. I think some of Borges's fictions have mixed both genres very successfully. There is a third possibility. There are some philosophical novels that are clearly and unmistakably more than just quoting or personifying philosophical problems. This type of philosophical novel is recognized as philosophical only post facto. These novels, in fact, are able to convince us that certain human problems, quandaries, and challenges constitute fundamental philosophical problems. This type of novel expands the horizon of philosophy, and in this sense it can be said that it contributes to philosophy without poaching or smuggling from it. Coetzee's philosophical novels belong to this later genre, for in them we may find both personification and quotation, but something else that is not dependent on a prior loan from philosophy. This generative character of Coetzee's literary production is what I seek to express with the term zoopoetics, or animal poesies. In fact, we must place Coetzee within the tradition of Plutarch, Montaigne, Orwell, C. S. Lewis and, most importantly, Franz Kafka, who poeticized and philosophized through literary animal creations.

Animal Looks and Smells:
The Ethical Gaze and Animal Proximity

Boyhood: Scenes from Provincial Life is not the first work where Coetzee broaches the question of animal suffering, but it is surely one of the most telling. *Boyhood* is not exactly a memoir, nor an autobiography, but rather a highly mediated and uncomfortably honest meditation on his childhood. The second paragraph of the first page talks about three hens, which were supposed to lay eggs, but which did not "flourish." The hens lived in a pool of stagnant water in the backyard, and they developed "gross swelling on their legs, like elephant-skin." After some consultation, his mother learns that they will return to laying eggs after "the horny shells under their tongues have been cut out. So one after another his mother takes the hens between her knees, presses on their jowls till they open their beaks, and with the point of a paring-knife picks at their tongues. The hens shriek and struggled, their eyes bulging. He shudders, and turns away. He thinks of his mother slapping stewing-steak on the kitchen counter and cutting it into cubes; he thinks of her bloody fingers."[12] Later in the same book, Coetzee recalls of "his" witnessing the routine practice of castrating the sheep and the regular slaughter of one of the sheep to feed people in the farm. Toward the end of chapter 11, where this memory is recalled, Coetzee writes:

> Sometimes when he is among the sheep—when they have been rounded up to be dipped, and are penned tight and cannot get away—he wants to whisper to them, warn them of what lies in store. But then in their yellow eyes he catches a glimpse of something that silences him: resignation, a foreknowledge not only of what happens to sheep at the hands of Ros behind the shed, but of what awaits them at the end of a long, thirsty ride to Cape Town on the lorry. They know it all, down to the finest detail, and yet they submit. They have calculated the price and are prepared to pay it—the price of being on earth, the price of being alive.[13]

These passages may be first in the ontogenesis of Coetzee's own consciousness. They are surely integral in the ascension to consciousness in "he" who is and is not Coetzee. They reveal two important aspects of Coetzee's relationship to the "animal question" First is his pronounced concern with the suffering of animals and how it is imprinted in his consciousness, as some of the earliest memories about his childhood. Second, and just as importantly, is the preoccupation with whether animals themselves are aware of their impending death. Are animals ever aware of their own death? In another passage, written chronologically earlier than those in *Boyhood*, in "The Narrative of Jacobus Coetzee" that makes up the second half of *Dusklands*, there is an important passage, vis-à-vis a certain Heideggerian philosophical view of death:

> We cannot count the wild. The wild is one because it is boundless. We can count fig-trees, we can count sheep because the orchard and the farm are bounded. The essence of orchard tree and farm sheep is number. Our commerce with the wild is a tireless enterprise of turning it into orchard and farm. . . . He

who does not understand number does not understand death. Death is obscure to him as to an animal. This holds true for the Bushman, and can be seen in his language, which does not include a procedure for counting.[14]

The animal does not understand death. It is impenetrable, inaccessible because it is boundless, countless, and immeasurable. The animals, like the Bushman, can't comprehend death because they do not understand quantity. These are very interesting suggestions if we put them in the light of what Martin Heidegger had to say about the dying of the human being and the mere perishing of animals. Humans alone die, while animals merely perish. For Heidegger, death is an event that is only meaningful to the human being because death is the culmination or end of an existential project. Death is meaningful because it is the closure of meaning projection. Animals, allegedly, do not project. They don't have a future. They are world poor.[15]

In *Waiting for the Barbarians* there is a scene in which one of the horses that is taking the magistrate to meet the "barbarians" lies down and refuses to go on, while other horses collapse in exhaustion. "That night one of the pack-horses refuses its feed. In the morning, even under the severest flogging, it will not rise. We redistribute the loads and cast away some of the firewood. While the others set out I stay behind. I can swear that the beast knows what is to happen. At the sight of the knife its eyes roll."[16] Sheep and horses "know" of their impending death. Do they see it? How do they see their death approaching? How do they experience their deaths? Is it an event of consciousness, and what form does it take? Whoever has been to a slaughterhouse knows that cows and bulls know that they are going to meet their death. The fear of death hangs in the air. Animals sweat fear. They can smell it in other animals and in humans. One must ask: Can they differentiate between the fear of other animals and humans? Is the sweat of our fear more pungent than that of a fellow cow? Or, is the smell of fear in animals more rank, more penetrating, more urgent? And if so, is this their language?

Ten years later in his novel *The Age of Iron*, we encounter a wonderful passage. The novel is a letter, written by a woman, a former professor and scholar of Romantic literature, who is dying of cancer, to her daughter, who now lives in the United States. In this novel there are many animals. There is the faithful dog that keeps company to Vercueil, a wino, homeless man, who is invited to move in with the dying Mrs. Curren. But there are also her cats and the stray dogs that visit Mrs. Curren when she sleeps in the park, as a homeless person, and acknowledge her dying and leave her in peace, in contrast to the kids who attempt to torture her and beat her as she lies on the ground moribund. Early in the book there is a very graphic description of the decapitation of chickens that parallels the earliest memory about the de-tongued chickens in his childhood. Still, the passage I want to focus on reads: "One must love what is nearest. One must love what is to hand, as a dog loves."[17] It is irresistible to hear echoes of Heidegger's differentiation between *zu-handen* and *vor-handen*. Derek Attridge, who has written a fascinating book on Coetzee's work, also hears echoes, if only unconscious ones, of Heidegger. Attridge thinks that Mrs. Curren's attempt to let go is analogous to Heidegger's notion of *Gelassenheit*.[18] The book ends when Mrs. Curren asks Vercueil, "Is it time?" The question is about whether it is time for her to die. The homeless man will do her a favor, as had been agreed earlier. She lies down, he lies next to her and holds her with "mighty force, so that the breath went out of me [Mrs. Curren] in a rush."[19] In her letter, she notes that as he lies next to her, for the first time she did not smell him. She smelled nothing. Was she unafraid? Was he unafraid? Do resignation and peacefulness have no smell? When we are happy, do we not smell it? Or do we simply lack a certain smell?

In his 1994 novel *The Master of Petersburg*, a fictionalization of Fyodor Dostoevsky's life, we hear the voice of a dog, or the distant barking of a dog in the guise of a human call, the voice of a son. Ivanov, a character in the novel, is woken up thinking he hears the calling of his son, Pavel, but as he comes out of his slumber, he realizes it is a dog howling in the distance.

> The dog howls again. No hint of empty plains and silver light: a dog, not a wolf; not his son. Therefore? Therefore he must throw off his lethargy! *Because* it is not his son he must not go back to bed but must get dressed and answer the call. If he expects his son to come as a thief in the night, and listens only for the call of the thief, he will never see him. If he expects his son to speak in the voice of the unexpected, the will never hear him. As long as he expects what he does not expect, what he does not expect will not come. Therefore—paradox within paradox, darkness swaddled in darkness—he must answer to what he does not expect.[20]

Ivanov goes to the dog, which has a chain tangled in one of its forelegs. "At his approach the dog retreats as far as it can, whining. It flattens its ears, prostrates itself, rolls on its back. A bitch. He bends over it, unwinds the chain. Dogs smell fear, but even in the cold he can smell this dog's rank terror. He tickles it behind the ear. Still on its back, it timidly licks his wrist."[21] He leaves the dog and does not free it from its chain. Yet, he is haunted by his failure to aid the dog. The dog could be an omen, a sign; the dog could stand in for something else. After all, he had thought the dog was his son calling him from his sleep. The text proceeds:

> He suspects he will not save the dog, not this night nor even the next night, if there is to be a next night. He is waiting for a sign, and he is betting (there is no grander word he dare use) that the dog is not the sign, is not a sign at all, is just a dog among many dogs howling in the night. But he knows too that as long as he tries by cunning to distinguish things that are things from things that are signs he will not be saved. That is the logic by which he will be defeated; and feeling its iron hardness, he is at his wits' end, like a dog on a chain that breaks the teeth that gnaw it.[22]

Here it is important to pause and notice that there are two moments of identification, which are matched by two moments of annunciation. Dogs smell fear, but it is Ivanov who smells the dog's "rank terror." The dog is tethered to a chain, in a stormy, dark, and cold night, abandoned twice, and fearful. Ivanov, in turn, feels as though he were tethered to the chain of the iron logic of the quandary of waiting for sings: the paradox of the annunciation, what Derrida calls the messianic. One can't wait for the messiah, for the messiah will come in the darkness of the night, unannounced, under the guise of the unexpected. Yet, not to look for signs is also to be unguarded to the arrival of the forthcoming, of the expected. The dog is not a sign for anything else, not his son, not the embodiment of ultimate responsiveness to the ethical appellation of the other. The dog is the dog, howling in the night. It is the dog terrified, suffering, hurt, barking, urging, requesting. The dog stands for the irreducible call of suffering, but also for the dog as a dog. The dog is this dog. It is to this dog that Ivanov has a duty. A dog whose howl is not heeded is one who suffers the disgrace of neglect.

Another of Coetzee's creation, David Lurie, the central character in his 1999 novel *Disgrace*, also communes with dogs. In Lurie's case, he communes with them at the end of their lives. Here we also come across the affirmation that dogs know their coming fate. Lurie works at an animal shelter, but also at a place where people bring the pets they can't provide for. He is in charge of putting them to sleep, and then disposing of their bodies. Lurie's, writes Coetzee, "whole being is gripped by what happens in the theatre. He is convinced the dogs know their time has come. Despite the silence and the painlessness of the procedure, despite the good thoughts that Bev Shaw thinks and that he tries to think, despite the airtight bags in which they tie the newmade corpses, the dogs in the yard smell what is going on inside. They flatten their ears, they droop their tails, as if they too feel the *disgrace* of dying."[23] Lurie learns to let himself be licked by these condemned and sentenced dogs: "Why should a creature with the shadow of death upon it feel him flinch away as if its touch were abhorrent?" A double disgrace, of having to die in this way, put down this way, and of having to be rejected as if it were unpleasant and disgusting. Lurie extends his hand and lets himself be touched by the love, or pleading, of dogs, which love what is present at hand, what is nearest.

It is in *Disgrace*, however, that Coetzee makes a parallel that has been very controversial, especially in its fullest expansion in *The Lives of Animals*, namely the analogy between what happened in concentration camps and what happens in slaughterhouses, or abattoirs. People bring their dogs to him because they do not know how to make provisions for them. There are too many. Dogs suffer from their own fertility. "When people bring a dog in they do not say straight out, 'I have brought you this dog to kill,' but that is what is expected: that they will dispose of it, make it disappear, dispatch it to oblivion. What is being asked for is, in fact, *Lösung* (German always to hand with an appropriately blank abstraction): sublimation, as alcohol is sublimed by water, leaving no residue, no aftertaste."[24] The work of disposing these dogs is one of *loesen*, of disappearing them, or taking care of them, of resolving them as a problem, and turning them into nothing. They are incinerated. In order to do that, their bodies have to be broken, their bones crushed and bent so that they fit in the chute of the ovens. Lurie finds the way their bodies are crushed and mangled abhorrent, hurtful. He finds this thoughtlessness, urgency, efficaciousness, and diligence disgraceful, dishonorable, and appalling. He takes on the role of also incinerating their remains, their corpses. "Why has he taken on this job . . . it would be enough to drop off the bags at the dump and drive away. For the sake of the dogs? But the dogs are dead; and what do dogs know of honour and dishonour anyway? For himself, then. For his idea of the world, a world in which men do not use shovels to beat corpses into a more convenient shape for processing."[25] Earlier in this passage of the book, Lurie asks himself about why he has become so sensitive to the suffering of this condemned animals: "Although in an abstract way he disapproves of cruelty, he cannot tell whether by nature is cruel or kind. He is simply nothing. He assumes that people from who cruelty is demanded in the line of duty, people who work in slaughterhouses, for instance, grow carapaces over their souls. Habit hardens: it must be so in most cases, but it does not seem to be so in his. He does not seem to have the gift of hardness."[26]

Disgrace, it can be argued, talks about four forms of disgrace, which I will discuss at greater length in the appendix to this chapter: the disgrace of a teacher who refuses to acknowledge and most importantly fails to apologize for his transgressions of certain protocols, the disgrace of the protagonist's daughter through rape, the disgrace of animal mass killing, and the disgrace of colonial/postcolonial history. Father, daughter, (post)colonial subjects, and animal (in this case, dogs) are disgraced. The dishonor, however, of the animals comes from the way in which they are *lösen*, resolved, dissolved, and solved into a nonproblem. Their disgrace is their killing. More specifically, the disgrace comes from the realization that their way of being disposed of has no effect on their executors. Their extermination does not enter the moral world, except perhaps that of Lurie.

J. M. Coetzee came to the attention of philosophers when he gave the 1996–97 Tanner Lectures: "The Lives of Animals" were lectures within lectures: lecturing about someone lecturing.[27] In them Coetzee introduced us to one of his most enduring creations, Elizabeth Costello, a fiction writer. These lectures, however, are very philosophical. As metafictional exercises, they are also metaphilosophical, that is, about the limits of philosophy. The first lecture is entitled "The Philosopher and the Animals," and the second is "The Poet and the Animals." The lectures, however, read like philosophical or Platonic dialogues. There are references to all kinds of philosophers, from Aristotle, Aquinas, Descartes, Bentham, Kant, Midgley, to Regan and Nagel. There are philosophical arguments about the putative ontological difference between animals and humans. One way to think about these lectures is to say that they are arguments against the academically imposed limits of philosophy, and the virtues of poetry and fiction. While philosophy is judged wanting, poetry is celebrated. While the former enthrones humans in an ontological and rationalistic exceptionalism, cutting us off from the ethical challenge of other animals, the latter does not just offer us ways to imagine others, but even provides us with ways to immerse ourselves phenomenologically in other life-worlds, even animal life-worlds. Still, Elizabeth Costello does not seem to carry the day. She is portrayed as having lost the philosophical argument, even if she may have won on the battlefield of the ancient struggle between poetry and philosophy. The *Lives of Animals* lectures went onto be incorporated, without the bibliographical apparatus which had made them even more of a genre oddity, in the book entitled *Elizabeth Costello*, which in its British edition was subtitled *Eight Lessons*. The "eight lessons" makes reference to the fact that the chapters that make up the book originated in lectures Coetzee gave at different times in different places on different occasions.

An even remotely fair engagement with *The Lives of Animals* and the way they fit in within the book *Elizabeth Costello* is beyond the scope of this chapter. Every page is full of extremely important philosophical and literary insights on the animal question.[28] I will, however, focus on two aspects of these richly suggestive lectures, or chapters, in *Elizabeth Costello*. The first concerns the comparison between what goes on in the slaughterhouses that feed the wealthy nations of the world and concentration camps, and the second concerns what Coetzee via Costello calls the "sympathetic imagination."[29]

The first lecture, entitled "The Philosophers and the Animals" begins, interestingly enough, with a reference to Kafka's story "A Report to an Academy" that tells of an educated ape, Red Peter, who delivers a lecture before a learned society. Costello claims that she feels like Red Peter, and more acutely now, as she is about to talk about animals and our dealings with them. The lecture turns quickly to preparing the "ground for the comparison" that she is about to make. She claims that the crime of the Nazis was to "treat people like animals."[30] The language of the stockyard, slaughterhouses, and abattoirs echoes loudly in our moral censure of the Nazis: butchers, they killed the Jews and Gypsies like sheep in the slaughterhouses. Elizabeth Costello then claims, and this commands lengthy quotation:

> Let me say it openly: we are surrounded by an enterprise of degradation, cruelty and killing which rivals anything that the Third Reich was capable of, indeed dwarfs it, in that ours is an

> enterprise without end, self-generating, bringing rabbits, rats, poultry, livestock ceaselessly into the world for the purpose of killing them. And to split hairs, to claim that there is no comparison, that Treblinka was so to speak a metaphysical enterprise dedicated to nothing but death and annihilation while the meat industry is ultimately devoted to life (once its victims are dead, after all, it does not burn them to ash or bury them but on the contrary cuts them up and refrigerates and packs them so that they can be consumed in the comfort of our homes) is a as little consolation to those victims as it would have been—pardon the tastelessness of the following—to ask the dead of Treblinka to excuse their killers because their body fat was needed to make soap and their hair to stuff mattresses with.[31]

I will not attempt to engage the question whether in fact the modern slaughterhouses for the carnivorous diets of the world are at all comparable to concentration camps in terms of what is here referred to as "the metaphysical" difference, namely that one is dedicated to killing and death, while the other is dedicated to life and nourishment. We could take recourse to Michel Foucault's concept of the biopolitical and make plausible the claim that slaughterhouses and concentration camps are not different qualitatively, that is, metaphysically, but that they lie within a continuum within which death is life and life is death. Nor will I attempt to engage the question of whether the mass killing of humans as a deliberate extermination is at all comparable to the mass killing of cattle, chickens, and pigs. Instead, I will focus on what I take to be Costello's point in making the comparison, as unsustainable and provocative as it may be.

Costello, I think, is interested in what makes Treblinka—a metonymic for the Holocaust—such a singular event, one charged with moral and theological connotations. For Costello, the issue is how it was allowed to happen, not that it happened, but that it could happen with so little protest from the German people. This is what is so horrifying, namely that there was not just ignorance, but a willful, deliberate, sought out, constructed, and elaborated ignorance. Costello avers: "In Germany, we say, a certain line was crossed which took people beyond the ordinary murderousness and cruelty of warfare into a state that we can only call sin."[32] In fact, the sin here is one of ignorance. People in the vicinity of Treblinka claimed that they did not know what was going on in the concentration camps, notwithstanding all the rumors and evidence. They said, it is claimed, that "while in a general way they might have guessed what was going on, they did not know for sure; said that, while in a sense they might have known, in another sense they did not know, could not afford, for their own sake."[33] They would not know because knowing would have exposed them to a moral command, a moral urgency to do something. "They lost their humanity, in our eyes, because of certain willed ignorance on their part."[34] It was ignorance that they imposed upon themselves in order to preserve themselves from the moral hazard of having to respond. Evidently, we must ask of Costello/Coetzee: What is worse morally, more ethically reprehensible? To will oneself into ignorance, or to know and not respond? But not responding is already a response. Not responding is a form of response even as it averts once's moral face away from the tragedy, the suffering, the killing taking place. Here we have to return to Coetzee's discussion of Gordimer's character Rosa. The issue is to be able to bring back into the moral ambit the question of these killings, of these deaths.

Later in the lecture Costello takes us closer to what lurks behind the comparison between the slaughterhouses of the overfed and the extermination camps of the racially pure. "The particular horror of the camps, the horror that convinces us that what went on there was a crimes against humanity, is not that despite a humanity shared with their victims, the killers treated them like lice. *That is too abstract.* The horror is that the killers refused to think themselves into the place of their victims, as did everyone else."[35] The horror is that the killers had utterly failed to sympathize with their victims. Their moral imagination failed because they failed to even attempt to think about what it must have been like to live in the squalor of those camps and to know that when one became infirm and useless, one would go up in smoke and fall to the ground as ash. The Nazi Germans horrify Costello/Coetzee because they did not say "It is I who am in that cattle car," but instead said, "It must be the dead who are being burned today, making the air stink and falling in ash on my cabbages."[36] What failed here was sympathy, which turns us away from the objects in the horizon of consciousness and toward the subject itself—the agent of sympathy. The failure of the moral imagination, the failure to extend sympathy to the condemned of the extermination camps, victims of the *Lösung*, that was exhibited by the people living around Treblinka is about them, it is about their own decision to move themselves outside the space of moral reason. Costello/Coetzee, I think, are suggesting that when we fail to even ask about what goes in the abattoirs of our culture, we are committing a similar horror: we fail to sympathize, to imagine ourselves in the position of those suffering—wailing, whimpering, reeking-with-terror animals.

We have already made a transition to the issue of the "sympathetic imagination." Costello, still within the first lecture, claims that there are "no bounds to the sympathetic imagination."[37] In order to illustrate she adduces the case of the fictional character she created in her hypothetical novel *The House on Eccles Street*, which had brought her fame. In this novel she thinks her way into the existence of Marion Bloom, a character that is alluded to by Joyce in *Ulysses*, but that Joyce certainly did not flesh out. If Costello could think her way into a nonexistent fictional character, in fact, to invent her with a complex and detailed subjectivity, why can't we think our way into the existence of existing beings? Costello then affirms: "If I can think my way into the existence of a being who has never existed, then I can think my way into the existence of a bat, or a chimpanzee or an oyster, any being with whom I share the substrate of life."[38] The sympathetic imagination, however, is not just about imaging our way into the lives of beings with whom we share life. This imagination has the function not of bringing us close to the idea of the animal. It is not about the animal itself, or the animal qua animal. It is about what happens between the animal and that person who imagines themself in the place of the animal. The sympathetic imagination is relational, but it returns to the subject from which it is projected.

Poetry, claims Costello in her second lecture, appropriately entitled "The Poets and the Animals," is the most apt, perhaps the only, form in which the sympathetic imagination allows us not just to imagine animals, or other forms of life, but also to commune with them in such a way that what the poet produces is not a catalog of ideas about the animal, but "a record of an engagement with him [the animal]."[39] This engagement, furthermore, is not just at the level of ideas, or the conceptual, at the level of rights and duties, but at a phenomenological level. Poetry, and all fiction in general, allows to "body forth" the animal. Poetry, in contrast to philosophy, argues Costello/Coetzee, allows us to imagine other animals in a unique way, namely by bodying their existences. Poetry and fiction allow us to world a corporeal and material animal world in relationship. Zoopoetics is a corporeal worlding of companionship between nonhuman and human animals, between putatively rational and allegedly irrational animals. Zoopoetics discloses for us the worlding of animal companionship. Zoopoetics also reveals to us that animals, pace Heidegger, are not world-poor because their world is our world, and our world has been formed with and through them.[40]

In his 1995 *Granta* essay "Meat Country," written in Austin, Texas, while Coetzee was a visiting professor there, he wrote: "The question of whether we should eat meat is not a serious question . . . Asking whether human beings should eat meat is on the same level of logic as posing the question, 'Should we have words?' We have words; the question is being posed in words; without words there would be no question. So if there is going to be any question at all, it will have to be a different question, one I have not begun to frame."[41] In the *Lives of Animals*, Costello claims, "The question to ask should not be: Do we have something in common—reason, self-consciousness, a soul—with other animals? (with the corollary that, if we do not, then we are entitled to treat them as we like, imprisoning them, killing them, dishonoring their corpses)."[42] Costello does not tell us, when discussing "The Philosophers and the Animals," what the question that we should ask is. The animal question is not about asking the right question, she seems to be suggesting. Rather, it is about poeticizing with them, through them, feeling their pain, not because we can know what that pain is, but because by imagining that unique, embodied suffering, we can be different, we can form part of a different world in which all suffering can be part of the moral ambit.

Fall from Grace: Appendix

By the time J. M. Coetzee was awarded the Nobel Prize in Literature in 2003 I had been already a long time devotee. I had devoured his *Waiting for the Barbarians* and *The Age of Iron*, had been totally enthralled by his autobiographical works, *Boyhood* and *Youth*, but *Disgraced* occupies a special place because it is the one about which I have had several very serious discussions with friends and students. In fact, one of those students who knew about my passion for Coetzee gave me as a gift the Penguin edition of Coetzee's Nobel Prize lecture. He inscribed it with the following dedication: "To Eduardo: Maybe it will make more sense the second time. With many thanks, as always, Martin." Martin Woessner, who went on to write a wonderful essay on Coetzee and philosophy,[43] and I had gone back and forth on what Coetzee's really weird lecture, "He and His Man," could mean when we had read it online. It opens with a quote from Daniel Defoe's *Robinson Crusoe*. I think that the text has four layers, made up of four standpoints: there is the standpoint of Crusoe's parrot, referred to as the "he" in the title. There is Crusoe, who is "his man." There is the standpoint of the fictions that Crusoe would have postulated had he been his own author. And then there is, possibly, Coetzee's own standpoint, of which we only have a glimmer. The text is cryptic, to say the least. But I came to the conclusion that Coetzee was performing at least two ideas that guide his writing. One is that authors are extensions of other writers. Most authors are invented by the books they read, to paraphrase Jorge Luis Borges. We know that Coetzee has written sequels, prequels, and versions of books by Defoe and Dostoevsky. His books are populated by characters, which are self-conscious acts of ventriloquism. The second idea, that I think can be culled from the Nobel Lecture, is that readers cannot be allowed to be lulled into the deception that all fiction seeks to instigate. The literary contract in which an author creates a world and the reader enters it departs from the putative agreement that the author has surrendered control over the world they created and now it has become independent. This is the literary contract: the author surrenders her creation, the reader makes of it what he will. It belongs to the reader in the way in which we inherit God's creation. One of the distinct aspects of Coetzee's work is how it relentlessly, unapologetically, even violently, shocks the reader into the realization that they are active participants in the fiction that they seek to consume passively. Coetzee's work is continuously returning us to the scene of a primordial encounter in which author and reader are embarking on what is a moral voyage: an author assumes responsibility for a tradition, a particular literary project, a world, some characters, who then become the guide for the author. Great writers are those who let themselves be guided by their characters. Great readers are those who allow themselves to be challenged by the world that is offered to them, but only if they become participants in how the story is to be made sense of. By now, I have read this lecture several times, and every time I encounter a different meaning, and a new reading emerges.

 I begin with this reference to Coetzee's Nobel lecture as a way to preface my remarks about Coetzee's philosophical depth. Coetzee is a philosopher's writer. He is not a philosopher's writer just because his fiction is ethically dense, intricate, and provocative. He is also an author who has written extensively on other writers and their philosophical meaning and ethical import. Coetzee has five or six books of collected essays, ranging from African literature, to contemporary Latin American, North American, and European literature. His essays betray a remarkable knowledge and understanding of twentieth-century philosophy. He is also someone who has studied linguistics and even computer programming. Each one of his books is an experiment in form and technique. He has experimented, successfully, with the diary form, the travel journal, the colonial outpost official reportage, and the epistolary forms. For instance, his *Diary of a Bad Year* combines three different narratives, each running horizontally and simultaneously on each page. As someone who is thoroughly familiar with the work of Todorov, Eco, Roman Jakobson, and Derrida, Coetzee is an author who knows how to play form against content and content against form. It is thus not surprising that more philosophers are paying attention to his work.

I want to turn to Cynthia Willett's essay "Ground Zero for a Postmoral Ethics in J. M. Coetzee's *Disgrace* and Julia Kristeva's Melancholic"[44] as a way to foreground some key themes in Coetzee's zoopoetics: the fall from grace of humanity and dignified embodied existence. Let me begin by stating that I think I half agree and half disagree with Willet's reading. I agree with her reading of *Disgrace* as a novel that sketches a post-Holocaust ethics of alterity, an ethics that is appropriately and succinctly captured in an earlier title of this essay, "Ethics of the Dog-Man," and which becomes even more evident in the provocative title it carries now as a published essay. On the other hand, I disagree with her attempt to use Kristeva to get us to an ethics of responsibility. Most of the analytical work in Willett's text was accomplished without Kristeva's philosophical apparatus. In fact, let me offer the following proforma argument: Kristeva's work runs counter to what Coetzee is trying to accomplish in this text. Coetzee is one of the most cerebral and anti-Freudian writers one can read today. This is not to say that there is no historical memory and unconscious and that his characters do not live out the dramas of suffered traumas. Coetzee's works are replete with psychic traumas, all of which have scarred psyches, both individual and collective. But his works are also populated by mangled, tortured, raped, desecrated, and disgraced bodies. Bodies that not accidentally tend to be those of women who have been raped, tortured, seduced, or who have succumbed to cancer and the allegorical terminal diseases that consume the bodies of women in colonial situations. In Coetzee's works the skin of human bodies is an evanescent surface on which colonial and postcolonial history has left its indelible mark. Through our suffering flesh we can see to our scarred souls. We are wounded animals, and like dogs, we whimper and lick our wounds. His fiction seems to say that we need neither Freud nor Lacan to see the evidence of wounded souls. Thus, I concur with Willett when she claims that "the novel [*Disgrace*] may well aim to expand our moral sentiment and, as it does so, call upon a nearly sublime duty to ourselves in regard to animals, but no standard moral element (neither moral sympathy nor Kantian reason) accounts for the full ethical force of the novel."[45] But I dissent when she claims "Kristeva and Coetzee belong together because they both pose the search for ethical meaning in the context of a deep and abiding solitude, one that leaves the subject a stranger in the world."[46]

In fact, I would argue that *Disgrace* is precisely about how the full *grace* of our humanity shines luminously when we respond to the ethical appellation of the other, when we return to ourselves from the other, through the other. This is precisely the ethics that Willett alludes to in the title of her paper, namely the ethics of those who let themselves be guided by the "pedagogy of the animal"—to allude to Kelly Oliver's book on this very subject[47]—who live close to their corporeality and reveal in their utter vulnerability that ethics is always a gift, from the other to oneself.

In order to make good on my proforma argument, I must offer, if only in brief, an overview of what I take to be *Disgrace*'s moral axes. The novel is deliberately entitled *Disgrace*, and the ambiguity in the title is also deliberate. Is *disgrace* here a verb or a noun? Does the title name a state or something that has been done? Something or someone may be a disgraced, but only after someone has been disgraced by someone or by a situation. Disgrace is relational and it leaves its trace. In *Disgrace*, we begin from a state of disgrace after having been disgraced, and from there, we ascend to ethical grace, to the gift of integral humanity. This, I postulate, is the moral trajectory of the novel. There are four states of disgrace, four acts of disgracing that lead to that state of disgrace, and four correlate paths of ascent that lead to grace by way of moral redemption. The first state of disgrace is that of ethical insouciance and sexual arrogance; as such, it is already a relational state of disgrace and disgracing. The second state of disgrace is also a relational state of disgrace. It is the disgrace of rape, the rape of the daughter before her vanquished, neutralized, and wounded father. The disgraced is raised to a higher power precisely because it is a rape before the "white" father who is not able to do anything. The third state of disgrace is that of the dogs who are abandoned to their "extermination" (*Lösung*) because humans cannot be bothered by them, by their numbers. "There are simply too many of them" (142). This disgrace is that of a perfunctory and officious death—thoughtless death. The fourth state of disgrace I will discuss later on.

Coetzee's novel begins, very tellingly, with the protagonist visiting his customary prostitute—-incidentally, Coetzee has written one of the best reviews of Gabriel Garcia Marquez's last novel, *Memorias de mis Putas Tristes* (*Memories of my Melancholy Whores*).[48] We are told that this weekly arrangement has allowed David Lurie, our protagonist, to "solve the problem of sex." David, we find out, has a putative "intimate" relationship in which Soraya, his prostitute, knows a lot about him, his needs, and his temperament. We also find out that he knows nothing about her, but he speculates that she may be a mother, because her body bears the traces of giving birth. One day he sees her walking with two boys. She is holding their hands. She is indeed a mother. And she has a life that he knows nothing about. He follows her, until he makes eye contact. Something is exchanged in that moment of eye contact. The next time they meet for their weekly session, Soraya announces that she has to go away to take care of her dying mother and that she does not know when she may be back. In fact, she disappears and has quit the escort service through which David had contracted her. He tries another "call girl" who is also called Soraya. But he is not satisfied. What does he do? He hires a private detective to track down his first Soraya. His detective finds her. He now has her telephone number. He calls her at her home and says: "This is David. How are you? When can I see you again?" (9). She answers that she does not know him and then adds, "You are harassing me in my own house. I demand you will never phone me here again, never." And then the text of Coetzee's novel proceeds, but we are not sure whether this is the author or David: "*Demand*. She meant *command*. Her shrillness surprises him: there has been no intimation of it before. But then, what should a predator expect when he intrudes into the vixen's nest, into the home of her cubs. He puts down the telephone. A shadow of envy passes over him for the husband he has never seen"(10).

I think these first ten pages of the novel introduce us to a disgraceful and disgraced man. I am not saying that David Lurie is disgraceful or disgraced because he is with a prostitute, or because he has resorted to a prostitute in order to solve the "sex problem." I think it is possible to have honorable relations, even relationships, with prostitutes. It is a disgrace that some women may have to resort to prostitution, but they are not disgraced or disgraceful. David Lurie is disgraced and disgraceful because he is caught solipsistically within the circle of his own desire. In fact, his desire is unearned. He lives off the effortless and paid-for simulacra of intimacy. His tenderness is bought. When he caresses her, he is caressing his own plenipotency. That he refuses to allow her privacy, her decision not to be with him in their artificial contract, is further proof of his arrogance, his hubris. It is this very same selfishness, solipsism, hubris, and plenipotency of unearned desire that blossoms into the scandal that leads to his fall from "professional" grace.

David Lurie proceeds to seduce one of his students, one who is not "the best student but not the worst either: clever enough, but unengaged" (11). Upon rereading the novel in order to engage Willett's provocative paper, it became even more noticeable to me how much of what transpires between David and Melanie, the "clever but unengaged" student, is less a seduction and more a thrusting of himself upon her. In one section, we have the description of what many of us would surely consider a rape. Still, we have the same situation as with his prostitute. He imposes himself upon his student and uses his professorial privilege to track her down, to find out her phone and home address. And then, after she begins to miss and fail his class because of her not coming to his class, he resorts to berating her for not doing her schoolwork. In an analogous fashion to how he tracked down and called "his" prostitute, he calls Melanie to his office and asks: "When will you return to my class-room to be my student?"

David Lurie is fired not because he has had an affair with one of his students, but because he refuses to publicly apologize, to confess that he abused his power, that he did something inappropriate. In any event, the description of the disciplinary hearing that Lurie faces is an amazing analysis of the vacuous morality that prevails in bureaucratic institutions. And we are left wondering who is more morally debunked: his colleagues who fail to see through the moral transgression, or Lurie who now hides behind his refusal to defend or give an account of himself.

There is a passage in this section of the novel, the section when Melanie's boyfriend confronts Lurie and then vandalizes his car, which requires that he spend "six hundred rand," that is significant. It is significant because it is the first time when we get a glimpse of the novel's deep theme. The passage reads: "After this *coup de main* [the vandalizing of his car] Melanie keeps her distance. He is not surprised: *if he has been shamed, she is shamed too*" (31, italics added). He has been shamed by the boyfriend, who through his act of vandalism has unmasked him as a pederast, as a seducer, as a sexual harasser. He has been shamed because his transgressions have been made public. But how has Melanie been shamed too? She has been shamed by his sexual predation. She has been disgraced by his use of his power and privilege over her. She has been shamed by his shameful behavior. He has dragged her down with him. A close reading reveals too that an attempt to fault Coetzee for not offering a strong female character to resist Lurie's sexual advances would be a misplaced criticism. The fact is that Melanie did try to stay away. She said no! She neither sought nor accepted with either a verbal yes or a physical embrace his sexual advances.

David Lurie, professor of English Romantic literature, twice divorced, frequenter of prostitutes, seducer of his own students, is a disgrace, is disgraceful, and is a disgracer of the humanity in him and those of others. His irresponsible desire, what I called his unearned desire, sequesters him in the prison of an ethical solipsism that he refuses to escape, that is, until he is forced by others to abandon it.

I have saved the fourth state of disgrace for last because it is a state in which all three states of disgrace I have discussed so far gather into a stage of historical, psychic, and embodied disgrace, and this is the disgrace of the inheritance of coloniality. *Disgrace* is a postcolonial novel is as much as it is a novel about the *(post)coloniality of power*—David Lurie lives his life on a stage that is demarcated by South African colonial history. His daughter's rape, by three black youths, is allegorical of the kind of violence that Lewis Gordon is trying to make sense of in his essay "Tragic Revolutionary Violence,"[49] which Willett quotes in her essay. This is the disgrace of the (post)colonial condition, about which Coetzee has written so much: that humanity has to be wrested from conditions of oppression, dehumanization, and disgracefulness by a violence that reduces both the colonizer and the colonized to further acts of disgrace. It is a disgrace that the flesh of the colonized and the colonizer is marked by the violence that reduces both to hate, resentment, retaliation, and counterretaliation. Coetzee points in the direction of South African colonial history softly, not in order to exculpate the violence of the colonized against the colonizer. Perhaps the rape of white flesh by black flesh is too legible and discernable an allegory not to allow us to fall into the trap of reinscribing the racist supremacist expectations. But Coetzee's narrative truncates this possible line of disavowal. Lucy, David Lurie's daughter, refuses to fall into and reopen the cycle of violence. She is in fact the true conscience of this novel. Not because her body is the surface on which men inscribe their plenipotency, but because she is the one that rises above her anger to love the child in her, and to learn to love from within the very condition that is fraught with all the danger of the coloniality of male power and white privilege. We are disgraced by the aftermath of colonialism, and we live in a condition of disgrace so long as we continue to trade in the currency bequeathed to us by its violence. Colonial disgrace gathers in itself the disgrace of male sexual violence, of female sexual victimization, and the many genocides and exterminations that the hubris as well as the moral indolence of the colonizer breed and necessitate.

At one point, as Lucy is telling her father David what she has to acquiesce to in order to be able to retain her house in her land, and thus live out her own dream. She says: "Yes, I agree, it is humiliating. But perhaps that is a good point to start from again. Perhaps that is what I must learn to accept. To start at ground level. With nothing. Not with nothing but. With nothing. No cards, no weapons, no property, no rights, no dignity. Like a dog. Yes, like a dog" (205). Suffice it to say that Lucy refuses to file a report with the police, but she also refuses to leave her house.

And how does this novel end? David Lurie, our protagonist, returns to work in the animal hospital where he takes up the work of euthanizing and incinerating the bodies of the dogs that he has put down. The last one to be put to death is the one dog with which he has developed a relationship, "Dreipoot"—three feet. Bev, the woman who runs the hospital asks, "I thought you would save him for another week, . . . are you giving him up? . . . Yes, I am giving him up" (220).

When David gives up Dreipoot, he has acknowledged a relationship, his relationship to this dog that brought him tenderness and licked his face and to which he sang and played the banjo. The disgrace that dogs smell in our shame is occasioned by the thoughtlessness, the officiousness, the perfunctory killing that does not attend to the appellation of the other (142-143). Would the concentration camps have taken place if gay people, Gypsies, and Jews had been "given up" by someone, some who have cared for them, whether in life or in death?

The ethics of the dog-man is the ethics of taking responsibility for all of our others, with whom and through whom we are raised from the disgrace state we suffer, because of the coloniality of history, the solipsism of our desires, and our disregard of other animals, to the grace of our full humanity—the grace of being a "good person" who has learned to be a good animal, as Adorno commanded with his categorical imperative of the good animal (216).

Chapter 2

Political Bestiary

On the Uses of Violence[1]

Omnis mundi creatura
Quasi liber et pictura
Nobis est et speculum

—Alan of Lille, *De Incarnatione Christi*[2]

The Bestiary

The most basic definition of a bestiary is a book of beasts, a kind of encyclopedia or compendium of the descriptions, and in many cases, pictorial representations, of fantastic, unusual, but sometimes quite pedestrian and common animals. The bestiaries did expose us to the exotic, but they did not stop there; they sought above all to offer a catalog of God's creation with a key to unlock its moral message. Bestiaries were eminently religious and spiritual works. The bestiary flourished during the twelfth and thirteenth centuries, and most of the extant ones were produced in England. They were as popular as the Bible and some of the breviaries that were also produced during the late medieval period.[3]

Bestiaries, however, had a pedagogical-spiritual function. They were used to educate Christians about the beneficence of God's creation, its moral design, and how that design was evident in all that was living. Thus, a monk reading and contemplating these beautifully produced books would be reading it at three different levels: first, the monk would read the bestiary literally, in terms of what it said about certain animals and the etymologies of their names; second, the text would be read as establishing a link between the Old and New Testaments, and how those links were embodied in the virtues and qualities of certain animals; finally, on a third level, the texts would be read so as to decipher the moral lessons that should become legible by linking these intertextualities. The theological, pedagogical, and spiritual function of the bestiary was succinctly formulated by the thirteenth-century English theologian Thomas of Cobham (c. 1236), when he wrote: "The Lord created the various creatures with different natures, not only for the sustenance of men but also for their instruction. There is no creature in which we cannot see some characteristic which leads us to imitate the Lord or some characteristic which induces us to avoid the devil; for the whole world is full of different animals, like a book filled with written words and sentences in which we can read what we should imitate or avoid."[4] Nature is God's book, and we just have to decipher its meanings and messages. The bestiary is an attempt to decipher the layered meanings of God's book in terms of animals. Yet, while the bestiary is a Christian device, its sources are far more ancient. In fact, the bestiary is the appropriation of an older practice. According to T. H. White, who translated *The Book of Beasts* from a twelfth-century Latin bestiary, the bestiaries' sources can be traced back to the ancient Greeks, specifically Herodotus, Aristotle, Pliny, Solinus, and Aelian.[5] White is surely right about these Greek thinkers having contributed to the tradition, but what is significant are the absences. He does not mention Homer, Plato, and Plutarch. In fact, before Aristotle could contribute to the development of what later became the *Physiologus*, Homer and Plato had already contributed to the foundations of what are in fact philosophical bestiaries. I would like to briefly discuss some key sections in Homer's *Odyssey* and some of Plato's dialogues that I take to be direct contributions to both the physiologus and the bestiary. I want to discuss these passages because of their overt ethico-political overtones.

Homer's Beasts

Odysseus begins the narration of his odyssey in book 9 of the *Odyssey* with the story of his encounter with Polyphemus, the Cyclops. Polyphemus is the son of Poseidon and the nymph Thoosa, who was child of Phorcys, lord of the barren sea. The story is well known. Odysseus and his crew land on the island where the race of the Cyclops lives. Odysseus visits the cave of Polyphemus, hoping to be offered hospitality, namely in the form of food and provisions for his voyage back to Ithaca. Here is what Homer tells us:

> We came to the land of the Cyclops race, arrogant lawless beings who leave their livelihood to the deathless god and never use their own hands to sow or plough; yet with no sowing and no ploughing, the crops grow for them—wheat and barley and grapes that yield wine from ample clusters, swelled by the showers of Zeus. They have no assemblies to debate in, they have no ancestral ordinances; they live in arching caves on the tops of hills, and the head of each family heeds no other, but makes his own ordinances for wife and children.[6]

This passage must be read with another one that occurs a few pages later, when Odysseus has introduced himself and in the name of Zeus asks for hospitality: "We of the Cyclops race care nothing for Zeus and for his aegis; we care for none of the gods in heaven, being much stronger ourselves than they are. Dread of enmity of Zeus would never move me to spare either you or your comrades with you, if I had no mind to it myself."[7] The Cyclops is your quintessential beast. They are living creatures, and thus, they are a sort of animal. They are above the human and below the gods, although they think themselves more powerful than the gods. They have no religion; no law—no ordinances—and most importantly, they do not cultivate the land, or create political and social alliances. They are lawless and pre-political, even anti-political. They are beastly precisely because they are lawless. They have no law, and they are outside the law and refuse to acknowledge any law. Their beastly nature is most dramatically manifested when the Cyclops proceeds to eat Odysseus's companions. So, he is both lawless and carnivorous, or rather anthropophagous. The beastly is that which both refuses the law and eats humans. The Cyclops, however, does not lack all *techne*, or technology. After all, the Cyclops has his sheep, which, as Odysseus narrates, he tends to with method and care. So, the Cyclops is a shepherd, but a lonely shepherd, an autarkic and lawless carnivore that has no fear of the gods, though he benefits luxuriously from the beneficence of the gods.

Polyphemus imprisons Odysseus and his companions, eating two of them each time he returns to the cave after pasturing his sheep. We know

52 | The Philosophical Animal

that Odysseus comes up with a plan to escape. The plan cannot involve killing the Cyclops, for otherwise they would be caught in the cave, which is closed by a giant rock humans cannot roll. The plan must involve making the Cyclops roll the rock, while also preventing him from seeking the aid of the other Cyclops. As readers may recall, the plan entails blinding the Cyclops, forcing him to leave the cave, to pasture his flock without sight. This is where Odysseus's next ploy comes in. When the Cyclops seeks to extract information from Odysseus, his name and where he came from, Odysseus tells him that his name is "Noman," "Noone," or "Nobody." As Adorno and Horkheimer have pointed out in their *Dialectic of Enlightenment*, this ruse has been metonymic of the relationship between nature and subjectivity.[8] To become subjects, we must deny our nature. I think that this reading is very plausible and insightful, but I want to offer another.[9]

At the heart of book 9 of the *Odyssey* is the juxtaposition between law and lawlessness, savagery and civility, the wild and the tame, the primitive and culture. And in the juxtaposition is the boundary that separates the two diametrically opposed worlds: the use of violence. Civilization is based on the proscription of violence and its sublimation and neutralization in ritual and through myth. To be human is to renounce violence, and in particular violence against other humans, and more specifically, to become human is to reject anthropophagi by entering into the circle of ritual and the sublimation of violence into sacred ritual. The Cyclops lack all of this, as they have absolutely no fear of Zeus. In this case, however, in order to survive before or against a lawless violence, humans themselves have to become lawless. Odysseus has to become no one, no man, that is, he has to abandon his fear of the gods, the interdictions against killing, by stepping outside the civilized order. To vanquish the Cyclops, Odysseus has to become like the Cyclops—he has to become no man. The Cyclops, thus, operates like a synecdoche for the lawless violence that is at the heart of the Greek political bestiary.

Plato's Bestiary

Plato's dialogues are full of allegories, metaphors, similes, and metonyms. One could argue that Plato's entire philosophy is captured in two key allegories. One is the allegory of the ring of Gyges, which is told in book 2 of the *Republic* (2.359a–2.360d). The ring of Gyges is a magical ring that allows whoever wears it to become invisible, sort of what happens with

Frodo when he wears the ring in Tolkien's *The Lord of Rings*. The question is whether we would chose to do either moral or immoral acts under the cover of invisibility. The moral of this allegory, or mythological device, is that morality must be based on something other than coercion or fear of retribution. We have to have an inner motivation toward morality. The other key allegory in Plato is also to be found in the *Republic*, and this is the allegory of the cave, which is probably one of the most descriptive and also metonymic allegories ever conceived. The allegory of the cave, as we know well, captures in one image Plato's ontology, epistemology, ethics, and ultimately, what he thinks philosophy is about. I want to suggest that there is yet another allegory in Plato's work that is as important, and this is what I will call the allegory of the philosophical dog. In fact, I would argue that we can discern a Platonic bestiary, that is, a catalog of beasts that Plato finds terrifying and objectionable. We can find references to this bestiary in the *Lysis*, the *Euthyphro*, the *Phaedrus*, the *Sophist*, the *Laws*, and most distinctly in the *Republic*. In the *Sophist*, an extremely important dialogue about the distinction between sophistry and philosophy, a dialogue that is pivotal in Plato's hagiography of Socrates, Plato compares the sophists to wolves. Let me quote:

> STRANGER [curiously, Plato does not assign a name to this speaker]: For all these reasons, Theatetus, we must admit that refutation is the greatest and chiefest of purifications, and he who has not been refuted, though he be the Great King himself, is in an awful state of impurity; he is uninstructed and deformed in those things in which he who would be truly blessed ought to be fairest and purest.
>
> THEATETUS: Very true.
>
> STRANGER: And who are the ministers of this art? I am afraid to say the Sophists.
>
> THEATETUS: Why?
>
> STRANGER: Lest we should assign to them too high a prerogative.
>
> THEATETUS: Yet the Sophist has a certain likeness to our minister of purification.

> STRANGER: *Yes, the same sort of likeness which a wolf, who is the fiercest of animals, has to a dog, who is the gentlest.* But he who would not be found tripping, ought to be very careful in this manner of comparisons, for they are most slippery things. Nevertheless, let us assume that the Sophists are the men. I say this provisionally, for I think that the boundary in dispute will prove to be an important one, should it ever be resolutely defended.[10]

Here the stranger is suggesting that the Sophists are comparable to the ministers of purification—those who help us detect error, deception, ignorance, deceit, and infamy—as wolves are to dogs. Evidently, wolves are fierce and not to be trusted, while dogs are both gentle and trustworthy. In the *Lysis*, an early dialogue, Socrates claims that he has a passion for friendship, to such an extent that he would prefer a friendship to the best cock or quail, nay, he would trade the best horse or dog for a good friend.[11] Socrates is willing to give up the best of the best, either a horse or a dog, for a good friend. So, the closest thing to a great, the greatest friend, is either a dog or a horse. In the *Euthyphro*, piety, as the art of attending to the gods, is compared to the training of dogs. If the former is for the benefit of the gods, namely piety, the other is to the benefit of the hunter. If one is for the benefit of the community, the other is for the benefit of the household. All of these comparisons and similes converge in the *Republic*, where the wolf is linked both to the Sophists and the dictator or tyrant, and the dog to the philosopher. The relevant passage in the *Republic* is in book 2, where Socrates compares the dog to the guardian of the state, that is, the philosopher:

> Would not he who is fitted to be a guardian, besides the spirited nature, need to have the qualities of a philosopher?
> I do not apprehend your meaning.
> The trait of which I am speaking, I replied, may be also seen in the dog, and is remarkable in the animal.
> What trait?
> Why, a dog, whenever he sees a stranger, is angry; when an acquaintance, he welcomes him, although the one has never done him any harm, nor the other any good. Did this never strike you as curious?

The point never struck me before; but I quite recognize the truth of your remark.

And surely this instinct of the dog is very charming; your dog is a true philosopher.

Why?

Why, because he distinguishes the face of a friend and of an enemy only by the criterion of knowing and not knowing. And must not an animal be a lover of learning who determined what is or is not friendly to him by the test of knowledge and ignorance?[12]

Much later in the *Republic*, Plato returns to the wolf, but now to compare it to the tyrant:

How then does the protector [of the state] begin to change into a tyrant? Clearly when he begins to do what the man is said to do in the tale of the Arcadian temple of Lycaean Zeus.

What tale?

The tale is that he who has tasted the entrails of a single human victim minced with the entrails of other victims is destined to become a wolf. Did you never hear it?

O yes.

And the protector of the people is like him; having a mob entirely at his disposal, he is not restrained from shedding the blood of kinsmen; by the favourite method of false accusation he brings them into court and murders them, making the life of man to disappear, and with unholy tongue and lips tasting the blood of his fellow citizens; some he kills and others he banishes, at the same time hinting at the abolition of debts and partition of lands: and after this, what will be his destiny? Must he not either perish at the hands of his enemies, or from being a man become a wolf—that is, a tyrant?

Inevitably.

This, I said, is he who forms a party against the owners of property.

The same.

After a while he is driven out, but comes back, in spite of his enemies, a tyrant full grown.

That is clear.

And if they are unable to expel him, or to get him condemned to death by a public accusation, they conspire to assassinate him secretly.

Yes, he said, that is their usual way.[13]

We can now see how a particular beast operates in Plato's bestiary. The wolf is the metonym for deception, deceit, fierceness, enmity, lawlessness, and predatory violence. More specifically still, the wolf is to the sophist as the dog is to the philosopher, as the tyrant is to the philosopher king. And even if the wolf may become a tyrant, the dog will never become a sovereign. The dog, in the guise of the philosopher is merely the guardian of the state, qua philosopher. Once the dog seeks to be more than that, it threatens to become a wolf. The philosopher is a faithful guardian of the state. The philosopher serves the sovereign by discerning between the enemies and friends of the state, something that the Sophist cannot and will not do.

Aristotle's Zoology

It would not be an understatement to claim that the scientific and philosophical study of animals begins with Aristotle. In fact, it has been claimed that science, as the methodical study of the causes of things and events, began with Aristotle. Before Aristotle wrote on ethics, politics, logic, and metaphysics, he had spent many years observing and gathering a wealth of information on different animals, from sea to airborne animals. Several of Aristotle's manuscripts from his fieldwork survive. In Latin they are known under the collective name of *Historia Animalium*, which sometimes is excerpted and published under the name of *Zoology*. This manuscript is made up of ten volumes. But in addition, we also have *Parts of Animals, Movement of Animals, Progression of Animals,* and *Generation of Animals*. In the *Corpus Aristotelicum* these works are listed under "Study of Nature." It is noteworthy that these works are collected next to those that also deal with the sky, the earth, as well as the soul, or *De Anima*. Aristotle's scientific works on the observation, classification, and chronicling of nature had an inordinate influence on what later became the tradition of the physiologus, which later is taken up in the Christian bestiary. Yet, this is not the place to go into any great detail about Aristotle's several volumes on animals. There are two things that I want to note that are important for our purposes here. First, in contrast to his teacher, Plato, Aristotle had worked closely for many years with animals, observing them, categorizing them, noting their differences and similarities. We could say that Aristotle was the Greek Darwin. Many of the treatises from his *Historia* and on *Generation of Animals* read like Darwin's journals and diary from his voyage on the Beagle. It is evident that Aristotle approached animals with a scientific attitude, which is less inclined to the fancies of imagination, flights of rhetoric, and loose similes. Yet, one of the reasons why Aristotle's zoological writings would be taken up, in many cases almost in plagiarized fashion, is that even Aristotle could not dispense with the inclination to rely on allegories, comparisons, parables, and morals. So, for instance, we can read in book 9 of *Historia Animalium*, in which Aristotle studies bees, wasps, and ants, the following: "Among the insect type of animals that are some of the most industrious, and to be compared with all the other animals, are the ant kind and the bee kind, also anthrines and wasps and virtually all that are kin to them . . . Now the working of the ants is on the surface for all to see, and how they all go on one path and put aside and store their food; for they work at night too when there is a full moon."[14] Aristotle devotes the next several pages to describing in the most surprising detail the behaviors of both ants and bees, which he holds evidently in high esteem. He talks about their work habits, their social structure and hierarchies, what they do when wasps attack them, whether they wage war on other species or only other bees or ants. Notwithstanding the descriptive and distanced language, Aristotle cannot but observe, or remark, on the well-ordered character of bee and ant societies. In fact, Aristotle repeatedly resorts to the language of praise, even encomium. Both bees and ants seem to personify discipline, respect, deference, frugality, cleanliness, and industriousness. While most of these works were devoted to an analysis of the structure and order of nature, Aristotle is also aiming at educating his readers about the virtues that we all should strive to inculcate in our fellow citizens and ourselves. In this way, animal behavior becomes a cipher for what we ought to strive to achieve among ourselves. Nature is a moral educator, or if not, then at the very least a moral text from which we can extract indispensable moral lessons.

While this is not a survey of what Greek and Roman philosophers had to say about animals that may have contributed to the development of the tradition of the physiologus and later the bestiary, I cannot not discuss very briefly Pliny the Elder and Plutarch, two key figures in the preservation and transmission of Aristotle's work on zoology. Pliny the Elder can be said to have invented the encyclopedia and the zoological compendium. His *Naturalis Historia*, or *Natural History*, is one of the few works to have survived in its entirety from the first century after the death of Christ. The work is made up of thirty-seven books, generally published in three thick volumes. The first books concern the physical description of the earth, as well as the mathematical theories that allow us to describe it. This is what we generally call cosmology. Books 3 through 6 deal with geography and the description of cultures. In these volumes, in fact, we find one of the earliest elaborations of the geographical theory of the races. Book 7 deals with the physiological description of humans. Books 8 through 11 deal with zoology. The next books deal with botany, agriculture, horticulture, and pharmacology, as well as mining and mineralogy. Pliny's *Natural History*—or the *History of Nature*, would be more accurate—is a veritable encyclopedia, gathering the most useful knowledge that was to be procured at the birth of our first millennium. For my purposes, I am interested in a particular passage in book 8 that describes elephants. Elephants are peculiar creatures, as they do not appear in the Hebrew Bible until quite late, yet they were used to personify and symbolize Christ.[15] In this way, we can see how Roman works about nature were appropriated and assimilated into a Christian sacred zoology and geography.

In discussing many of his topics, Pliny combines description with narratives that involve the particular animals, plants, or mineral under discussion. This is what today we would call intertextuality and web linking. So, in his discussion of elephants, Pliny moves back and forth between describing the behavior of elephants to recording stories where they appear. Here are two examples:

> Elephants always travel in a herd; the oldest leads the column and the next oldest brings up the rear. When going to ford a river they put the smallest in front, so that the bottom may not be worn away by the tread of the larger ones, thus increasing the depth of the water. Antipater states that two elephants employed for military purposes by King Antiochus were known to the public even by name; indeed they [the elephants] know their own names. It is a fact that Cato, although he has removed the names of military commanders from his *Annals*, has recorded that the elephant in the Carthaginian army that

was the bravest in battle was called the Syrian, and that it had one broken tusk. When Antiochus was trying to ford a river his elephant Ajax refused, though on other occasions it always led the line; thereupon Antiochus issued an announcement that the elephant that crossed should have the leading place and he rewarded Patrochus, who made the venture, with the gift of silver harness, an elephant's greatest delight, and with every other mark of leadership. The one disgraced preferred death by starvation to humiliation; for the elephant has a remarkable sense of shame, and when defeated shrinks from the voice of its conqueror, and offers him earth and foliage. Owing to their modesty, elephants never mate except in secret; the male at the age of five and the female at ten; and mating takes place for two years, on five days, so it is said, of each year and not more; and on the sixth day they give themselves a shower-bath in a river, not returning to the herd before. Adultery is unknown among them, or any of the fighting for females that is so disastrous to the other animals—though not because they are devoid of strong affection, for it is reported that one elephant in Egypt fell in love with a girl who was selling flowers, and (that nobody may think that it was a vulgar choice) who was a remarkable favourite of the very celebrated scholar Aristophanes."[16]

Pliny's elephants are paragons of moral virtue, which they have not by instinct but by self-reflection, a sense of modesty. Where there is modesty, that is, the possibility of shame, there is morality. For Pliny, elephants exhibit in the highest form the combination of both the elemental and elaborated dimensions of moral existence. These elephants exhibit shame, fear, courage, but also modesty, gratitude, and love. Above all, they know themselves not just in their shame or modesty, but also because they recognize their name. They know who they are because they recognize their name. They have a name and thus, they have a sense of "I."

Some of these themes are echoed in another extremely important source for the bestiary, Plutarch. Plutarch was a Roman historian, biographer, essayist, and moralist, who influenced the development of Christian neo-Platonism through his own works on Plato and Socrates. Among his numerous works we have fifteen volumes of what is called Plutarch's *Moralia*—or moral writings. These books cover everything from love, courage, and ire to whether sea or land animals are more rational, and whether it is acceptable to eat meat. There is a particularly wonderful essay that brings us full circle to Homer's Odysseus. The essay is presented as a dialogue among Circe, Odysseus, and Gryllus. Circe is the sorceress who turns Odysseus's crew into swine in book 10 of the *Odyssey*. As in book 10, Odysseus pleads before Circe to convert his men back to human form. In Plutarch's playful dialogue, his men refuse to be turned back to humans. Circe cannot turn them back if they do not want to be returned to their human form. Odysseus disbelieves Circe and asks to talk to them. Enter Gryllus, one of Odysseus's men who engages him in a most instructive discussion about why they would rather stay as swine. There are two particular passages that I want to briefly discuss. They are:

> GRYLLUS: At this moment, then, you are conceding the point that the soul of beasts has a greater natural capacity and perfection for the generation of virtue; for without command or instruction, "unsown and unploughed," as it were, it naturally brings forth and develops such virtue as its proper in each case.
>
> ODYSSEUS: And what sort of virtue, Gryllus, is ever found in beasts?
>
> GRYLLUS: Ask rather what sort of virtue is not found in them more than in the wisest men? Take first, if you please, courage, in which you take great pride, not even pretending to blush when you are called "valiant" and "sacker of cities." Yet you, you villain, are the man who by tricks and frauds has led astray men who knew only a straightforward, noble style of war and were unversed in deceit and lies; while on your freedom from scruple you confer the name of the virtue that is least compatible with such nefariousness. Wild beasts, however, you will observe, are guileless and artless in their struggles, whether against one another or against you, and conduct their battles with unmistakably naked courage under the impulse of genuine valour. No edict summons them, nor do they fear a writ of desertion. No, it is their nature to flee subjection; with their stout heart they maintain an indomitable spirit to the very end. Nor are they conquered even when physically overpowered; they never give up in their hearts, even while

perishing in the fray. In many cases, when beast are dying, their valour withdraws together with the fighting spirit to some point where it is concentrated in one member and resists the slayer with convulsive movements and fierce anger until, like a fire, it is completely extinguished and departs.

Beasts never beg or sue for pity or acknowledge defeat: lion is never slave to lion, or horse to horse through cowardice, as man is to man when he unprotestingly accepts the name whose root is cowardice. [Slavery (*doulei*) as though derived from "cowardice" (*deilin*)] And when men have subdued beasts by snares and tricks, such of them as are full grown refuse food and endure the pangs of thirst until they induce and embrace death in place of slavery.[17]

The passage is fairly transparent and does not require too much glossing. Animals, in contrast to humans, have a greater aptitude for virtue because they cannot deceive. Their relationship to virtue is not mediated by either calculation or fear. The following passage is also particularly important and it comes at the very end of the dialogue:

GRYLLUS: . . . I scarcely believe that there is such a spread between one animal and another as there is between man and man in the matter of judgement and reasoning and memory.

ODYSSEUS: But consider, Gryllus: is it not a fearful piece of violence to grant reason to creatures that have no inherent knowledge of God?

GRYLLUS: Then shall we deny, Odysseus, that so wise and remarkable a man as you had Sisyphus for a father[18]

In fact this last line should read: "If those who do not know God cannot possess reason, then you, wise Odysseus, can scarcely be descended from such a notorious atheist as Sisyphus." This is a very provocative ending because Plutarch is now making reference to the Cyclops whose bestiality and brutality were related to his lack of fear, or reverence, for the gods.

Animals, Plutarch seems to be suggesting, are more virtuous, not just because they lack the kind of calculative cunning that leads to duplicity, perfidy, and deception but also because they are without fear or knowledge of the gods. They are virtuous, or rather, they are moral despite their lack of fear of God. Put in a positive way, to be truly moral and virtuous requires that one act morally and virtuously from an inner motivation and not from fear or subordination. Plutarch's beasts are not just rational, but they are moral in the way Kant defined the moral worth of moral actions: namely in that they are done out of duty and respect for the moral law untethered to either threat or reward.

The Good Animal versus the Demonic Beast

At this point it would make sense to exegete the relevant entries in some bestiaries concerning some of the animals we have discuss thus far, namely the wolf, the dog, the bee, and the elephant. It is noteworthy that the longest entries in Latin and French bestiaries are devoted to these creatures, along with the horse.[19] But I will only discuss, briefly, the wolf, the dog, and the elephant. In the twelfth-century bestiary translated by White, we read that the wolf is so called from the Greek *lykos* because of their bite and because "they massacre anybody who passes by with a fury of greediness."[20] Wolves are known for "their rapacity, and for this reason we call prostitutes wolves, because they devastate the possession of their lovers."[21] Most interestingly, we read in this bestiary, "the devil bears the similitude of a wolf: he who is always looking over the human race with his evil eye, and darkly prowling round the sheepfolds of the faithful so that he may afflict and ruin their souls."[22] And "its eyes shine in the night like lamps because the works of the devil are everywhere thought to seem beautiful and salubrious, by darkened and fatuous human beings." [23]The power, abilities, and behavior of the devil, furthermore, are already anticipated in this creature that resembles it the most: "Because a wolf is never able to turn its neck backward, except with a movement of the whole body, it means that the devil never turns back to lay hold on repentance."[24] To be evil thus is not to be able to repent. The Christian wolf, in fact, resembles the Platonic wolf, which as we noted was compared to both the tyrant and the Sophists for their cunning and for their embellished and attractive use of rhetoric. The beauty of the eyes that shine in the darkness is similar to the beauty of the rhetorician that deceives the people.

As with Plato's philosophical dog, so with the Christian dog. For Plato, the dog embodied the truth of philosophy, namely the ability to distinguish the friend from foe of the polis and the sovereign. In the

Christian bestiary we read: "Now none is more sagacious than Dog, for he has more perception than other animals and he alone recognizes his own name. He esteems his master highly."[25] Dogs are known for their loyalty, to the point that they rather die than betray or abandon their masters. But their sagacity is based on reason. Dogs marry virtue with reason. The dog "shows his sagacity in following scent, as if enunciating a syllogism. 'Either it has gone this way,' says he to himself, 'or that way, or, indeed, it may have turned twisting in that other direction. But as it has neither entered into this road, nor that road, obviously it must have taken a third one!' And so, by rejecting error, Dog finds the truth."[26] This then makes almost inevitable the following comparison: "In certain ways, Priests are like watchdogs. They always drive away the wiles of the trespassing Devil with admonishment—and by doing the right thing—lest they should steal away the treasury of God, i.e., the souls of Christians."[27] Priests resemble dogs in another way. Their speech is like a dog's tongue and their barking. "The tongue of a dog cures a wound by licking it. This is because the wounds of sinners are cleansed, when they are laid bare in confession, by the penance imposed by the Priest. Also the tongue of a puppy cures the insides of men, because the inside secrets of the heart are often purified by the work and preaching of these learned men."[28] The Platonic philosophical dog has become the Christian priestly dog; one was the guardian of the sovereign, the other the savior of God's treasury, the souls of the flock. As in the Greek zoological imaginary, the dog is the nemesis of the wolf.

Now the elephant, about which we heard from Pliny the Elder, here is what the bestiary has to say: "There is an animal called an ELEPHANT, which has no desire to copulate."[29] But when they do copulate, they do with great discretion, to the point that as the bestiary notes, "they copulate back-to-back" because of their modesty. But they are also extremely intelligent, have long memories, and are loyal and faithful, like the dog. The virtues of modesty, sexual abstinence, and filial devotion make them a unique cipher for the sacrament of marriage. As our bestiary notes: "The Elephant and his wife represent Adam and Eve. For when they were pleasing to God, before their provocation of the flesh, they knew nothing about copulation nor had they knowledge of sin."[30] And "they never quarrel about their wives, for adultery is unknown to them. There is a mild gentleness about them, for, if they happen to come across a forwandered man in the desert, they offer to lead him back into familiar paths."[31] The elephant, precisely as the representation of both Adam and Eve, is also the cipher of the second Adam, Jesus Christ. The elephant is the divine messenger par excellence:

> When the Big elephant arrives, i.e., the Hebrew Law, and fails to lift up the fallen, it is the same as when the Pharisee failed with the fellow who had fallen among thieves. Nor could the Twelve Elephants, i.e., the Band of the Prophets, lift him up, just as the Levite did not lift the man we mentioned. But it means that Our Lord Jesus Christ, although he was the greatest, was made the most Insignificant of All the elephants. He humiliated himself, and was made obedient even unto death, in order that he might raise men up.[32]

What I have not noted yet is that just as the dog is the nemesis of the wolf, the elephant is the nemesis of the dragon. The dragon, like the wolf, represents the devil. Most of the numerous representations of the elephant also depict menacing dragons.

These three animals, as well as the horse and the bee, which we don't have the time to discuss, have a relationship to truth, to violence, to the sovereign, and to salvation or beatitude. Their relationship is semiotically and metaphorically juxtaposed. The dog is to the priest, as the elephant is to Jesus, while the wolf is to the false prophet, as the dragon is to the devil. In this parallelism we find that some animals lead to truth, renounce violence, and are guides to salvation. In the other case, the bestial animals use violence without measure and reason, deceive and lie, leading astray and to perdition. While the text in bestiaries laid out interpretations that interlink ancient texts with the Bible, the images and representation used all semiotic devices to inspire horror, revulsion, and even violent outbursts against the represented evil.

It is thus not coincidentally that many of the bestiaries that survive bear the traces of violence done against the representations of evil, iniquity, and sin. So, as Alixe Bovey notes with respect to the Tiberius Psalter, in particular in his discussion of the image of St. Michael killing a dragon, "So potent was this image of the confrontation between Good and Evil that a viewer physically attacked the image of the dragon, leaving small irregular slashes in the surface of the page. Indeed, every image representing evil in the Psalter has been treated the same way, with small yet distinct scratches piercing the parchment page. This kind of defacement is common in medieval manuscripts, where the face of evildoers (particularly the tormentors of Christ), devils and demons frequently show signs of being smudged and scratched."[33]

The Sovereign Beast

The moral economy and semiotics established by the bestiary continue to inform much of our discourse about political power, the enemy, as well as those we take to be the protectors of the social order. For instance, Hobbes's *Leviathan*, from 1651, arguably one of the most important treatises of politics to inform English political philosophy, makes very explicit reference to bestiaries or to the biblical beasts. What is peculiar about Hobbes's *Leviathan* is not just its iconography, but also the reference to the beast. Hobbes refers to *Leviathan* only three times, and each time with different overtones. In one case, *Leviathan* refers to the automaton that is artificial and made. In another case, it refers to the biblical beasts of the whale, crocodile, and dragon. In yet another case, *Leviathan* refers to the composite man that is represented in the cover image of the book, a giant man made up of many small individual men.[34] Hobbes thus combines three allegories: the beast, the automaton or robot, and the giant men. With this conflation of three allegories Hobbes intended to say that the state is a beast, the work of men, but also an artifice. As Hobbes scholar Patricia Springborg put it: "The metonym of Leviathan was the synecdoche of the state."[35] What is significant in Hobbes's iconography, however, is how he plays off the biblical and Christian imaginary of the beastly and monstrous against the obvious violence and power of the state. The state is in fact a divinely ordained monster, necessary for the preservation and salvation of humanity.

If we had space, we could also discuss the work of Immanuel Kant, which also makes reference to animals, in particular the bee, thus picking up the allegory of the bee as the model citizen, which was present already in Aristotle's work but that found its most elaborate articulation in Bernard Mandeville's *The Fable of the Bees* from 1732. And, if we had more time, we would have to include a discussion of Carl Schmitt's fascinating book from 1942 *Land and Sea*, which has the subtitle of *eine weltgeschichtliche Betrachtung*, that is, a "world-historical consideration."[36] Yet, this provocative book is really a combination of a modern bestiary with reflections on war, world history, and the tools of waging war. In this book Schmitt relates the basic elements of the cosmos—namely, earth, water, air, and fire—to mythological beasts: thus water is to the leviathan, as land is to the behemoth, as fire and air is to either the dragon or the phoenix.[37] Each beast stands for a form of military power: sea power, land power, and air power combined with fire power. Like Hobbes, Schmitt thought that the state was a beast, or beastly, but unlike Hobbes, he thought that each beast also stood for the unique kind of state that arose out of a particular ability to wage war and thus to take, partition, and work the land.[38] What is remarkable is that already in 1942 Carl Schmitt had anticipated the defeat of Nazi Germany by the phoenix of the US and English air forces.

What I wanted to analyze in this chapter, in short, was animals, political power, and violence by discussing beasts, the guidance of the sovereign, and the ways in which certain forms of violence are inherent or endemic to certain kinds of beasts. How we have imagined animals, whether angelic or demonic, has allowed us to articulate the limits of sovereign political power and its inherent violence. If the animal is the metonym for the nonrational in us, the beast is the synecdoche for the lawless violence of a sovereign power that turns on its subjects.

Chapter 3

Heidegger's Bestiary

The Speechless and Unhistorical Animal

Can one, even in the name of fiction, think of a world without animals, or at the very least a world poor in animals, to play without playing with Heidegger's formula, discussion of which waits us, according to which the animal is "poor in world" [*weltarm*]? Does animality participate in every concept of the world, even of the human world? Is being-with-the-animal a fundamental and irreducible structure of being-in-the-world, so much so that the idea of a world without animals could not even function as a methodological fiction? What would being-with-the-animal mean? What is the company of the animal? Is it something that occurs, secondarily, to a human being or to a *Dasein* that would seek to think itself before and without the animal? Or is being-with-the-animal rather an essential structure of *Dasein*? And in that case, how is it to be interpreted and what consequences are to be drawn from it? Those are the questions that we will encounter again in dealing with Heidegger's text on the world and the animal, the animal that is poor in world [*weltarm*] and the *Dasein* is world-forming [*weltbildened*]. As we shall see, this question will be nothing other than that of the being-world of the world. What is the world? What does one call "world"? And is the presence of life, or animal life, essential or not to the mundanity of the world? The scope of this question will be clearer later on.

—Jacques Derrida, *The Animal That Therefore I Am*[1]

68 | The Philosophical Animal

Introduction

The veritable explosion of books on animals and philosophy may tempt us into affirming that a new philosophical topic has been discovered, or at the very least, taken up seriously and judiciously by philosophers. Yet, the volume of publications is not a good index of either the history or relevance of any philosophical theme. The so-called question of the "animal," or to use Derrida's corrective of "animals," is as old as the question what is the human? What does it mean to be human? As has been argued at least since Homer, the human is a distinct type of animal that recognizes its animality by drawing a line of distinction vis-à-vis other animals. We are the animal that is anxious about its animality. We are the animal who asks what it means to be an animal, and whose animality is always in question. We are the animal whose next of kin is another animal and who dejectedly realizes it is too far from God. We are the animal, as Giovanni Pico della Mirandola put it, who is without an abode, a place in the great chain of being. We are the animal without a specific habitat. We are born thrown into a world that is partly already there but which remains to be built. We are the homeless animal; but we are also, as Nietzsche put it, the mangled, unfinished animal. We are the animal, thus, which is yet to be domesticated. We are the undomesticated animal, to echo Peter Sloterdijk's provocative formulation.[2]

In this chapter I want to approach the question of the animal in a far more sober and circumscribed fashion by reconstructing Martin Heidegger's contribution to the "question of the animal(s)." I will filter this reconstruction through the trope or lens of the bestiary. As I argue throughout this entire book, every reflection on animals is part of either an implicit or explicit bestiary. In the following, more concretely, I aim to, first, use the trope of the bestiary to elucidate the political effects of Heidegger's reflections on animals; second, I will offer an overview of three key texts by Heidegger from a decade of work, from the late 1920s to the late 1930s, which according to orthodox Heideggerian chronologies traced the temporal span for his famous *Kehre*. This *Kehre* marks the turn from the analytics of Dasein to the thinking of the *Ereignis of Seyn*, the eventuality of the appropriation of Being. Yet more specifically, in the following I will claim that Heidegger's phenomenology of animality, which is corollary to his phenomenology of Dasein, says more about humans than animals; that in Heidegger's thinking, the questioning of the animals is profoundly implicated with the questions of "polemos," nation, state, and

Volk; and that consequently, we have to learn to see Heidegger's bestiary as a bellicose, martial, and political bestiary.

Bestiaries

Before we turn to the analysis of Heidegger's texts from the 1930s, I must provide a brief discussion of bestiaries. As was discussed in chapter 2, but expanding on what I presented there, a bestiary is a book of beasts, a kind of encyclopedia or compendium of the descriptions, and in many cases, pictorial representations of fantastic, unusual, but sometimes quite pedestrian and common animals. Bestiaries sought to expose us to the exotic, but they did not stop there, they sought above all to offer a catalog of God's creation with a key to unlock its moral message. They were used to educate Christians about the beneficence and beatitude of God's creation, its moral design, and how that design was evident in all that was living. Thus, a monk, or a prince, who would read and contemplate these beautifully produced books would be reading at three different levels: *first*, a monk would read the bestiary literally, in terms of what it would say about certain animals, and the etymologies of their names; *second*, the text would be read as establishing a link between the Old and New Testaments, and how those links were embodied in the virtues and qualities of certain animals; finally, on a *third* level, the text would be read in terms of the keys it offer to decipher the moral lessons that should become legible by linking these intertextualities. Bestiaries were hypertexts, linking the wisdom of the Greeks, with the religious doctrines of the Old and New Testaments, with what Christians postulated to be the most noble moral virtues endorsed by God. Indeed, as I noted in chapter 2, the bestiary is the Christian version of the Greek *Physiologus*. It could be claimed that C. S. Lewis and Tolkien's books, written during a profound crisis of Western culture, draw on the Christian bestiary to offer a diagnosis of the cultural malaise.

I want to argue that we can offer a typology of bestiaries, that is, that we can agglutinate under a group of rubrics that reveal their divergent and specific aims:

1. Philosophical, such as those we find in Aristotle's works on animals: history, parts, and of the motion of animals. We can certainly read Plato's *Republic* and the *Sophist* as bestiaries. Hobbes's *Leviathan* and *Behemoth*; Carl Schmitt's

Land and Sea. Nietzsche and his "blond beast," but all the other animals that populate his corpus. Of course, Heidegger, as I will argue, and more recently, Derrida, Agamben, Haraway, and Coetzee.

2. Religious: the ones that we take to be paradigmatic, those one can find in the British Library, but also all the religious texts that allegorize the Devil as a beast.

3. Political: again, Plato's *Republic,* Aristotle's *Politics,* Hobbes, Rousseau, Heidegger, Derrida, Agamben, Schmitt.

4. Imperial: Sepulveda, Vitoria, Hegel, Kant, and more recently, the discourses on terrorists as vermin, as plagues, as an infestation to be cleared.

For the moment let me whet your philosophical appetite by claiming that the "imperial bestiary," in many ways, was already present in Herodotus's *Histories*, but assumed a very explicit shape and intentionality in the imperial bestiaries of European colonization, and anticipates what I would call the "bestialization machine of the biopolitical state." If we understand the biopolitical state as that type of state that makes live and kills in order to make live, that is to say, it makes live by killing and kills by making live, then the beast is the trope or figure of that which must be killed with absolute impunity so that society may be protected. The distinction between the bestiary and the bestialization machines is that while the former aimed to give us a moral map of living creatures, of course providing invidious distinctions, the latter has a very deliberate goal of inventing "the beast," "the beastly," so as to warrant its eradication, extermination, cleansing. What I have here called the "bestialization machine" is that which Primo Levi and Eugene Kogon describe so well in their essays and books on the Nazi concentration camps. I want to flag here Jeffrey Herf's *The Jewish Enemy* as the best illustration of the way in which bestiaries were transformed into "bestialization machines" by a biopolitical state.[3] Yet, similar rhetorical strategies that are found in the Nazi book of beast are to be found in the counterterrorist manuals of the armies of the US, Soviets, and Israelis. How we draw the line of differentiation between humans and animals may lead to the "animalization" of other human animals. From animalization to bestialization is a short step. Indeed, as long as we see the animality of the human as either a burden or an intractable dimension of human existence, we are already on the slippery slope toward bestialization, and even worse, toward verminization, to use Derrida's term. In other words, the "anthropological machine" is always a "bestialization machine."[4]

Heidegger's Animals

Here I'd like to begin with a quote from Stuart Elden, who has written perhaps one of the most comprehensive analysis of Heidegger's expansive bestiary: "The range of animals discussed is extensive. Notably there is the bee and the lizard on the rock, and there are the incidental mentions of frogs, chaffinches, the bird of prey, domestic pets like the dog, amoebae and infusoria, fish, moles and worms, dogs and flies, the moth that flies into the light, and sea-urchins—a veritable bestiary."[5] Indeed, Heidegger has extensive and numerous references throughout his work to animals, but before I turn to the three texts I want to discuss, let me begin with a brief discussion of Heidegger's seminal work, *Being and Time*, from 1927. We can offer a thumbnail sketch of this work in the following way: *Being and Time* aimed to develop an existential analytic of Dasein because Dasein is the ontological keyhole through which we can peek at Being. Dasein's mode of existence is already ontological, that is, in its mode of being it already discloses something about Being as such. The existential analytics of Dasein turn into a hermeneutics of existence because the mode of existence of Dasein is precisely always as an act of interpretation. Dasein is the type of entity whose existence is always in question and whose existence does not have an a priori meaning. The meaning of our existence is always entwined with the anxiety about that very existence. This analytics and hermeneutics of Dasein gravitate around three key axes:

1. Temporality/historicality—Dasein is determined by its finitude, which is foremost manifested in our anxiety about our mortality. Dasein is mortal.

2. Worldhood—Dasein exists only in a world. Its being is always a being with others amidst, or in the middle of, a world that discloses beings. Dasein's existence is always a temporal reaching out into a world that is both already given and still to be accomplished.

72 | The Philosophical Animal

> 3. Language—Dasein experiences, exists, only in and through language. Logos is not logic, but word. Like Dasein's world, language is the ether, so to say, in which Dasein dwells. Dasein does not own language, rather language owns Dasein.

These key themes of temporality, worldhood, and language are essential for what Heidegger will have to say about animals in his later works. Nonetheless, in *Being and Time* Heidegger mentions animals three times: *first*, with respect to death, where death is taken as a basic phenomenon of life, and that all animals die (human die, animals merely perish); *second*, with reference to the fact Dasein moves in the domain of Being in which we also find plants and animals—Dasein exists in the same horizon of being as plants and animals (Dasein is an organic living being); and *third*, with respect to the problem of whether the sensibility of animals is constituted by "time." In other words, Heidegger asks, whether the way in which animals sense the world is determined by temporality in similar or dissimilar ways to how Dasein senses it.[6]

An extremely interesting, and provocative, aspect of Heidegger's reflections on Dasein and animals is the following. In section 11 of *Being and Time*, Heidegger introduces a fascinating and hitherto unanalyzed contrast between "primitive" and "advanced" Dasein. If Dasein is ontological, how does it admit that its form of being has a history? Dasein is historical, but this distinction seems to suggest that its ontological structure is itself historical; in other words, this ontological structure is itself result of a historical process. This in turn raises the question of how does this ontological structure relate to the fact that this structure is part of the domain of being of the living, that is, the result of a process of biological evolution. We could say at this point that Heidegger formulates the problem, or recognizes the challenge, but does not offer, at least in *Being and Time*, answers. Furthermore, it could be said that his turning to the animal question in later writing is an attempt to resolve the aporia introduced in this section.

Now I can turn to the three texts that I think are particularly significant for our purposes in this investigation:

- *The Fundamental Concepts of Metaphysics*, S/W 1929/1930: GA 29/30

- *Sein und Wahrheit* S/W 1933/1934: GA 36/37—translated as *Being and Truth*

- *Logic as the Question Concerning the Essence of Language,*
  S 1934: GA 38

Let us being with *The Fundamental Concepts of Metaphysics*, from 1929, two years after *Being and Time*, and a year after the Davos encounter with Ernst Cassirer. This course has become famous because of provocative formulations about humans and animals that Heidegger introduces there. Paragraph 42, which begins with this formulation: "The Path of comparative examination of three guiding theses: the stone is worldless, the animal is poor in world, man is world-forming."[7] This paragraph, however, proceeds to discuss the problem of the human in terms of the distinction between man and God. Man like God stands over against the world. Like God, man is other than its world. Man has a world, and although he is part of it, he can still take distance from it, which is why man has a "picture," a "view" of the world. Heidegger then notes:

> As we said, man is not merely a *part of the world* but is also master and servant of the world in the sense of "*having*" world. Man has world. But then what about the other beings which, like man, are also part of the world: the animals and plants, the material things like the stone, for example? Are they merely parts of the world, as distinct from man who in addition *has* world . . . We can formulate these distinctions in the following theses: [1] the stone (material object) is *worldless*; [2] the animal is *poor in world*; [3] man is *world-forming*.[8]

Here I want to focus on the way in which the animal is poor in world. The animal does not lack a world; rather its world is poor, deprived, limited. The animal has a world that is as elemental as it can be. As we read, we discover that this world is poor because the animal lives, exists, in this world not by doing and acting, but by behaving, by being driven by its instincts. The world of the animal is determined beforehand by its instinct. In other words, the world of the animal is the kind of world that this particular animal can experience. It is not only poor in world. It can only have its kind of world. It could be said, in fact, that animals have too much world, too much of a very specific and predetermined type of world. In contrast, humans, who have no world, can fashion their world (in fact, Heidegger will claim something like this ten years later in GA 85). Heidegger then claims:

> Who forms the world? Man according to our thesis. But what is man? Does he form the world in the way that he forms a choral society, or does he form the world as essentially man? Is this "man" as we know him, or man as one whom for the most part we do not know? Man insofar as he himself is made possible by something in his being human? Could this making-possible precisely consist in part in what we are proposing as world-formation? For it is not the case that man first exists and then also one day decides amongst other things to form a world. Rather world-formation is something that occurs, and only on this ground can a human being exist in the first place. Man as man is world-forming. This does not mean that the human being running around in the street as it were is world-forming, but that the *Da-sein in* man is world-forming. We are deliberately employing the expression "world-formation" in an ambiguous manner. The Dasein in man *forms* world: [1] it brings it forth; [2] it gives an image or view of the world, it sets it forth; [3] it constitutes the world, contains and embraces it.[9]

This passage is important because man, the human, is defined as that type of being that forms worlds in three ways: it creates them, and it creates or produces images, or representations, of them, in such a way that Dasein can survey them as a totality, as the other of itself; and third, once it constitutes them, Dasein can embrace them, or take possession of a world. For the moment, we can say that the animal has its habitat, whereas the human makes it, imagines it, represents it, and then possesses it by embracing it. At the same time, this passage is provocative for it claims that what is world-forming in man is something that determines its essence as human. The world-forming capacity of the human is prior to our humanity. What is world-forming in the human is Dasein, the ontological structure that determines the essence of every human. When Heidegger claims: "This does not mean that the human being running around in the street as it were is world-forming, but that the *Da-sein in* man is world-forming," we must ask what whether there can be humans who lack Dasein. A plausible and evident reading would be that the average human being is not an exemplar of the world-forming man that Heidegger has in mind, "but that the Dasein in man is world-forming." The "but" that divides the sentence could also mean that the average human lacks Dasein, or that Dasein has not yet taken possession of them.

Another reading could be that Dasein is a structure that is different from the human, and that the human can become world-forming when Dasein takes possession of it. Can we thus not conclude that not even the human has a world so long as it is not owned, taken possession, by Dasein? It may be that man remains an animal poor in world so long as it is not taken possession by Dasein. Is this the distinction between animals and humans, namely that the former can't be possessed by Dasein while the latter may be, but not necessarily so?

For the moment, let me summarize. In the 1929 course, Heidegger's method is to compare three types of beings that have or do not have world, or have it in a privative way, in order to arrive at the meaning of worldhood. Worldhood, as Heidegger notes, is the accessibility to the being of beings. Dasein, however, alone produces worlds in such a way that the being of beings appears "as" and in their own being. Dasein alone is the type of being that can relate to the being of beings in terms of *als* ("as") in such a way that their being is given in their own terms. The *als* is the freedom of the being of a being to appear as itself. In 1929, the difference between humans and animals gravitated about the worldhood of world. This worldhood, however, is determined by the world-forming power of Dasein. The animal is poor in world because the world of the animal does not allow the being of beings to appear in its own terms. Things are for it, for the animal, only in terms of their instincts. Entities are what they are in accordance with its "driven performing," and as such the truth of their being never comes forth. That Dasein in man is world-forming means that Dasein is quasi-Divine.

Let us turn now to the rather famous and highly debated course from academic year of 1933–34, when Heidegger is most mired in his Nazism. The course was published in 2001 in German in the *Gesamtausgabe* (GA as it is now commonly referred to) and appeared in an excellent English translation by Gregory Fried and Richard Polt in 2010. This course was given during the time Heidegger was rector of the Freiburg University, at the time when he also gave some of his most enthusiastic and univocal endorsements of the Nazi regime. This course begins with the following striking formulations:

> The German people is now passing through a moment of historical greatness; the youth of the academy knows this greatness. What is happening, then? The German people as a whole is coming to itself, that is, it is finding its leadership. In

> this leadership, the people that has come to itself is creating its state. The people that is forming itself into its state, founding endurance and constancy, is growing into a nation. The nation is taking over the fate of its people. Such a people is gaining its own spiritual mission among peoples, and creating its own history.[10]

These, however, are prefatory remarks to a series of philosophical claims that are perhaps even more striking than those we just quoted. That the German people were going through a "moment of historical greatness," is precisely the kind of temporal eventuality that opens up something entirely new. Something essential and epochal is disclosed by these moments of historical greatness. But who and what is at stake in these moments? What is being determined? What is being decided in these moments of historical epochality? For Heidegger, at least at this time in history, the coming of the German people to itself, finding its leadership, and creating its state, in which it preserves itself, is nothing but the very fundamental question of a people's *Being*. The quest for the *Being* of the nation is no easy task. It involves a "demanding, quarreling, and honoring" that together constitute the "great restlessness" in which the German people decides its fate. The *Being* of the German people is "this restless conjunction of the joining-in that honors amid the enjoining that demands. We are, insofar as we seek ourselves in demanding, quarreling, and honoring. We seek ourselves insofar as we ask who we are. Who is this people with this history and this destiny, in the ground of its Being?"[11]

In other words, the question of what is the nature of the historical greatness turns out to be a question about determining the "who" of the people being challenged in the moment of epochality. Historicality leads us to the who of a people. Alone a people, a nation, that can ask itself radically who, what, it is, can live historical greatness. What is historical is secondary, or follows from the more fundamental question of "who?" But asking this question, about "who" the German people are, is really a question about something more fundamental. Heidegger writes: *"This questioning,* within which our people holds on to its historical Dasein, holds it through the danger, holds it out into the greatness of its mission—this questioning *is its philosophizing, its philosophy.* Philosophy—that is the question of the law and structure of our Being. We want to make philosophy actual by asking this question, and to open this questioning by posing the *fundamental question of philosophy.*"[12] What we have then is the following: the fundamental question of philosophy and the fundamental event of our history are one and the same because the fundamental question of philosophy is the fundamental question about the nation, its state, its preservation. But these questions come down to one question: who is this nation? Who are we, the German nation? In asking about its "who"—who we are as a German nation—the German people does its philosophizing. This questioning after its being, is its philosophy. Philosophy at its most essential turns out to be nothing more than the asking about the "who" of a people. Essential, radical, epochal philosophy, can only be *philosophized* by historical people, whose historical Dasein is preserved in its philosophizing. Here Heidegger is out-Hegeling Hegel himself.

For Heidegger, in 1933, philosophy is but the "incessant questioning struggle over the essence and Being of beings,"[13] but this history that is always historical is nothing but the asking after the essence or being of a people. For this reason, philosophy dissolves into the questioning of a people that responds and heeds the call of its destiny, its history. The fundamental questioning of philosophy is nothing else than the fundamental eventuality of a people's history, which has dared to ask about its "who?" This "who" is critical, because it is decisive, it is determining, it is the result of a decision. To ask "who?" is to ask something about decisions, about determinations, about boundaries, negations, about temporality. The question of "who" opens up the horizon of temporality. This becomes explicit in the second half of the lecture course, titled "On the Essence of Truth." There we turn to the question of the animal, again, but now from the standpoint of the relationship among the determination of a "who," temporality, and language.

For Heidegger, as many already know, the question on the essence of truth is a fundamental question. Truth, evidently, is the truth of being. Yet, in the same way that beings, that is. entities, are not Being, and Being is not an entity, truth is not simply correspondence, or the adequacy of a claim or statement about things or a state of affairs to those things or how things are in the world. Before there is correspondence and adequacy there has to be something that enables truth in this derivative way. Truth as *aletheia*, as a clearing and disclosure, is more primordial, but this event of disclosure or opening up takes place only in and through language. We could say that for Heidegger the essence of truth is the essence of language. What is the essence of language? What is language? Is it something that humans have that makes them different from animals? Do animals have language. What is the source of language in humans? Can we be human without languaging?

In this lecture course Heidegger takes up this line of thinking in distinctive ways. Like truth that as disclosure is prior and more originary than truth as correspondence, language is not simply naming, designating, denoting. Here is some vintage Heidegger: "Do human beings speak only because they want to designate and offer information about something—a thing, a being—so that language is a tool for the designation and presentation of information? Or do human beings in general have something to give information about and to give a name to because insofar as they speak, that is, are able to speak? Is language an imitation—albeit a richly developed one—of beings as a whole, or are these beings as a whole, as beings, *made powerful and unfolded only and through language*?"[14] The rhetorical structure of this question can lead only to one answer. Of course language is not imitation, and language is not a mere tool that we use like trained monkeys to point at bananas or plastic toys around the cage of our world. Before pointing, wanting to share information, there has to be the manifestation of what is to be pointed at. Entities can be pointed at, information can be given about them because they have already been "made powerful and unfolded" in language. Speaking is a modality of language, so long as it is a mere imparting of information and a signaling to an entity in the world. Speaking is derivative and thus not a proper way to arrive at the essence of language. What is it derivative of? What is prior to language as speaking? What about silence? What about not speaking? "Do human beings speak because they want to declare and communicate something, or do human beings speak because they are the entities who can keep silent? In the end, is the originary essence of language the *ability to keep silent*? And what does that mean? Is keeping silent merely something negative, not speaking, and simply the outward appearance of noiselessness and quiet? Or is keeping silent something positive and something deeper than all speaking, whereas speaking is not keeping silent and no longer keeping silent and not yet keeping silent?"[15] The essence of language turns out not to be the ability to speak, but to be able to keep silent. More fundamental than being able to say something is being able to keep quiet, to remain silent. Silence is not privative, or negative, that is, the mere absence of speaking. Silence is like the nothing that Heidegger discusses in his lecture "What Is Metaphysics?" (*Basic Writings*). The nothing that nothings is but the silence that silences—for silence here is generative—it is prior to speaking. Indeed, as Heidegger claims in 1934 in this lecture course: "*The ability to keep silent is therefore the origin and ground of language.*"[16] We are getting close to animals, for animals can be said to have a language, but can they keep silent? Another quote: "The attempt to trace back the essential origin of language to keeping silent seems at first to run contrary to everything that we said at the start about human beings and language when we distinguished the human being from the animal. The animal cannot speak, because it does not have to speak. So the animal is in the happy position of being able to keep silent, and the fact shows this quite evidently. Animals certainly do not talk; therefore, they keep silent—indeed, they are silent all the time."[17] Heidegger is here pursuing a reduction ad absurdum. If animals keep silent, "they are silent all the time," does that mean that they have a "higher capacity for language than the human being"?[18] Or is their being quiet the same as human silence? Evidently, animal silence is not the same as human quiet. The animal can't be quiet because it can't speak. It really can't keep quiet. It is in fact speechless, although it can communicate, for animals do signal and point. Why is silence the "origin and ground of language"? We should keep in mind here what Heidegger will write in this "On the Essence of Truth" (*Basic Writings*), namely that essence of truth is the truth of freedom, namely the letting be of Being as beings. The ground of truth is language, but language before it is either communicating or keeping silent is a freedom, that is decisiveness, determination, resoluteness (*Entschlossenheit*). This resolve that is freedom clears and gathers, opens up and circles. In this course this is formulated thusly: "Keeping silent is gathering, the gathering of one's entire comportment so that this comportment holds to itself and so is bound in itself and thereby remains properly oriented and fully exposed to the being to which it relates. *Keeping silent: the gathered disclosedness for the overpowering surge of beings as a whole.*"[19] This keeping silent is really a letting things appear as themselves. But this letting them come forth is predicated on what Heidegger calls the "*originary reticence of human Dasein*, a reticence by which Dasein brings itself—that is, the whole of beings, in the midst of which it is—into words."[20] This passage, which comes close to end of this particular section of the course, which is entitled "On Truth and Language," must be read in tandem with the opening passage of this very paragraph, which is meant to amplify this claim "*This bond to the superior power of Being* is for us the *deepest essence of human beings*."[21] The passage reads:

> Because and *only* because human beings are of this essence, they exist *in language*, and indeed there *must* be something like human *language*. The animal does not speak because it

cannot speak. And it cannot because it does not need to speak. It does not need to speak because it does not have to. It does not have to because it does not find itself in *the urgent need to speak*. It does not stand in such a need because it is not *compelled by need*. It is not compelled because it is *closed off to the assailing powers*. Which powers? *The superior power of Being!*[22]

Animals can communicate, signal, show, and even provide information, as Heidegger notes—bees after all can convey information about the whereabouts of honey, and Labrador retrievers can bring us to the shot duck. But their communicating is not language. The communication of animals is no different than the prattle of *Das Man* (the they, the mass). The buzzing of bees is no more language than the cacophony of human voices in a shopping mall or a beer hall. "Human Dasein" (*menschlichen Daseins*), an expression that should stop us in our tracks, can ascend from the meaningless boisterousness of the "average human running around in the street" so long as they allow themselves to be "overpowered" by Being. Whereas in "What is Metaphysics?" the essence of truth is the essence of freedom, here the essence of truth is tethered to the fundamental reticence of Dasein in the human, not the human itself, but the Dasein in man. This reticence is the ground of language, which is the ground of truth. Animals, and certain modalities of humanity, are incapable of truth so long as they are not overpowered by the "superior power of Being."

We can now turn to the course from the summer of 1934, *Logic as the Question about the Essence of Language*.[23] We need to begin with the fact that this course had been originally announced as "Der Staat und die Wissenschaft" ("State and Science"). One can assume that the course was meant to pick up some ideas that Heidegger had articulated in his famous *Rektoradsrede* from the prior summer, and of course, from the line of argumentation he had developed in the first part of the course from the 1933–34 academic year that we discussed above.[24] Heidegger is alleged to have begun this course with the words "Ich lese *Logik*"—which again, is alleged to have surprised and angered some Nazi functionaries.[25] Purportedly, Heidegger did this to dissuade Nazis from attending his lecture course. The published book, based on students' manuscripts but not from one of Heidegger's own, does indeed begin with an etymological discussion of "Logic." As we read, however, we discover that Heidegger did not leave behind all intentions to discuss "the state," or for that matter the question of the who of a nation, in order to plunge us in the icy water of logic.

Indeed, Heidegger begins properly, after the little detour through an etymology of the word *logic*, with the following affirmation: "We stand before the shaking up of logic, which we do not undertake [in] 1934 perhaps with the purpose of an arbitrary '*Gleichschaltung*,' but which we have been working on for ten years and which is grounded on a transformation of our *Dasein* itself, a transformation, which means the innermost necessity of our proper historical task."[26] One may interpret this as Heidegger attempting to differentiate his project from that of what we can may call oxymoronically "vulgar Nazis." It is interesting that here Heidegger talks about "an arbitrary '*Gleichschaltung*,'" as if to suggest that there may be another kind: essential, fundamental, necessary, metaphysically compelled, overpowering, determining, and so on. Take any of Heidegger's key words and you may have what is inchoate in this formulation. In any event, if we were unclear about what Heidegger may have meant, insinuated covertly, with the expression of an "arbitrary synchronizing, or bringing into line and harmonizing [?]" a striking passage will dissolve any ambiguity:

> This question [the question concerning the essence of the human being] is not the kind that it springs only as a clever sudden idea from the astuteness of an individual, but behind it and before it stand overpowering necessities. Even these do not always work, so that even the event of the World War in no way has touched on or furthered the question concerning the human being. Victors and vanquished, for the time being, have fallen back into their old condition. Hence, the World War as historical power of our planet has won nothing at all, nor decided anything [Der Weltkrieg ist also als geschichtliche Macht für die Zukunft unseres Planeten noch gar nicht gewonnen, noch nicht entschieden]. It will not be decided by the question of who has triumphed, but it will be decided by the trial, which the *Volker* are facing. The decision is reached, however, through the answer, which we give to the question of who are we, that is, through our being.[27]

Reading this should make one shudder. From what standpoint can one, anyone, claim that a calamity, a disaster, a carnage so monumental as World War I was not decisive, nor had won anything for humanity and that it had said nothing, or contributed nothing to our understanding of the human being? But perhaps more astonishing is the effect that this affirmation, coming from the most famous German philosopher at the time, must have had on the young students gathered in his lecture hall, most possibly decked in military uniforms, with the likelihood that Heidegger himself would have been wearing a military jacket with the Nazi pin on his lapel, as we see him in photographs from this period.

On Page 50 of GA 38, Heidegger addresses the Sturmabteilung (SA) in his lecture—very interesting indirect communication with the national socialists in his classes, who apparently were not persuaded to stay away from an esoteric course that appeared to be about "logic." Indeed, this course is peculiar in that the editors have allowed, or have not edited out, the outbursts from the audience. In this sense this course is more a transcription than a manuscript. Through the text there are parenthetical expressions "[*Trampeln*], *stomping*" that signal approval or confirmation of something Heidegger had just said. This course turns out to be a jeremiad that picks up on his Rector's Address from the past summer. He challenges students to identify with the task of the state, to take up their scientific work in the university as another way to contribute to the winning of the nation. For in taking up the task of the university, "we will the will of the state."[28]

The course then turns to a question that is familiar to us now, namely the question of what it means to be a people, who are "we" who recognizes itself as a "people." And before I turn to what Heidegger has to say about animals and Negroes, and peoples without history, I must momentarily bring attention to a passage that come toward the end of the conclusion of Heidegger's reflections on the "who" of the people. The passage reads:

> We are *a Volk*, not *the Volk* . . . We said, the We is a We that is after the manner of a decision. Now, however, it is precisely not placed in our will whether we belong to the *Volk* or not; that, to be sure, cannot be decided through our passing of a resolution. For, that is always already decided, without our willing, based on our descent, about which we are ourselves are not decided. Citizenship [*Staatsangehörighkeit*], one can perhaps will, but belongingness to a *Volk* never. What is the purpose, therefore, for a decision here?[29]

Then, Heidegger asks: "Two intermediate essential questions arise here: 1. What is a people? 2. What is a decision [or what does a decision mean]?

We will see that both questions are entwined."³⁰ Indeed, the being of a people is its decision for itself, but it is a decision that is determined by its history. To be a people is to decide its history, its fate. This is already familiar to us from Heidegger's discussion of temporality and history in chapter 5 of *Being and Time*. What is important in these remarks, remarks that are being made in the shadow of the Nuremberg Race Laws (1935) that deprived Jewish people of German citizenship, is that one may "perhaps want [*vielleicht wollen*]" citizenship, but one may "never" will to belong to a people.

The question of peoplehood leads us to the question of history and historicity, which is why we will discuss animals and unhistorical peoples. The essence of history is going to reveal to us the nature of the being of the human, for "history is the being of the human," it is the "distinctive character of the human being." The human being is distinctly temporal. Its temporality is history. Nonetheless, here is the key passage that links history and peoplehood: "If we now take up the questioning concerning the essence of history, one could think that we have arbitrarily decided what history is, namely, that history is that which is distinctive for the being of the human being. One could object, on the other hand, that there are human beings and human groups (Negroes like, for example, Kaffirs) who have no history, of which we say that they are without history."³¹ It would not be idle to ask: is being without history like being poor in world? Indeed, this is what Heidegger means. And this becomes explicit in the sentences that follow immediately:

> On the other hand, however, animal and plant life has a thousand year long and eventful history. Fossils give an instructive evidence of this. Yes, not only life, under which we include the animal and the plant, but the entire earth has its history. We do track this history, for example, the changes of the earth's crust. The geologists track the history of the earth in its ages. There is, therefore, history also outside the human region; on the other hand, within the human region, history can be missing, as with Negroes. Therefore, history would be no distinctive determination of the human being.³²

If Negroes have history, then history would not be a "distinctive determination of the human being"!! And yet, we do know that there is something like a "history of the planet." So, what we call natural history—under which Heidegger invites us to include the history of life of animal life, plants, and Negroes—must be different from the history that is proper to human Dasein. The temporality that differentiates these different types of history is distinguished in the following way:

>   Flow   Movement (process)   Happening
>
>   (Earth)   (life)   (human being)

Thus, the temporality of the earth is determined by a flow (*ablauf*) of the tides of time, so to say; that of life by a movement or process (*Bewegung*) of birth, decay, and succumbing; and that of the human by a happening or event (*Geschehen*), which truly temporalizes. Events are the happening of history. They temporalize history.[33] Historicality is truly eventuality, the possibility of a happening. In contrast, everything else is a raw, or derivative, form of history.

> Even nature, the animate as well as the inanimate, has its history. But, how do we come to say that Kaffirs are without history? They have history just as well as the apes and the birds. Or do earth, plants, and animals possibly have after all no history? Admittedly, it seems indisputable that that which goes by, immediately belongs to the past; however, not every that passes by and belongs to the past needs to enter into history.
>
>   What about the revolutions of the propeller? These might rotate day after day—yet, properly nothing happens thereby. If the aircraft, however, takes the *Führer* from Munich to Mussolini in Venice, then history happens. The flight is a historical happening, but not the running of the engine, although the flight can only happen while the engine runs. And, yet, not only the meeting of the two men is history, but the aircraft itself enters into history and is perhaps later someday set up in the museum.[34]

Here history is epochal eventuality, the making of history by a decision, the decision of a people to step into its history thus opening itself up to its history. Here properly human history is decisiveness. This is summarized for us by a sketch that Heidegger must have drawn on the blackboard (see figure 3.1).[35]

Heidegger's Bestiary | 85

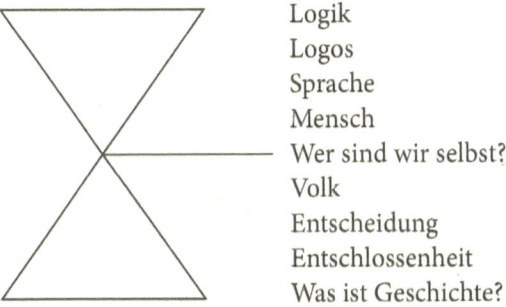

Figure 3.1. "What Is History?" *Source*: Martin Heidegger, *Logik als die Frage nach dem Wesen der Sprache*, GA 38 (Frankfurt am Main: Vittorio Klostermann, 1998), p. 97.

In 2020 Vittorio Klostermann published what had been thought to have been lost, namely Heidegger's own manuscript of these lectures from 1934. This manuscript does contain a very similar image as the one shown above (see figure 3.2). However, the order of the words is reversed.[36]

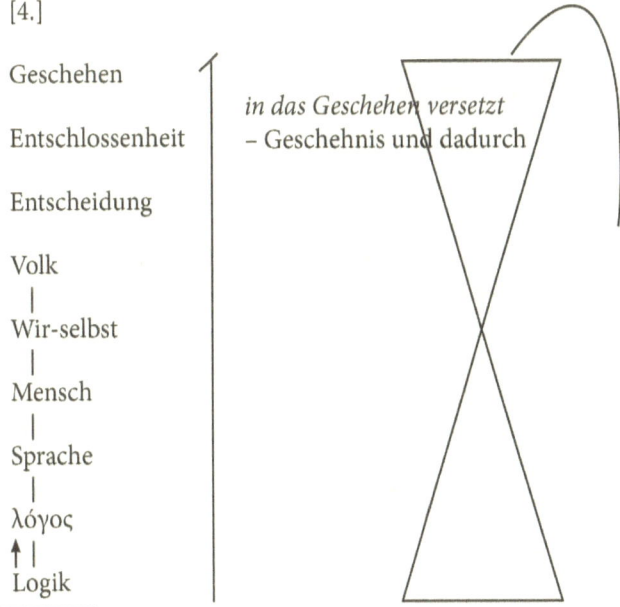

Figure 3.2. "The Event in History." *Source*: Martin Heidegger, *Logik als die Frage nach dem Wesen der Sprache*, GA 38A (Frankfurt am Main: Vittorio Klostermann, 2020), p. 177.

In other words, the question of logic turned into the question of the essence of language, which turned out to be a question about the essence of human Dasein. This question in turn is none other than the question of who we are as a people. For the human being cannot but be a member of a people. To ask who am I as a human is to ask what does it mean to be a member of historical collectivity? This question, however, is already the question of who a people is: who am I? is most fundamentally the question who are we? But this is the question of "a people," and this question is nothing other than a question about a decision. A question about one's being is but a decision about the being of that people. This decision is made possible by resoluteness, decisiveness in the face of what is the challenge of truth. Thus, we have that history is this: the resolute decisive decision about the fate of a people. Getting there, however, required that many humans and people be exiled from history, in fact, that they be assimilated to the status of "ahistorical animals."

The course that had been announced as "State and Science," which masked itself as a course on logic as the essence of language, turned out to be indeed a course on the "state" and philosophy at the service of the state. In a passage close to the end of the book, entitled "The State as the Historical Being of a People," Heidegger writes:

> Because the being of the historical *Dasein* of the human being is grounded in temporality, that is, [in] care, therefore, the State is essentially necessary—the State, not as an abstract, and not [as] derived from a right [that is] invented and relative to a timeless human nature that is in itself, but the State as the law of the essence of historical being, by virtue of whose decree the *Volk* first secures for itself historical duration, that is, the preservation of their mission and struggle over its mandate. **The State is the historical being of the *Volk*.**[37]

This passage, in fact, allows us to complement Heidegger's drawing from page 97 of the GA, with a sketch that would look something like this:

> The Human Being—*Menschlichen Dasein*
> A People—*ein Volk*
> Time—*Zeit*
> History—*Geschichte*
> Being—*Seyn*
> The State—*Der Staat*

The state, in which a people gathers and preserves itself, is the historical being of a people. We must then ask about the state: Is it an expression of Being, as such? Do we have here in fact a political ontology that grounds the state on the very structure of human Dasein? Heidegger's bestiary is in fact the reverse side of his political ontology. His veiled reflections on animals have turned out to have had very explicit and momentous political implications. His bestiary, it is clear, has been a bellicose, polemical, agonistic bestiary.

Recapitulating: Political Ontology as a Genocidal Bestiary

Although we have excluded a discussion of another of Heidegger's important texts on the question of the animal, namely GA 85, we have, I hope, enough material to arrive at the following conclusions. For Heidegger animals, plants, and certain humans are:

- Worldless—even if they are poor in world, that is, their world is a mere environment
- Speechless—even if they communicate they don't talk, because they don't have language
- Ahistorical—even if they are in time, their timing is not epochal eventuality—a happening
- Affectless (without affect)—they are prisoners of their bodies and surroundings (this is made clearer in GA 85)

What non-Dasein living beings are, however, is determined almost through diametrical juxtaposition by what Dasein is, namely:

- Language.
- It is through language that Dasein temporalizes.
- But this Temporalizing is at base a decision.
- Decisions are grounded in Resoluteness, which is the way a "we" historicizes.
- In history, Dasein is its mit-Sein; for it is in history that Dasein produces a self to self-relation.

88 | The Philosophical Animal

- History, however, or for the same reason, is a struggle out of resoluteness.

- This resoluteness is preserved in the state. The state is the temporal embodiment of the decision of a people.

- The state is a people come to itself in its decision—it is the responding to its fate. The state is the answer from a people asking who it is, out of its decision to be itself.

The consequence of these juxtapositions is the exiling of animals, plants, and certain humans from the world, from language, from history, and even from affect. This is consequent on the fact that animals, plants, and certain humans cannot temporalize. Inasmuch as these cannot temporalize, they cannot transcend either. This is made clear toward the end of this lecture course, when Heidegger summarizes: "Language is the ruling of the world-forming and preserving center of the historical *Dasein* of the *Volk*. Only where temporality temporalizes itself, does language happen; only where language happens, does temporality temporalize itself."[38] Thus, insofar as plants, animals, and certain humans—to keep to this euphemism—do not temporalize, they cannot experience death as death. It is in light of this decade of work on worldhood, temporality, and language that we can begin to make sense of the following claims, which he will make after World War II: "Agriculture is now a motorized food-industry—in essence, the same as the manufacturing of corpses in gas chambers and extermination camps, the same as the blockading and starving of nations [it was the year of the Berlin blockade], the same as the manufacture of hydrogen bombs." And another equally chilling claim, made shortly after this one:

> Hundreds of thousands die en masse. Do they *die?* They succumb. They are done in. Do they die? They become mere quanta, items in an inventory in the business of manufacturing corpses. Do they die? They are liquidated inconspicuously in extermination camps. And even apart from that, right now millions of impoverished people are perishing from hunger in China. But to die is to endure death in its essence. To be able to die means to be capable of this endurance. We are capable of this only if the essence of death makes our own essence possible.[39]

Here a passage from 1957 on the "Nature of Language" would be relevant. There he writes: "Mortals are they who can experience death as death. Animals cannot do so. But animals cannot speak either. The essential role between death and language flashes up before us, but remains still unthought."[40] Perhaps we should conclude that all those living beings, which dwell along human Dasein in the region of the living—plants, animals, and certain humans—do not truly die. They merely perish. They merely succumb. All those gypsies, Black Africans, gays, Jews, etc., who died in the concentration camps did not die, for they did not get possessed by the "superior power of Being." When one reads all of these lecture courses together, one is not far from thinking that Heidegger's bestial bestiary is but a bestiary of extermination, a genocidal bestiary—a political ontology of extermination.

II
Not Yet Human

Chapter 4

Habermas on Human Cloning
The Debate on the Future of the Species

Shallow are the souls that have forgotten how to shudder.

—Leon Kass, "The Wisdom of Repugnance"[1]

Life in a moral void, in a form of life empty even of cynicism, would not be worth living.

—Jürgen Habermas, *Die Zukunft der menschlichen Natur: Auf dem Weg zur einer liberalen Eugenik?*[2]

A New Brave World

Recent scientific breakthroughs in biotechnology have unleashed a wave of reflections, debates, and speculations that range from the usual doomsday rhetoric about a genetic Brave New World to the celebratory technophilia that portrays any attempts at regulation as ways of blocking our deserved path to a more humane and perhaps even more just future society. In the views of one group we face a more brutal and sophisticated form of eugenics, now aided by the discourse of neoliberalism and commercialized medicine, but, as adamantly and forcefully, another group argues that just as the green revolution driven by biotechnology can solve world hunger, genomics can solve the problems of social delinquency and poverty. The hypothetical situations that both groups appeal to quickly turn into science fiction scenarios of what is not just probably going to happen but is even inevitable. In fact, it has become difficult to discern science fiction from fact, hypothetical situation from situations already in the works at laboratories. As it should be expected these debates have spilled over into every imaginable sphere of human reflection and concern. Political theory, legal theory, moral theory, social philosophy, psychology, the history of science, the philosophy of technology, disability studies, even art; the list is interminable indeed, and each one of these horizons of human reflection has been impacted by the possibilities, and improbabilities, unleashed by biotechnological breakthroughs that were epitomized in the cloning of Dolly the sheep. Every one of these fields has been impacted to its core because biotechnology and the techniques of genetic intervention that it makes available to doctors have *qualitatively* altered our self-understanding as human beings. Scientific and technological developments have reached such levels of sophistication, stylization, and specialization that we must now speak not simply of a *quantitative* accumulation, but of a *qualitative* breakthrough. For the first time, our own human essence, or nature, has become available to direct technological manipulations. What is at stake is no longer the accommodating of a technological breakthrough to our self-understandings, and sociopolitical realities, but of reflecting on our own self-understanding as a species in the light of a technological breakthrough that puts in question what it means to be human. Once technology was used to fashion the intransigent natural world in our image and in accordance with our plans and desires. Now we have become our own object of technological manipulations—we have become our own tools. For this reason, biotechnology and its application to humans, genomics, demand that we reflect on what it means to be human in an age in which human nature is up for grabs.

Jürgen Habermas has intervened in this dialogue with a forceful, timely, and provocative text: *Die Zukunft der menschlichen Natur* (*The Future of Human Nature*).[3] The book appeared in the fall of 2001 amidst the celebration and debate concerning his having been awarded the Peace Prize of the German Booksellers Association.[4] The text also appears on the coattails of another German debate, namely the debate that was not a debate between Peter Sloterdijk and Habermas. I think it is important to keep in mind the Sloterdijk (non)debate in the background as it determines, in my view, the very nature of Habermas's response.[5] In other words, while Habermas's *Die Zukunft der menschlichen Natur* is not a frontal and explicit confrontation with Sloterdijk, it is an implicit and tangential rejection of what he represents. At the beginning of his text Habermas explicitly dismisses the hyperbolic rhetoric of self-styled Nietzscheans who juxtaposed a "hypermodernity" to a "hypermorality" that is too redolent of the old German ideology of the German mandarins.[6] In contrast to these posthumanists, Habermas suggests that we should reflect at a lower level of abstraction, one that is more in tune with our reflexive modernity. At this level we can consider the practical impact that genetic intervention, and here Habermas is particularly interested in stem cell research and preimplantation genetic diagnosis (PGD), will have on the moral self-understanding of future generations who would be at the other end of PGD interventions; more specifically, what are the consequences for political modernity if we are allowed to proceed with the optimization and instrumentalization of the species that all forms of genetic intervention entail. In the first part of this chapter I will give an account of some of the central arguments that Habermas develops in order to reject a liberal eugenics. In a second part, I will articulate some objections to and criticisms of Habermas's position. I will conclude in the final part with some positive formulations that move the critique and dialogue to a different level of argumentation.

The Debate over the Ethical Self-Understanding of the Species

Some preliminary remarks on Habermas's fascinating text are necessary. First, while the book does not carry anywhere in either its title or subtitle the descriptive *Kleine Politische Schriften*, which we have come to associate with Habermas's polemical texts, this is clearly a political text. It is not strictly a philosophical or sociotheoretical piece. The philosophical arguments, or the reference to philosophical arguments and texts, in this lengthy essay are presented only in order to support political arguments about how we should treat genetic interventions from a legal-political standpoint. Second, while the text is not strictly philosophical, it advances some new theses that will surprise many of Habermas's readers. In fact, some of the arguments against genetic interventions and screening will endear Habermas to many of his critics, particularly those who have been pushing him to be more attentive to the corporeality of ethical subjects. The polemical force of the text, however, eclipses the provocative philosophical arguments that resemble perhaps too much the philosophical anthropology that Habermas used to espouse in his earlier years, when he was working on an anthropological-cognitive grounding of knowledge interests. In other words, there are some very peculiar arguments that may lead us to think that Habermas might have taken another philosophical turn, in this case away from a postmetaphysical philosophical paradigm, back toward a quasi-Aristotelian metaphysics of substances and essences disguised as an ethics of the species. I will return to this point later. For now, I will offer what I take to be a sympathetic reconstruction of Habermas's main arguments.

It is Habermas's view that a serious and public debate about whether we should ban all PGD has not taken place.[7] Citizens have surrendered to the cynical perspective that developments in medicine and biotechnology are driven by the market and the liberal credo that decisions relating to reproduction should be left to citizens' private discretion. Thus far any kind of public debate has been stalled because of the assumption that the medical disciplines and technologies are aiming to enhance the range of reproductive technologies available to individuals. Yet, Habermas urges that we surrender neither to cynicism nor to the self-insulating metaspeculations of the posthumanists, à la Sloterdijk. We must be able to develop principles and norms that will allow us to make normative decisions about what should and should not happen with respect to the optimization and enhancement of humans. The tragedy would be to face a world in which any decisions about what we want for ourselves and our children will be preempted by the faits accomplis of technologically driven transformations to the human genome. Yet, Habermas is also sensitive to the difficulties we face when seeking to develop any kind of argument that may entail banning or curtailing access to technologies that might mean the decrease in pain and suffering brought on by congenital diseases. Indeed, there is no neon line that separates medical interventions that seek to eliminate disease from those that merely seek to enhance the life of patients. The same is true of genetic screening and gene therapy.

In the face of these challenges, Habermas argues that our failure to have a serious public debate about genetics, and its slow normalization and percolation into everyday medicine, impacts directly and perniciously on our self-understanding as moral subjects, and consequently will have adverse effects on the very foundations of our liberal political culture. Habermas therefore is interested in developing arguments against liberal eugenics, not just, or merely, because he is interested in the hypothetical status of clones and genetically enhanced humans, but, most importantly, because our failure to deal seriously with the ethical and moral implications of the use of genetic technologies on ourselves will alter the very nature of our liberal political culture. This line of argumentation should not come as surprising. One of the central claims of Habermas's work on political philosophy is that there is a relationship among our moral intuitions, juridical norms, and political principles. It is these relationships among the moral, the legal, and the political that allow Habermas to argue for the normative character of politics and its entwinement with rights, which are enshrined in constitutions. Some might even claim that Habermas has brought morality and law together so closely that he has actually collapsed them. Nonetheless, in the same way that there is a normative content to juridical norms, there is a normative dimension to the liberal, constitutional, rule-of-law state. Alternatively, there is a parallelism between the law, morality, and political liberalism, in such a way that each one reflects in a different style certain basic normative intuitions that can be referred back to the very structure of communicative interaction. At the basis of communicative interaction, or at its heart, we find the autonomy of the reasoning, dialogic person, who expresses and lives her or his autonomy precisely in the form of giving reasons and always having the prerogative to say yes or no to the speech acts of others. The autonomous moral subject is protected by rights, and these rights in turn are maintained by autonomously acting public agents. It is this core of political liberalism, which refers back to the basic moral autonomy but also to the vulnerability of the human person, that is threatened by the prospects of cloning and genetic enhancement. Insofar as the autonomy of persons is undermined by the self-optimization and self-instrumentalization that genetics makes available to us, our political and moral modernity are also threatened.

We have to be clear. Habermas is not concerned with the legal status of future human beings who might have been "produced" by means of PGD, or genetic enhancements.[8] He is concerned with the moral self-understanding that we would be expressing, if silently, because of tacit assent to allow a liberal eugenics to go unchecked, and with the moral self-understanding that future post-clonal and eugenic post-humans would have of themselves.[9] With respect to the former, Habermas is aware that there are few convincing arguments that can be deployed in favor of bringing about a banning of PGD. Again, the lack of arguments against PGD has to do with our inability to provide clear criteria for discerning between positive and negative eugenics. Here, however, Habermas thinks there is a way in which we can begin to delineate criteria if we think of our future children as second persons in a dialogue about what medical interventions they would accept. The suggestion is that in the absence of clear criteria we should in all instances abstain from thinking of our children in the form of third persons, or rather as entities totally at our disposal. To treat our future children, and future generations, as third persons is to instrumentalize them entirely, and when we do that we fail to treat them as members, if only virtually, of our moral communities. Only if we treat our children or future generations as second persons in a virtual dialogue can we check whether they would assent to our decisions regarding the use of PGD on their genotype. In other words, only if we are able to countenance arguments in which our future generations could hypothetically consent to our modification of their genotype is it acceptable for us to proceed with it.

Our treatment of future generations as second persons in a virtual or hypothetical argument about what we should do or should not have done in the way of genetic interventions is entwined with our particular mode of relationship to other members of the moral community. Future generations are part of our moral community, although in the form of a future anterior, or as virtual participants. Cloning and genetic modifications of the human genotype are not the only limit cases where this taking of future generations as moral counterparts has come to the foreground. One may even go a step further. One of the virtues of postconventional moralities is that they expand the moral community before which we are accountable not just horizontally and synchronously, but also vertically and asynchronously. We have become responsible for the past, as well as the future. We are responsible for what our antecessors did, but also for what we do, or fail to do, and how it affects future generations. We are responsible to the future for our acts of commission and omission. What is important here, however, is that when we relate to members of our moral community, which is without boundaries and includes all potential discourse partners, we presuppose what Habermas calls "relational symmetry," which in turn is related to human dignity.[10] Human dignity is the name for the inviolability that delimits interpersonal relations. Where there is a moral community, there is a community in which mutual respect is enshrined in the idea of the inviolability of every person. But this inviolability is only as good as its symmetrical assignation. Where there are some who are available to the interests of others, the former are violable, or rather, expendable and disposable; and where this is the case, we do not have relational symmetry, but asymmetrical misrelationality or disrelationality. It is inviolability that moral norms seek to protect.[11]

Moral norms emerged, in the social history of humans, as compensatory mechanisms for human neoteny, or exogeny, that is, the fact that human are essentially unfinished and premature. Humans, essentially, are born frail, incomplete and, one may say, mangled and totally at the mercy of the inclemencies of the outer world and at the mercy of the generosity or callousness of other humans. As Habermas writes: "The normative regulation of interpersonal relations may be seen as a porous shell protecting a vulnerable body, and the person incorporated in this body, from the contingencies they are exposed to. Moral rules are fragile constructions protecting *both* the physis from bodily injuries and the person from inner or symbolic injuries."[12] The person emerges as autonomous through intersubjective relations, that is, socialization. We are socialized into autonomy by being nurtured from utter dependence to independence, or relative independence. Autonomy, however, only stabilizes or attains self-consciousness within a "network of undamaged relations of mutual recognition."[13] Autonomy is attained at the culmination of a process of socialization that takes over and sublimates physical fragility, vulnerability, and neoteny into mutuality and codependence. It is for this reason that autonomy is always matched by solidarity, independence by empathy, self-determination by avowed dependence. It is for this reason that the dependency, or recognition, that is the other side of autonomy explains why "one can be hurt by the other."[14] Autonomy, in this sense, is an always-tottering accomplishment, which grants to moral beings a respite from their bodily fragility and symbolic injurability. For this reason, we can see why symmetrical relationality is an achievement, the result of a project of socialization, and the result of deliberative tending to. When we treat members of future generations as second persons, we are treating them as members of our moral community, if only in *foro hypoteticus*. For this reason we are of necessity required to be mindful of the moral integrity of future children. When we intervene in the genotype of a future child, we are in fact violating their bodily and moral integrity. Here, in very broad strokes we have a postmetaphysical and (post)secular argument for rejecting liberal eugenics, which expands on the fundamental insights of discourse ethics, and a discourse theoretical approach to political liberalism into the area of human reproductive technologies.

Habermas's proposal is suggestive, although perhaps not entirely convincing. It is certainly not clear whether our future generations would agree with our decisions not to allow the enhancing of them, thus depriving them of better chances for living. They might be extremely thankful to us for having spared them the debilitating effects of some congenital disease. Yet, they might also resent us for not having granted them longer life-spans, higher IQs, more muscular bodies, and so on. Indeed, the discursive criterion, which requires that we entertain a hypothetical argument with future generations, seems only to displace the temporal locus of our quandary from the present to the future. The quandary would remain, for even future generations would still not know whether a particular genetic intervention would have been undertaken to cure or simply to enhance. Let us take the following example: even future generations will have to face the challenge of having to decide whether to optimize the health of all the members of society, by decreasing the cases of, let us say, breast cancer and obesity. In some cases neither disease counts as profoundly debilitating, although it does impact on the lives of individuals and the overall expenditures of society on medical care for these cases. One may go a step further: future generations might be under more pressure, both because of lengthened life-spans and decreasing availability of social and natural resources, to maximize their health and decrease their vulnerability to disease and disability. In other words, future generations might fault us, as we fault our parents and preceding generations, for not having taken into account sufficiently the needs of coming generations.

One does not have to become postmodern, or take in tow all the doomsday lingo of posthumanists, to acknowledge that disease and health, the pathological and the normal, are functions of cultural conventions. If we think of "health as the silence of the body," to paraphrase Georges Canguilhem, then we need to ask what counts as this silence. Clearly, this silence would be something, such as not to be hindered by our bodies from pursuing a fulfilling life project that could grant our existences a theme, a coherence, a narrative that we could allow us to say that we lived our lives well, lives that were not misspent or damaged. Yet, does not this silence also mean, perhaps, not dying too young, not losing one's hair too soon, not having too debilitating PMS, not being able to focus one's attention enough to follow both the logic of a computer program and the differential equations of a physics problem? What counts as a disease, what counts as the silence of the body? For the moment, one thing is certain, that we do not know whether the new genetics will enhance the autonomy of subjects, or whether the enhancement of humans will alter irreversibly our self-understanding as moral persons. In Habermas's view, however, we have a banister to guide us in the nearness of this moral abyss, and this is provided by an ethics of the species (*Gattungsethik*).

By an ethics of the species I take Habermas to mean that we all share as living human beings certain fundamental commitments to the preservation of the species and to living in accordance with the "species being" of human beings. Habermas does not use the term "species being," for obvious reasons. Yet, this can help us give a name to two aspects of the human being that Habermas thinks are the points of departure for any conception of what it means to be a member of the species. The first aspect has to do with the fact that as humans each of us has a body that is grown and not made. In other words, each of us is given a body by nature, but this body is not given to us either by others or ourselves. This body is an inner nature, one that is given to us by our human condition. In juxtaposition, there is a social body, one that comes to constitute a second nature, which is given to us by a cultural world. To be a living human being is to have two bodies: a body that is grown and suffers, and a body that is given or that we give ourselves, against which we struggle but that can also be reinscribed and negotiated. To be human is to take up the challenge of the contingency of our bodily nature, realizing that this is a factum with which we must struggle and come to terms. The second aspect has to do with the fact that as living human beings each of us is a body and has a body (this is the distinction between *Korpersein* and *Korperhaben* that Habermas takes from Helmut Plessner). The Dasein of the human is such that no human can be without a body, that is, that the human identity is entwined with the body. Yet, we also have a body in such a way that we can imagine ourselves in another body. We have a dual relation to our bodies: we cannot be without them, yet our Dasein is not exhausted by their existing. Biotechnology, genetic modifications of our genotype, and PGD entail for Habermas a disruption of this "species being," of this simultaneous corporeal contingency and ineluctability of the human being. An ethics of the species commands a respect, or mindfulness, for how our moral identities are tied in with what we could here call the "fallenness" (*detrope* and *Geworfenheit*) of human corporeality. To be a living human being means our becoming conscious of and attaining to moral autonomy by departing from the inescapable fact of the genetic lottery that grants each one of us our bodies.

Undoubtedly there are persons who will contest this discourse-theoretical approach to the challenges entailed by genomics. Indeed, that there might be dissent and challenge is not an unexpected event, but rather is already a permanent feature of our modern societies, as Habermas acknowledges explicitly. Political liberalism, of the deliberative and constitutional character that Habermas espouses, is precisely desirable because it seeks to protect differences of ethical perspectives while simultaneously maintaining a commitment to some basic moral norms, such as the moral norm that all moral partners must be treated as equals. Discourse ethics pairs up with deliberate democracy because together they preserve commitment to moral universalism with an avowed respect for the individual prerogative to choose a coherent and meaning-granting life-plan. Deontological and procedural political liberalism offer themselves as the epitome of modernity because they enshrine universalism as well as attentiveness to the singularity of the individual. As was already adumbrated above, autonomy is the other side of acknowledged dependence. Alternatively, autonomy is the outcome of symmetrical relationality that is mindful of the need for undamaged, that is, uncoerced and nonstrategic, relations of mutual recognition. But, how can we convince anyone to accept the proposal of discourse ethics, without at the same time already appealing to the assumptions of discourse ethics? And here, Habermas introduces the argument that a commitment to a moral outlook is itself the result of a prior ethical commitment. But to quote Habermas: "Under the conditions of post-metaphysical thought, the ethical self-understanding of the species, which is inscribed in specific traditions and forms of life, no longer provides the arguments for overruling the claims of a morality presumed to be universally accepted. But this 'priority of the just over the good' must not blind us to the fact that the abstract morality of reason proper to subjects of human rights is itself sustained by a prior *ethical self-understanding of the species*, which is shared by all *moral persons*."[15] In other words, local and ethical traditions that project particular ethical self-understandings cannot trump, or override, the claims of a universalistic moral outlook that has been recently enshrined in the universal declaration of human rights. Yet, and simultaneously, this very delocalizing and disembedding effect of modernity on ethical traditions is undergirded and underwritten by an ethical understanding, namely an ethical idea that assigns a specific ethical content to the very idea of the moral subject. Moral universalism is itself an ethical value, a substantive value that assigns to human beings particular qualities and properties that are not just formal, but substantive. To be treated as a member of a moral community requires that one's bodily and personal integrity be respected; otherwise there is no moral community.

Do We Really Need an Ethics of the Species to Halt Our Slide down the Slippery Slope?

The Future of Human Nature: On the Way to a Liberal Eugenics? is certainly vintage Habermas, that is, Habermas at his best as a philosopher at the service of the public. He has intervened with a very suggestive and actually informative proposal about how to reframe the issues about cloning and genetic modifications of humans. He has also in the process further refined his definition of discourse ethics and has expanded his ideas about moral autonomy in the direction of corporeal fragility. These are major clarifications and accretions to a moral theory that is gaining ground and adherents. Yet, I discern a series of disquieting assumptions, which put in jeopardy the gain in other areas, and, most importantly, these faulty and highly questionable assumptions might suggest a metatheoretical turn that calls into question the postmetaphysical character of the universal pragmatics and the theory of communicative action, with its subsidiary proposals for a theory of the state and a discourse ethics.

The first and most glaring problem with the argumentation developed by Habermas is that he seems to operate on an unspoken but discernible genetic determinism. Genetic determinism is ideology, and not science. There is already enough evidence to demonstrate that a living organism is not reducible to its genetic code. In fact the genetic code acts as a decoder molecule of other more important biochemical processes. The genetic code of a living organism is only a part of a complicated biochemical system in which environment and a secondary level of replication of proteins are as important, if not more important. For this reason, Richard Lewontin, who was the world-renowned Alexander Agassiz research professor at Harvard University's Museum of Comparative Zoology, has coined the term *triple helix* to foreground that it is not the genes that determine the living organisms, but the interaction among gene, organism, and environment that gives rise to a unique living entity.[16] Genotype, phenotype, and what we now call the proteome make up the matrix that sustains the life of organisms.[17] From the standpoint of protein and molecular evolution, proteins are prior to the DNA, and some genetic archaeologists speculate that DNA is at the service of proteins, a kind of memory bank. Genetic determinism has reversed this order of priority: proteins are at the service of DNA, phenotype and proteome at the service of genotype. It is this web of interdependence between three areas of highly variable and unstable interaction that explains the fact that genetic twins can turn out to be so different. As Barry Commoner put it in his article: "DNA did not create life; life created DNA. When life was first formed on the earth, proteins must have appeared before DNA because, unlike DNA, proteins have the catalytic ability to generate the chemical energy needed to assemble small ambient molecules into larger ones such as DNA. DNA is a mechanism created by the cell to store information produced by the cell."[18] Genetic determinism is the social Darwinism of the twentieth century, but is also unacceptable pseudoscience.

Let us grant Habermas that he in fact is not assuming any form of genetic determinism, that he in fact buys all the scientific criticism of a crude ideology; would his other arguments stand nevertheless? I think most of Habermas's arguments would still stand and remain valid even if we cleansed them of their covert genetic determinism. I want to turn now to Habermas's elaborations of an ethics of the species. The intuition, I take it, is profoundly noble and one that I am much in sympathy with. Yet, to ground an ethics of the species on the dual notions of biological determinism, as well as the distinction between what is given to us by nature and what we grant to ourselves by way of technology and culture, is to assume that we must accept the genetic lottery of nature as a fact of life and that technology has aimed only to manipulate and transform nature. There are two highly questionable assumptions here: first, that if we seek to intervene in our bodies by making them less "arbitrary" we are converting ourselves into our own creation; and second, that we would be betraying our human nature were we to attempt to transform what is grown into what is made. These two assumptions are reducible to one essential distinction, between inner and outer nature, between the biological and the cultural, between what is grown and what is made, or between what is created and what is invented. This is a very important distinction because on it ride many important issues concerning, for instance, our ability to grant patents on genetically modified organisms that are not really invented or made, but that are reshufflings of already naturally given genomic material.

Still, I want to argue that the distinction between the natural and the created, inner and outer nature, is one that is cultural and not ontological, and it is one that waxes and wanes with technological and scientific, as well as conceptual or *weltanschaunglichen*, shifts. In other words, what is taken to be "inner" nature, or the grown, is that of which technology already has cordoned off as untouchable. The biological in the sense Habermas suggests here is that of which we can say that technology should not touch it, but at the very instance of our making that pronouncement, we already know and acquiesce that technology has contaminated it. Another way of putting it would be to ask: how much is today's *Homo sapiens* a result of nature and a product of culture (i.e., technology, science, and deliberate intervention in its nature by cultural means)? We could argue along with Engels that the hand evolved because of the invention of the tool, and that the invention of agriculture and the use of fire made of us the animals that we are today. Pigs, cows, and horses exist in nature, true, but not like those we have domesticated, bred, selected, and pedigreed. In fact, we could argue that the cows and horses known to us are unlike those we may be able to find in nature, and in a strict sense they are unnatural, they are created, rather than found or discovered.[19] One day, in fact, after a meteorite or an atom bomb throws this planet into a dark ice age, the planet will be repopulated by the plants and animals we bred, created, and synthesized over centuries, and some future posthumanoid will call them "nature."[20] The fact remains, we have created ourselves in the process of domesticating nature, and in the process of domesticating nature we have transformed our own nature. The domestication of nature has been the domestication of our nature; the humanization of nature, has been the denaturalization of humanity. It is this malleability, and this ceaseless intervention into our natures, that has been epitomized in a central doctrine of the Judeo-Christian tradition, a tradition that informs the romanticism of the Enlightenment and the French and American revolutions, and that informs the invention of the social sciences that fuel so much social engineering and meliorism. I am referring to the doctrine of *imago Dei*, namely that humans have been created in the likeness of God.[21] It was Giovanni Pico della Mirandola who gave the most succinct and eloquent articulation of this essential doctrine when he said that humans are like God because they have no place in the natural order, and because they are, like God, creators, but creators not just of things in the world, but of themselves. Like God, furthermore, humans are initiators of the new, and as creators they introduce novelty into the cosmos.[22] It is this latter version of the *imago Dei* doctrine that we find reflected in Hannah Arendt's concept of natality, a notion that Habermas appeals to in this text, although with other goals in mind.[23] Nonetheless, there is a profound ambivalence in this doctrine introduced in Genesis. We are to be like God, but we can never surpass him. Yet, the imperative is there: tend to, shepherd, toil, and transform, but also create. Is not then an ethics of the species, in this tradition, an ethics of the imperative of self-creation and self-transformation?

Admittedly, this is only one aspect of Habermas's arguments against PGD and genetic self-optimizations. The others have to do with the moral self-understanding of future generations. These arguments can be summarized into two main groups. One claims that genetically altered and engineered persons will not see themselves as authors of their life histories; the other, that they will not think themselves equals vis-à-vis other generations because their autonomy will have been undermined by our allegedly having preempted their futures through our genetic interventions.

With respect to the first objection we could say that a rejection of genetic determinism might take care of this concern. In other words, even if we were to intervene genetically, and screen future generations, they would not be more determined than we ourselves have been. There is no asymmetry between their having undergone screening and our not having been screened. Genetically engineered persons have to face the "fallenness" of their existence just as much as we have to. A clone is no less responsible for their life histories than we are. A life history is never determined by a genotype; this latter provides only the putty, as it were, from which we fashion our meaningful life plans. To put it in the laconic sentence voiced by Ethan Hawke's character in the 1997 film, *Gattaca*: "There is no gene for fate." But I would add, and perhaps more correctly, "There is no gene for human freedom." Habermas is too quick to assimilate manipulation of the genotype with the determination of a life history because he also seems to think that there is a correspondence or symmetry between bodies and life histories. While his elucidations about the interdependence between bodily integrity and symbolic recognition for moral autonomy are welcome, they do not entail ipso facto that we are our bodies. The ancient philosophical mystery of our relationship to our bodies is no less solved by genetic engineering than by the cyberpunk lubrications about minds that can be downloaded into hard drives.[24] A clone, or a GM human, will be no more its body than we are our nature-given bodies. By the same token, its life history is as much its own to squander or to make exemplary. In fact, Habermas's argument is so profoundly counterintuitive as to make me wonder whether I have missed the real argument. For, faced with a life to live, a clone or a GM human would be no less responsible, and no more irresponsible, than any one of us gene simpletons, or us *in-valids* to use again the nomenclature introduced by Andrew Niccol's film *Gattaca*, unless of course we are thinking that their whole lives are written in their genetic code, an assumption that is indefensible.

The second argument is even less defensible. There have been, and will continue to be, generational asymmetries. And much though we all have engaged in a sort of wishful thinking about having been born in the wrong place at the wrong time, we are always children of our time. We, today, in the 21st century, are in profound asymmetry with earlier generations, even two and three generations ago, not to compare with twenty generations back. Take the fictional characters in Bernhard Schlink's short stories, who struggle over the issues of how to relate to their parents and their grandparents, and to those parents' and grandparents' cooperation, witting or unwitting, with the Nazis.[25] The post-1960s generation could claim that they are in an asymmetrical relationship with their preceding generations, and they might resent and even despise their parents for what they failed to do, or for doing what they should not have done. Imagine a young American coming to terms with his parents' and grandparents' and great-grandparents' participation in the bombing of Hiroshima and Nagasaki, Jim Crow, and slavery. The younger generations, and future generations, will always suffer a painful consciousness of asymmetry vis-à-vis past generations and, of course, future generations. Can genetic screening and genetic optimization of future generations create a caesura between generations deeper than that created by Auschwitz, the Gulags, and Hiroshima? Is it not true that we are always mortgaging the future of future generations, thus perpetuating the asymmetry between generations?

These objections still do not touch what I take to be the core of Habermas's concern in this spirited secular argument against genetic interventionism, namely a defense of political modernity: "The attempt to rely on legal means to prevent 'liberal eugenics' from becoming normalized, and to ensure the contingency or naturalness of procreation, that is, of the fusion of the parents' sets of chromosomes, would then express something quite different from a vague anti-modernistic opposition. Rather, seeking to guarantee the *conditions* under which the practical self-understanding of modernity, may be *preserved*, this attempt would itself be a political act of self-referential moral action. This conception, to be sure, is more consistent with the sociological concept of *modernity having become reflective*."[26] In other words, what is at stake in our blithe acceptance of a liberal eugenics is the very nature of modernity. For as we saw, making ourselves disposable to ourselves alters fundamentally our moral self-understanding in ways which Habermas thinks undermine, if not destroy, the very foundations of modern political modernity. In light of this, a rejection of liberal eugenics by legal means (i.e., legislation) becomes a "political act" that seeks to preserve the structure of political modernity. The preoccupation is certainly warranted, and we should not dismiss Habermas's concerns. Yet, many of the ways in which we can argue for a response to cloning are not necessarily betrayals of political modernity. One may envision responses in fact that make a virtue of political modernity and that might actually end by commending something like deliberate genetic screening and manipulation. I will present two arguments that one may see as being exemplary of the kind of reflexive modernity that Habermas praises, and which, nonetheless, end up on the opposite side of the court.

For the sake of brevity, let me turn directly to a principle that Peter Singer has developed in a suggestive article entitled "Shopping at the Genetic Supermarket." The principle reads: "For any condition X, if it would be a form of child abuse for parents to inflict X on their child soon after birth, then it must, other things being equal, at least be permissible to take steps to prevent one's child having that condition."[27] Peter Singer calls this the "preventive principle," and with it Singer formalizes intuitions we all share, whether as parents or not, namely the intuition that we are under an obligation to prevent harm from coming to not just our children but others as well, especially if this harm can be crippling and dehumanizing. This preventive principle, furthermore, "simply says that prenatal diagnosis and selective terminations [abortions] are permissible if they are a way of avoiding a condition that it would be child abuse to inflict on one's child." Indeed, parents are liable for child neglect and abuse. The moral intuition has in fact been translated into legislation and a catalog of rights—rights that we are able to appeal to when there have been cases of egregious medical malpractice or even simple medical neglect. The responsibilities parents must assume vis-à-vis the welfare of their children have expanded with our increased knowledge about potential dangers and imminent hazards. In turn, our legal systems have grown and became more detailed and explicit about what kinds of things we are liable for precisely in order to give a legal representation of our increased moral responsibility. Many bemoan this legalization of our moral world, but Habermas is certainly not one of them. Yet, I want to take Singer's argument a step forward by combining it with some Habermasian insights.

Negative duties, of the sort that say "You should not kill," "You should not cause pain," "You should not prevent anyone from developing her abilities," etc., are duties "that have as their content the protection of the integrity of a person as a freely acting being."[28] These negative duties, always matched by positive rights, give expression to core intuitions of the liberal tradition: "The integrity of the person seems to be adequately protected only by the general, unconditional, and negative duties that assure everybody the same zones of inviolability of subjective freedom by imposing obligations to refrain from certain actions."[29] Habermas acknowledges this tradition, but pushes further, for it is couched on the monological and individualistic concept of the moral and legal subject. In Habermas's view, the core intuitions of liberalism are better served by an intersubjective and communicative reframing of duties: "To these core duties belong only those that can be understood as aspects of the general demand: 'Act with an orientation to mutual understanding and allow everyone the communicative freedom to take positions on validity claims.'"[30] These duties are

> fundamental because they are oriented to respect for the integrity of communicatively acting subjects. But these norms do not just have the force of purely negative duties. In behaving truthfully I do not merely *refrain* from deception but at the same time *perform* an act without which the inter-personal relation between performatively engaged participants in interaction dependent on mutual recognition would collapse. The norms that prescribe the fulfillment of the necessary pragmatic presuppositions of communicative action as a duty are strangely indifferent regarding the distinction between negative and positive duties: by showing respect for another person, I at the same time protect the vulnerable core of his person.[31]

And it is for this reason that negative duties are also and simultaneously formulated in positive terms. The fundamental duties of moral interaction are directly linked with the preservation of the symbolic and bodily integrity of moral agents. Thus, I want to claim that if we take Singer's "preventive principle," which merely formalizes fundamental intuitions about our duty not to allow suffering to come to other human beings, and translate it into the Habermasian language of communicative freedom and psychical and symbolic vulnerability, we will end up with a duty to ensure the well-being of other human beings. In other words, we are not only at the very least *allowed* to seek to prevent harm from coming to any other human, but we are *commanded* to seek the well-being of others, especially if this well-being is within our power. This argument covers our duties for future generations, and in this way, we may say that the temporal arrow points in the direction of the future. But what about the argument concerning what future generations might have to say about what we did or did not do for them?

There will always be an asymmetry between generations, as we already remarked, but what are our duties toward future generations? I want to appeal to Rawls's idea of justice and his elucidation of this idea of justice with reference to two principles: the principle of "equal right to the most extensive basic liberty compatible with a similar liberty for others," and the principle that "social and economic" inequalities are to be arranged in such a way that: "(1) they can be expected to be to everyone's advantage; and (2) they are attached to positions and offices open to all."[32] For the moment, I want to focus on Rawls's fascinating reading of the difference principle with respect to the issue at hand, that is, how future generations would see genetic modifications and PGD. And here, I will quote Rawls, since he makes it unnecessary to interpret him and unlikely that one may misunderstand him:

> A caste system, for example, tends to divide society into separate biological populations, while an open society encourages the widest genetic diversity. In addition, it is possible to adopt eugenic policies, more or less explicit. I shall not consider questions of eugenics, confining myself throughout to the traditional concerns of social justice. We should note, though, that it is not in general to the advantage of the less fortunate to propose policies which reduce the talents of others. Instead, by accepting the difference principle, they view the greater abilities as a social asset to be used for the common advantage. But it is also in the interest of each to have greater natural assets. This enables him to pursue a preferred plan of life. *In the original position, then, the parties want to insure for their descendants the best genetic endowment (assuming their own to be fixed). The pursuit of reasonable policies in this regard is something that earlier generations owe to later ones, this being a question that arises between generations.*[33]

This is glossed by Gregory Pence in the following way: "To the argument that we should not attempt to improve the human race, Rawls provides a framework for a cogent reply: if we were in the social contract—taking the long view of millions of people over many generations—and we did not know which generation we would inhabit when the veil lifted, we would choose to make the later generations as genetically talented as possible, compatible with the equal liberty of each to procreate in preceding generations."[34] Thus, we not only have a negative duty not to inflict suffering, or to prevent the conditions that might bring suffering to someone, but we have the additional duty to seek the welfare of our moral counterparts. If we have the duty to prevent a harm that may be construed as child abuse, then we have a duty to seek the welfare of our children in such a way that they might not face conditions in which they could not pursue their life projects. At the same time, if we understand justice as fairness, a fairness that is circumscribed by the maximization of liberties to all, and the tolerance of inequalities only if they are to the general advantage of all, then we are also under the obligation to seek to enhance the life chances of future generations. Both insights allow us to conclude that we can embrace, and should even endorse, both PGD and even certain forms of genetic optimization. Here, then, it is no longer a matter of seeking to bar liberal eugenics legally, but rather of seeking to develop policies and legislation that would grant to all the equal access to the benefits of genomic technologies. And to seek to develop these policies is not a mere capitulation to commercial, medical, and scientific faits accomplis, but rather a legally enacted political act of self-referential modern postconventional moral consciousness.

A Luxury That We Cannot Afford

Jürgen Habermas has already noted in a postscript to the *Future of Human Nature* that there are extreme differences between the German and the US reception and treatment of questions concerning genetic manipulation and cloning. For German thinkers, the uses of eugenics by a totalitarian regime are still fresh memories. In the United States, perhaps the homeland of state-run eugenics programs, philosophers do not operate under the assumption that the government is bent on using genetics and gene technology to control and select the population. We need to be sensitive to these two distinct life-world contexts. Yet, Habermas has also offered an argument that appeals to our Western moral intuitions and traditions, and most concretely, he has articulated his rejection of any form of pre-implantation genetics diagnostics in terms of arguments about the future of our political identities.

I think, however, that Habermas falls prey to the criticisms he seems to be leveling against the Nietzscheans in Germany. Although he has sought to move the debate on human cloning, and related genomic technologies, to the more concrete level of the moral and the political, rather than the metaphilosophical, I think he has not made enough of a radical move in the direction of the concrete and pressing. Habermas himself remains at too high a level of abstraction. In fact, and this is my main criticism, Habermas's type of argumentation in this book reminds me too much of the kind of argumentation that we are seeing in the United States, the kind that seeks to moralize an issue that in many ways requires more of our legal and political attention.

The moralizing of the critics of cloning or genomics is a luxury that intellectuals of the First World nations can afford. It is a luxury, furthermore, that instead of clarifying the dangers present at hand, conceals and obfuscates them. Cloning, genomics, cell therapy, genetic diagnostics, and all genetically enhanced reproductive technologies are but a branch of a larger technological revolution. Jeremy Rifkin has rightly pointed out that the biotech century that we are facing is the product of the "information revolution."[35] The possibility, and imminent achievement, of human cloning is only one of the many possible results of a major techno-scientific revolution. The most pressing, and perhaps dangerous, hazards and challenges presented to us by the information revolution, of which the biotech revolution is only a branch, have to do with the erosion of the civil rights of citizens, on the one hand, and the transformation of agriculture by genetic modified crops, on the other. The information revolution has made it possible for governments to enhance their surveillance technologies, to have almost unimpeded and, most importantly and frighteningly, unmonitored access to citizens' private lives and public lives. While some speculate about the threats to personal integrity and inviolability because of future potentials for cloning, at this very moment somewhere in Berlin and Washington, state functionaries and engineers at the service of the security services of the state are devising even more ingenious ways to mine data from the web, from the data banks of hospitals, from public libraries, from cyberspace purchases, and from web browsing. A new wave of constitutionalization is under way given the impact and strain of information technologies.

The response should not be to shut down the web, nor should it be a mere acquiescence to the new technologies of surveillance by the state. Rather, a new civic activism should be inaugurated.

The second group of challenges has to do with the biotechnologization of world agriculture. The problem, however, does not concern merely the application of biotechnology to agriculture. It also concerns the development of a global legal regime that is imposing intellectual property rights over genetically modified organisms as a way to force a new type of colonialism. The dual challenges are unprecedented. On the side of the biotechnologization of agriculture we have the decrease in the genetic diversity of crops, the potentially disastrous unleashing of superweeds, and the altering of the life cycles of the fauna and flora that serve as the eco-niche that sustains agriculture. Presently, the acreage of genetically modified grains is growing worldwide. As of 2001, more than 80 million acres of genetically modified soybean have been planted, along with 20 million acres of corn. In fact, as is noted in an article in *National Geographic*, "More than 60 percent of all processed foods on U.S. supermarket shelves—including pizza, chips, cookies, ice cream, salad dressing, corn syrup, and baking powder—contain ingredients from engineered soybeans, corn, and canola."[36] Yet, we have had no public discussion, not even a constitutional hearings, nor even less a presidential commission, on genetically modified crops. Many of these GM crops, or so-called Frankenstein seeds, have been rushed to the market without appropriate testing, and even against the loud protest of European, African, Indian, and Mexican farmers and government officials. Genetically modified crops are a fait accompli—we are eating them without either our knowing or our assent. But as more and more acres of land are planted with GM crops, fewer are the corporations, or agribusinesses, in charge of the world supply of seeds. In 1995, twenty-four corporations held more than 50 percent of the combined market share of agribusiness. Of these twenty-four corporations, eight were multinationals. Since 1995, there has been an even greater consolidation as Monsanto, Dupont, and the Holden Foundation move to buy smaller multinationals.[37] But this monopolization of agricultural biotechnology in a few transnationals is exacerbated by the imposition through the General Agreement on Tariffs and Trade (GATT) and the World Trade Organization (WTO) of intellectual property rights (IPR) that make it possible for these very same multinationals to impose and police the use of their GM seeds.[38] The acme of obscenity of this new regime is Monsanto's attempt to introduce what have been called "Kamikaze seeds," seeds that have only one life cycle, thus making it necessary for farmers to have to keep buying seed every planting cycle. In this way, a new and more sophisticated form of colonialism, what I would call genetic colonialism, is being unleashed, one that puts the weapons of a legal regime and technoscience at the service of the multinationals of the industrialized nations of the so-called First World. The foundations of political modernity are being undermined not because we may allow human cloning, or because we may allow genetic screening, but because the information revolution has spawned new technologies that challenge our notions of privacy and accountability, and redefine the very terms on which we negotiate our life-worlds; at the same time this information revolution has transformed agriculture and cattle husbandry, accelerating humanity's transition from being predominantly rural to now being in the main urban dwellers, turning the production of food into another commodity. In this way, an amazing reversal has taken place: Once capitalism depended on nature, and the colonization of foreign lands, to procure the raw materials of production. Now transnational capitalism produces nature, and the poorer nations of the world must come to it to find what is "natural" at a price. The problem with the moralizing discourses about human cloning is that their talk about "playing God," whether overt or covert, is a "distracting irrelevance."[39] What we need is a renewed discussion about who owns what, and who has access to what, and whether we can use the authority of constitutional law and democratically enacted legislation to make of the "information revolution" a social cornucopia and not a Pandora's box.

Chapter 5

Communicative Freedom and Genetic Engineering

[The humanization of nature] . . . is to be understood in three ways. First, the human being humanizes nature; that is, he transforms it into what is self-serving for himself and thereby creates, in an interknitting of the transformation of nature and the development of the human personality which requires more exact clarification, the cultural shaping of his nature. Second, the human being humanizes nature within himself in the course of the long civilizing process that has been engaged in by the human species. Lastly, the human being himself is a humanization of nature, being an upstart out of the animal kingdom; in the human being nature becomes humane.

—Axel Honneth and Hans Joas, *Social Action and Human Nature*[1]

The Biotech Century and Political Modernity

The biotechnological revolution unleashed by both the prodigious advances in information systems and the convergence of science and technology over the last century, thus giving rise to what is now called technoscience, has raised a series of questions that pertain to our most fundamental beliefs about human nature. These questions have in turn cast doubt on the nature of political modernity. The biotech revolution has allowed us directly to intervene in the processes of the production of biomass and bioplasm. While most of humanity's phylogenetic history has been lived as toilers of the land, growers of crops, always entailing an industry of breeding, crossbreeding, selecting, nurturing, and preserving plant and animal diversity, it is only in the last century that what was haphazard and always at the mercy of the inclemencies of the chaotic patterns of weather could be industrialized. This industrialization of agriculture in the second half of the twentieth century was called the green revolution. This revolution, so pronounced the agribusiness of the industrialized nations, would spell the end of famine and the beginning of an age of crop superabundance. No children would go hungry in the age of industrialized agriculture. In tandem, although not visibly related, the same century saw the transnational use of medicine to eradicate pestilence, plagues, and epidemics. We forget that the last century's human cruelty was matched by the blind and devastating fury of microbes and viruses, some of which were only eradicated by transnational efforts (smallpox, influenza, malaria, cholera, etc.). Societies became populations to be carefully tended to and monitored by the biopower of the health state; the state became the general doctor of society. Medicine became socialized, normalized, politicized, and highly scientized, precisely because its benefits had to be maximized and its costs minimized. Both medicine and agriculture, and concomitantly animal husbandry, have undergone unprecedented processes of scientization and industrialization (i.e., technoscience) with the introduction of "bioinformatics."

What bioinformatics allows us to do is to take to a higher level the industrialization of agriculture and the socialization of medicine: both have been turned over to a new conceptual paradigm and a new technological regime. Life is information, and this information itself is manipulable, spliceable, rewriteable, translatable, and, in the end, commodifiable. The biotech revolution entails the informatization of life, and the commodification of all information, and thus the commodification of all forms of life. Life is information, information is a commodity, a commodity is an object of exchange, defined by exchange value; life, then, becomes defined by an exchange value, no less nor more important than any other type of information that might be produced and accumulated by the biotech transnationals that oversee the production of life in the age of biotechnology.

This brief characterization of the biotech revolution allows us to get an idea of the kind of questions it has raised about our human essence: as living beings are we equally reducible to information as any other form of bioplasm in the biosphere? Can we dispossess our genetic information as we dispossess our information profiles that our "smart" Mastercards and Visas carry embedded in their microchips and magnetic strips?

Should we not seek to remove crippling congenital diseases? Should we not make publicly available genetic screening kits that allow us to make more informed decisions about what kind of children we would like to give birth to? And, if we can allow, and in fact urge, the generalized use of genetic screening tests and devices (just as we allow pregnancy tests and morning after pills over the counter), why should we not also allow genetic enhancing techniques that seek not only to remove the dysgenic but also actually select the eugenic? Can we really discern the boundary between negative and positive eugenics in other than purely cultural conventions that recognize the arbitrariness of the decision not to excise from one's genotype certain characteristics and potentialities? These questions, until very recently only countenanced in the realm of the purely speculative and the sole domain of science fiction, already give an indication how questions about "our human nature" presage questions about our political modernity. If our human nature is so malleable, so disposable to our unalloyed will, is human dignity then an anachronistic notion? And if there is no human dignity, on what grounds can we advocate the respect and preservation of human rights? If political modernity is the marriage of freedom and reason, in which they are in a perennial dialectical tension, but in which the freedom of individuals is at the mercy of instrumental goals of creators and engineers, and reason is held hostage to a technological might, then is not this very political modernity in jeopardy? In making ourselves our own creations, are we not also endangering our most important project: the project of political modernity, in which the freedom of the many is balanced with the freedom of the individual, in which negative and positive freedoms are precariously balanced in a political freedom obtained through democratic self-legislation?[2]

It is this group of questions about the fate of our nature and the project of political modernity that are the heart of Jürgen Habermas's book *The Future of Human Nature: On the Way to a Liberal Eugenics?* I already discussed this book in chapter 4, focusing more on certain political aspects of the essay on "liberal eugenics." In this chapter, in contrast, I want to focus on the more philosophical aspects of the book, and more specifically, I want to draw attention to the centrality of the concept of "communicative freedom" as it relates to "intersubjective liability" and "corporeal injurability."

The book, to repeat, was published toward the end of 2001, shortly after Habermas had received the Peace Prize of the German Association of Booksellers, and it is made up of two texts. The first one is a short lecture that Habermas gave on the occasion of receiving the Dr. Margrit-Egnér Prize given to him by the University of Zurich in 2000. The second text, which makes up three-quarters of the book, is based on the reworked Christian-Wolff Lecture that Habermas gave on June 28, 2001, at the University of Marburg. The first lecture carries the telling title of "Begründete Enthaltsamkeit: Gibt es postmetaphysische Antworten auf die Frage nach dem 'richtigen Leben?' " which may be translated as "Justified Abstinence: Are There Postmetaphysical Answers to the Question What Is the 'Correct Life?' " The second text is titled "On the Way to a Liberal Eugenics? The Debate Concerning the Ethical Self-Understanding of the Species." I linger over the titles of the chapters, because they already tell us much about Habermas's argumentative goals: on the one hand, to argue for a self-limitation, or abstinence, in the face of the possibilities opened up by genomics and genetic engineering, notwithstanding the inability to provide postmetaphysical answers to the question about what is the correct, or right, way of life. On the other hand, Habermas wants to develop arguments that reject an already operative and taken-for-granted form of liberal eugenics that is based on the primacy of negative rights, which furthermore and most importantly threatens to undermine the very nature of political modernity because it unwittingly leads to an alteration of the ethical self-understanding of the species.

These are two argumentative fronts that are related to two general principles in Habermas's discourse: ethics and his notion of deliberative democracy—that modern postconventional moral theories must be, and can only be, oriented by a deontological and cognitivistic construal of moral norms, and that political rights admit, and require, rational justification, which is matched by, albeit not equivalent to, moral norms—that is, both moral norms and political rights have a normative dimension grounded in the societal differentiation of value spheres (the aesthetic, the scientific, the political, and the moral).

In this chapter, however, instead of seeking to reconstruct all of Habermas's arguments, and whether they withstand scrutiny, I will attempt to recover the conceptual core of Habermas's intuitions. I take it that many of Habermas's arguments in this book will shock both sympathetic and contrarian critics of his philosophical stance. They will shock his sympathetic critics because Habermas seems to be retreating from his hitherto unflinching defense of a deontological approach to moral questions, and they will shock contrarian critics because Habermas seems to be acquiescing to pressures to acknowledge the corporeality of ethical agents and to the entwining of questions of the good life with questions of the just life. I am less interested here in determining the extent of Habermas's retreat from his deontological views and his ceding to quasi-Aristotelian and neo-Hegelian perspectives on questions of ethics and morality. I would like to reconstruct, and perhaps rescue, Habermas's intuitions in terms of seven main arguments, or steps. In a final section, I will use Habermas contra Habermas to develop a different, although not inimical, line of argumentation with respect to preimplantation genetic diagnosis (PGD) and genomics.

Corporeal Integrity and Moral Identity

Habermas's text is extremely rich and filled with suggestive digressions. For this reason I would like to focus on seven arguments which I will proceed to list in a way that does not necessarily follow the order of presentation in the printed text, but which I think captures the logic of argumentation. *First*, preimplantation genetic diagnosis (PGD), and any form of genetic engineering, undermines, nay it is a direct affront to, our notions of bodily integrity. Both PGD and genetic engineering transform what is given to us by nature, into what is manufactured by us, or what we grant to ourselves in terms of a technology. In this way, our bodily integrity is undercut; for our bodies, which were given to us by the lottery of nature, become something we grant to ourselves in terms of production.

Second, both PGD and genetic engineering contribute to the collapse of the distinction between *having a body* and *being a body*, and in this way, our relationship to personal identity, and thus to moral identity and autonomy, has been undermined. To be a body is not the same as having a body, and it is precisely their nonconvergence that allows us to accomplish our personal identities. We are our bodies, but they do not exhaust us, since we are always more than our bodies. Genetic manipulations fuse being a body and having a body, for the body that we have is the body that we give ourselves: intention and product become one.

Third, insofar as both our bodily integrity and our personal identities are undermined, so is our freedom. Freedom is grounded in not just symbolic, or reciprocal, recognition by others, but also by the preservation and recognition of our bodily integrity. Freedom of the person is freedom of their corporeality, that is, freedom is a dual recognition, namely of the person as a communicative co-subject, but also as a bodily, corporeal being.

Insofar, then, as both my bodily and personal identity are undermined, so is my freedom. Thus, communicative freedom is grounded in both corporeal and symbolic integrity.

Fourth, my freedom is further undermined as my right to an open future is foreclosed by both PGD and genetic engineering; in other words, any kind of genetic manipulation is a foreclosing of an undetermined future due to the lottery of nature. If we can design human beings, then we, allegedly, are also determining their future, and in this way, their freedom to be what they would make of their life is undercut.

Fifth, insofar as the freedom of future human beings is in question because of our genetic manipulation and intervention, both their and our moral identity is in question: theirs, because they would not have a ground on which to construct their moral autonomy—for this would have been preempted by our closing off their future; and ours because we would have treated other human beings, even if only future ones, as means and not as ends, as objects and not co-subjects. Future generations would have become slaves to our instrumental choices, and we would have become slaves of our technological might that has vitiated any kind of moral restraint or abstention. Genetic manipulations and interventions challenge the moral identity of contemporary humanity as well as that of future human beings.

Sixth, such a challenge to our present and future moral identities means that we are stepping over into an intolerable moral vacuum because not even cynicism has a place in a world in which anything is possible precisely because it is within our power.

Seventh, and finally, insofar as we have failed to raise the kinds of moral questions that we have been discussing, and insofar as we have acquiesced to the faits accompli of technologically driven social revolutions, we have failed to fulfill our responsibility to and for future generations, and in this way, we might have irreparably broken the continuity between generations that guarantees the preservation of civilizational accomplishments. Future generations will look back at us with disbelief and resentment. Future generations might begin to think of themselves as a different species, not only because of what we might have done to them in terms of optimizing them to the point that they might no longer resemble us, but precisely of what we did to them that they themselves would not do to their moral counterparts.

In the face of these challenges, Habermas offers three counterarguments. In the face of the gravity of the kinds of challenges that genetic intervention entails, a purely deontological and postmetaphysical standpoint does not suffice, for it is the very future of the human species that is at stake. In this case, we must ascend to an *ethics of the species* (*Gattungsethik*), in which we depart from the fundamentals of the human species, and not from the procedural standpoint of the adjudication of moral norms. In this case, it is a matter of the preservation of those conditions that render morality possible, namely bodily integrity and moral identity. An ethics of the species can guide us in the near moral vacuum opened up by the prospects of boundless genetic manipulation and optimization. Related to an ethics of the species is the ethical grounding of the moral point of view. That is, prior to a commitment to the abstract, universalistic, deontological justification of moral norms, we must opt for an ethical stance toward humanity. In other words, the standpoint of justice is posterior to an ethical standpoint that is oriented by substantive values, that is material values: namely corporeal integrity and moral identity. And thirdly, in the face of a possible collapse, or demise, of the project of political modernity, a political act of self-determination must be taken that rejects all genetic manipulation. Such an act is not a mere political fiat, but an ethical self-affirmation in the form of a political act: political will at the service of ethical self-preservation. In this way, liberal eugenics is rejected in the name of political modernity. Grounded or justified abstention and self-limitation are not a retreat behind modernity, but a very affirmation of the project of political modernity. And the debate about the ethical self-understanding of the species is not anti-modern speculation, but precisely a debate about the very prospects of freedom and reason in an age of unrivaled commodification of humanity.

Natality, Futurity, and Genetic Engineering

Now that I have given a sympathetic reconstruction of Habermas's main arguments, I would like to assess whether they are defensible, even in terms of his own sources and presuppositions. PGD and genetic engineering are no more affronts to bodily integrity than are any other kind of medical interventions, such as pacemakers, synthetic organs, prostheses, the inoculations of vaccines, the introduction of fluoride in potable water, the close scrutiny of levels of vitamins, fats, proteins in foods, and the surgeon general's prescription of certain minimal levels of nutrition. One may argue that these medical interventions do not modify our "bodily integrity" in the way that genetic engineering does, because they are not aimed at design, but merely "fixing" or healing. But are not also diets, visiting the doctor regularly, receiving vaccines, and operations to receive implants or to have tumors removed forms of design?

Perhaps what is at issue is that we might be altering the germ line, that is, the entire human genotype, in such ways that its acquired, or eliminated, traits can be passed on. But then, this is a different issue than a matter of whether bodily integrity has been affronted. The issue is whether we have a right to pass on and impose on our descendants traits we selected for ourselves but in which future generations were not taken into account. It is not clear that genetic engineering represents a qualitatively new order of engineering, one that puts in question the very foundations of human identity. There is indeed a higher level of risk because we may be introducing into or removing from the human genome traits whose presence or absence is not clear. In Hans Jonas's view, there are two elements of genetic engineering that make it different from other forms of engineering: that experiment is the act of intervening in life—for we are experimenting with life—and that these intervention or changes might have an irreversible character.[3] These two characteristics, namely technological intervention and irreversibility, however, have less to do with the fact that it is simply engineering and more than it pertains to the biological, what is given by nature; for anything having to do with organisms is ipso facto a modification of their being and an irreversible act.[4]

On another level, we are talking about the bodily integrity of human beings who do not exist, people who have not yet been born and who would grow up, and be socialized, in their engineered bodies. What is the relationship of these yet-to-be humans to their bodies, in contrast to our own relationship to our bodies? I can say that if someone came along and took one of my organs or limbs without my consent, my bodily integrity would be shattered, even if I would still remain myself, although now in an altered sense. On the other hand, I have the right, of course, to "donate" one or many of my organs. In the former case, damage to my symbolic identity is devastating, because it is not voluntary. In the latter case damage is minimal or nonexistent because it is self-willed. Is having been genetically engineered like having one's organs stolen, or given extra organs or super-organs? Yet, what if I had been born with a faulty kidney, or a very weak heart, or a misshapen limb? What would my relationship to my body have been? What is the difference between having one's body altered before consciousness, before we acquire and build up a unique identity, and having it altered after acquiring that consciousness? Even if I had one of my limbs, even one of my senses (let us say vision), removed or damaged beyond repair after having acquired a certain identity, I could still reconstitute my personal identity to deal with the damage done to my bodily integrity. It is a unique characteristic of humans that their identities are not only corporeal, but also symbolic, and that this symbolic identity is negotiated, maintained, avowed, or refused on almost a daily basis. Genetic engineering does not alter these ontological-existential questions. We may say that existential questions will also haunt the genetic clone, for they will still have to choose their lives, practice their freedom.

Here we have already touched the second point. PGD and genetic engineering no more contribute to the fusion of "being a body" and "having a body" than anything else we have done or can do to ourselves as corporeal entities. Even genetically engineered humans would have to assume responsibility for their existences, no matter how closely we may have engineered their bodies. Their freedom would never be impaired, even if their horizon of choices has been altered. So long as human life continues to be biological life, and so long as this biological life assumes the form of a metabolic organism, there will always exist the gap between being a body and having a body. All organisms, where being organic means establishing a metabolic self-sustenance, have a dual relationship to their material substance. As Hans Jonas puts it: though they are "dependent on the availability of this substance, the organism is nonetheless independent of matter's particular identity. Its own functional identity does not coincide with the substantial identity of its material components, which nevertheless constitute it completely at any given moment."[5] Only after the next evolutionary step has been taken, in which consciousness gets uncoupled from its biological substratum, will the abyss between *Leib* (being a body) and *Körper* (having a body) be bridged,[6] and when this breakthrough takes place, the issue of genetic engineering will be moot, for we would have begun a new age in which the living would have become mechanical, and the mechanical would have become living (the cyborg, of which recent nanorobots are their primordial zoa).[7]

Even in a genetically modified future, human freedom will still remain a mystery, or one of those perennial philosophical questions about which future philosophers will still be wondering. Only the most extreme form of genetic determinism can be a point of departure for thinking that the freedom of future humans will be impaired or constrained by genetic manipulations of their genome. But genetic determinism is ideology.

There is no gene for human freedom, as I claimed in the last chapter. In fact, in light of Habermas's own understanding of communicative freedom, freedom is something we are socialized into, and it is something that is granted intersubjectively. Freedoms, both negative and positive, are social achievements, preserved and assured by institutions that relate to corporeal integrity, but are not reducible to it.[8] The freedom of future genetically engineered humans will be determined not by their genes, but by the kinds of political institutions we develop and which they inherit.

For similar reasons, we must reject the idea that genetic engineering entails a closing off of the open future of genetically modified humans. Human futurity—or "natality," to use Hannah Arendt's expression—is related to human freedom; in fact, human freedom is the ability to initiate, to begin anew, and to be a beginning for a new action. Action is the social counterpart of natality.[9] Future generations would still have to assume charge of their existences, live out their freedoms, and engage in action. But, we might object, is knowing that one has been genetically engineered not a burden, knowing too much, in such a way that like Oedipus, we are led to bring about our own fate. Is not human freedom based on a basic ignorance about what is fated to us? But do we not all, regardless of whether we have been genetically enhanced or not, suffer under the burden of knowing both too much and too little? Only if we subscribe to an extreme form of determinism can we accept that genetic modifications entail closing off the open future of genetically engineered humans.[10] Genetic engineering or not, the question whether action is determined, and our choices preestablished, will remain a perennial metaphysical problem.

The moral identity of future generations is not more in danger because of our genetic optimizations than it is because we are extinguishing biodiversity, irreparably transforming the biosphere, exhausting sources of potable water, and failing to make provisions for renewable resources for future generations, and most directly determining, because we failed to prevent genocide and close the gap between the poor Third World and the wealthy "First World." For the distance between future genetically enhanced generations and us is less than that between the poor of the world and the average citizen of industrialized nations. Note, for instance, that the income differential between the fifth wealthiest and fifth poorest was 30 to 1 in 1980, 60 to 1 in 1990, and 74 to 1 in 1995. In just over forty years, this differential has more than doubled. Biotechnology, unsupplemented by genetic engineering, can only increase these disparities. The rupture in moral identity from generation to generation is inevitable, and in fact a necessary condition of the very moral formation of humanity. Every human being must negotiate from year to year, decade to decade, their moral portrait. Analogously, cultural life-worlds can only persevere to the extent to which they allow for the processes of cultural transmission to be submitted to the dual processes of rejection and acceptance. The moral identity of future generations is something that they will negotiate in light of their own tasks, some of which they will have inherited from us and some of which they will impose on themselves.

Would our own moral identities have been severely damaged either because we had made a choice to pursue genetic engineering, or because we failed to even undertake public deliberation of its possible adverse consequences? Is humanity, as such, at any given moment, morally accountable for its identity? Is humanity, as such, at any given moment, capable of being ascribed a moral identity? Humanity is embodied in a heterogeneity of societies—societies that are formed by particular types of cultural life-worlds, which are, in turn, horizontally and vertically shot through with heterogeneity. At most, we may be able to speak of the morality of particular societies, and even then, this putative moral identity is not given a priori but is a topic of deliberation. Habermas himself has argued this in the context of the *Historikerstreit*. And as he put it in his Sonning Prize acceptance speech, "Beyond guilt that can be ascribed to individuals, however, different contexts can mean different historical burdens. With the life forms into which we were born and which have stamped our identity we take on very different sorts of historical liability (in Jasper's sense). For the way we continue the traditions in which we find ourselves is up to us."[11]

The moral burden for the possibly disastrous effects of genetic engineering cannot be foisted on humanity per se, but are liabilities that only certain contemporary societies have taken on. And even when these liabilities can be attributed only to particular societies, it is up to their citizens to evaluate and take up these moral burdens through a public debate. It is here where I see the strength of Habermas's public intervention concerning the possibly disastrous effects of PGD and genetic engineering, namely by urging us to engage in a broader, more deliberate discussion about the benefits and hazards of a seemingly qualitatively different form of engineering that may alter the very nature of humanity.

We have no less stepped over a moral abyss for thinking that we may be optimizing ourselves through genetic engineering than for having failed to do enough, or anything at all, for the growing disparity between the poor and the rich. One may argue, in fact, that while the former is actually a function of our moral scruples, the latter is a failure of our moral nerve. At the same time, no matter how much deliberation we bring to the question of genetic modification of the human genome, future generations will assuredly challenge our own moral self-presentation. And it is in this question that is always the prerogative of our contemporaries and future humans to challenge our moral self-presentations and portraits that sustain the vitality of cultural forms of life.

Finally, we cannot know in advance whether our acts of omission or commission with respect to genetic optimization of the human species will be a failure or fulfillment of our duty to future generations; for it is not clear yet that the benefits are greater or less than the hazards. To close paths for future biotechnological developments would certainly be a failure of our responsibility to future generations. To abstain deliberately from allowing irreversible changes to take place is perhaps the minimal duty to allow our descendants to have the prerogative to repeal and recall such self-imposed limitation. As Eric Lander, director of the genome center at MIT's Whitehead Center, phrased it: "I would have a ban in place, an absolute ban in place on human germ-line gene therapy. Not because I think for sure we should never cross the threshold, but because I think that is such a fateful threshold to cross that I'd like society to have to rebut the presumption someday, to have to repeal a ban when it thought it was time to ever try something like that."[12] This minimalist ethics of self-limiting abstention is the very least we can do for future generations. And neither a philosophical anthropology nor an ethics of the species are necessary to ground it.

Postmetaphysical Thinking and Post-Occidentalism

The transition to a postmetaphysical paradigm in thinking, we can argue along with Habermas, was augured and brought about by intraphilosophical, and intraintellectual logics of transformation: from identity thinking to procedural reason; from the philosophy of consciousness to the linguistic turn; from the exorbitant claims of *theoria* to the deflationary rethinking of philosophy qua its redefinition as a helper of the social and natural sciences.[13] This very transition, however, must also be understood in terms of historical experiences: the discovery of the New World, the

Reformation and the concomitant confessional wars, the discovery of historical cultures, and above all, the discovery of humanity as an object of study (ethnography and anthropology).[14] A postmetaphysical orientation in thinking is not only a conceptual imperative, but also the product of world-historical experiences that have rendered all cultures equally close to the universal, and thus, equally distant from universalistic claims (in the way that Kant and Hegel once hoped to argue).[15] I want for the moment to focus on two central lessons learned from this transition to a postmetaphysical orientation in thinking and the life-world. The first one is the recognition of the need to respect cultural differences, and hence the need to move from a substantivist, that is, metaphysical and ontological, to a proceduralist construal of reason.

Proceduralist reason does not prejudge whether a particular embodiment of reason is more or less rational than those from which we think or reason ourselves (again as Kant, Hegel, and even Marx presupposed). A postmetaphysical understanding of reason means that reason is understood in terms of norms of justification and adjudication, that is, practices of reason-giving and -testing. Inasmuch as reason is procedural, it is also situated and embedded in historical contexts of praxis and tradition. One may argue then that procedural reason is post-Eurocentric or anti-ethnocentric, and in this way seeks a dialogue not just among the disciplines and sciences, but also among cultures and traditions. Procedural reason opens itself up to the transcendental from within, and not from the *sub specie aeternitatis* standpoint of universal reason. The second lesson has to do with the launching of the project of political modernity, which by many accounts is still underway and still in the process of being clarified. As was intimated early on, the project of political modernity has to do with the attempt to dialectically balance the claims of reason with the claims of freedom, that is, rational freedom. Another way of saying this would be to claim that freedom must be legitimated through a process of rational deliberation, and that this deliberation is only possible if humans have been empowered by political liberties. Political power has authority because it is deliberated; it has been rationally enacted. And this power is at the service of the political liberties of citizens. In the name of freedom we can always contest power, and power requires that it be legitimated, lest it turn tyrannical and thus a refutation of freedom: reason and freedom meet in a precarious balance.

An attempt to ground a political response to the challenges of PGD and genetic engineering on an ethical self-understanding of societies, and, furthermore, to attempt to justify a political act that rejects genetic engineering in the name of an ethics of the species are two argumentative moves that betray these two central lessons. On the one hand, to ground an ethical response to the challenges presented to us by genomics in terms of an ethics of the species, the acceptance of which is the precondition for the proceduralist and cognitivist postconventional morality that is the hallmark of modern societies, means that we have retreated behind the post-Eurocentric, or anti-ethnocentric, aspect of postmetaphysical reason. The argument for the acceptance of an ethics of the species masks the imposition of a Western understanding of what is essential to be human. There is no need to rehash here the plurality of cultural perspectives on what makes humans distinctive, or nondistinctive, from other living species. It truly would be disastrous in an age of "dialogical cosmopolitanism,"[16] or what Walter Mignolo has called "critical cosmopolitanism"[17] to smuggle under the mantle of an ethical imperative an ethnocentric blackmail: either you are moral, by accepting our ethical values, and reject genetic engineering, or you are not, because you reject our ethical values, and thus you cannot ascend to the moral, and thus are doubly written off from the moral register. Such ultimatums and threats to be blacklisted are redolent of the worst forms of Eurocentrism. In an age in which globalization movements from below, such as feminism, peace, anti-nuclear weapons, environmental and green movements, have emerged from a transnational, postnationalist, and transcultural syncretistic consciousness, such theoretical gestures create dissonance.

On the other hand, the response to the challenges posed by genomics cannot be properly met with ethical tools, but with political tools. An ethical articulation of genomic challenges obfuscates their legal and political character. What is at stake is a balance between the communitarian rights of societies and the negative rights of citizens. An ethical presentation of the issues involved in genomics threatens to conceal the dimensions related to the negative rights of citizens to determine their own "correct life." It is these negative rights that Habermas glosses over when he invidiously convokes the name of a liberal eugenics followed by a question mark (as he does in the subtitle of his book). We may understand the Hippocratic Oath as a response to the judgment nature passed on us and the death we unleash on each other. Life for the human being is not just a metabolic process. It is, above all, a social activity. If metaphysics is born with graves, as Jonas has written so beautifully, justice was born with the question of life: its preservation, sustenance, and growth. For the human being, life is a question of justice: the right to life, before it is a right to the "correct form of life," is a right to life itself. This right to life is what is at the heart of the universal declaration of human rights.

The benefits granted by reproductive technologies and genomics were developed precisely to enhance this right to life. But, at the same time, we can neither say what the content of that life should be, nor can we dictate how that life should be led and lived. For this reason, the dominion over the living, and life, is a negative, nonprescriptive type of biopower. So long as everyone's right to life is ensured and protected, the way that life is lived, and the form that life takes, cannot be controlled, prescribed, or proscribed. And it is this self-constrained and abstemious biopower of political modernity that explains the simultaneous, and seemingly disparate, tendencies in contemporary modern culture, namely the simultaneous acceptance of the culture of self-optimization with the culturalization of disability; that is, just as we are understanding of people's desire to want to prevent the transmittal of genetic mayhem, we also are equally understanding of the desire to nurture life not marked as diseased, but as challenged and requiring our care and solicitude.[18] A culture in which disability is seen as culture, and not solely as disease to be eradicated, is perhaps the epitome of what Habermas has so eloquently defended in most of his work: communicative freedom. In communicative freedom injurability (dependency) and integrity (autonomy) are synthesized into political autonomy.[19] For this reason, justice is the other side of solidarity, as Habermas himself has argued: freedom and compassion, liberty and dependency are entwined in our political project of modernity.[20] And it is this communicative freedom that an ethics of the species and a political self-affirmation of political modernity motivated by an ethical perspective put in jeopardy.

Chapter 6

We Have Never Been Human, or How We Lost Our Humanity

From Habermas and Derrida to
Midgley and Haraway by Way of Agamben[1]

> If the question of the relation of nature and history is to be seriously posed, then it only offers any chance of solution if it is possible to *comprehend historical being in its most extreme historical determinacy, where it is most historical, as natural being, or if it were possible to comprehend nature as an historical being where it seems to rest most deeply in itself as nature.* It is no longer simply a matter of conceptualizing the fact of history as natural fact *toto caelo* (inclusively) under the category of historicity, but rather to retransform the structure of inner-historical events into a structure of natural events. No being underlying or residing within historical being itself is to be understood as ontological, that is, as natural being. The retransformation of concrete history into dialectical nature is the task of the ontological reorientation of the philosophy of history: the idea of natural-history.
>
> —Theodor W. Adorno, "The Idea of Natural History"[2]

Imago Dei and Philosophical Anthropology

It is not arbitrary that the chairperson of the President's Council on Bioethics, Leon R. Kass, has turned his attention to the book of Genesis in the so-called Old Testament. Leon Kass, a Straussian neoconservative, who was also influenced by one of Heidegger's children, Hans Jonas, and who often appeals to Heidegger's philosopheme of the *Gestell*, has been advocating a bioethics predicated on a form of philosophical anthropology that seeks its roots in biblical stories about the origins of humanity. Over the last two decades Kass has been arguing against the corrosive, nay apocalyptic, effects of all forms of reproductive technologies. Early in the 1970s, he prophesized that in-vitro fertilization would open the way to the end of sex, the family, stable gender roles, and the stability of Western society as such. Artificial reproduction, that is artificial sex, he anticipated, would lead to the "abolition of man," in that memorable phrase popularized by the Christian moralist and writer C. S. Lewis.[3] We must forgo discussion of what is real human procreation, that is, natural sex, as opposed to artificial or technologically assisted sex. Even in Genesis we find traces of artificial sex. But this is a discussion for biblical scholars. In 2003, Leon Kass published a gargantuan book entitled *The Beginning of Wisdom: Reading Genesis*, which is a lengthy commentary on Genesis.[4] Above all, however, this book is philosophical anthropology disguised as biblical exegesis. The goal of the text is to argue that in the allegedly oldest book of Judeo-Christian wisdom literature, we can find insights into what it means to be human, not just spiritually, but also, and most importantly, biologically. In order for Kass to argue that we must reject all forms of technological intervention into human reproduction (although he does waver when it comes to extremely debilitating diseases), he appeals to a basic human nature. In fact, over the last two decades he has been pursuing what was called early in the twentieth century philosophical anthropology.[5] The goals of this enterprise are to derive fundamental insights about social and cultural aspects of human existence from the alleged basic biological structure of the human being. Thus, from sexual difformism philosophical anthropology wants to derive the invariance and pervasiveness of gender roles across history and human groups, as well as insights about the alleged normality of heterosexism, or an existential analytics that says that human Dasein must come in two, which like electrical plugs, must fit nicely into each other. The philosophical anthropological project, however, is not merely descriptive; it is also and perhaps most importantly, prescriptive. The idea is to read down and backward into the essential structure of the human being, in order to then derive some ontic-ontologically grounded normative principles. If artificial insemination violates natural sex, then we must proscribe it. If gene therapy circumvents sexual reproduction, then it must be banned, as it violates the most fundamental aspect of human nature, and precisely what makes us human, namely that we are children of "natural" sex. In Leon Kass's case, he is now complementing his quasi-Heideggerian philosophical anthropology, mediated via Hans Jonas, with a biblically derived and buttressed insight into what it means to be human. Biblical exegesis cum philosophical anthropology, however, is a covert form of foundational ethics.[6]

Genesis, however, is less a stable and univocal text and more the region of millenarian encounters. Much of Christianity emerged precisely out of an attempt to make sense of one of the central doctrines, or *Lehre*, in Genesis, namely the "teaching" of the divine creation of the human being. In Genesis, we are told many things about original sin, arrogance, fratricide, divine wrath, deception, and so on, but two doctrines therein elaborated have been determining for Western culture: first, that human were created in the "image of God," and this is what has been called throughout history as the doctrine of *imago Dei*; the second, that God "created them," man and woman, as distinct, nonreducible, nonsubstitutable, beings. For the moment we will forgo discussion of the second point, as important as sexual difference may be for the definition of the human being. The doctrine of *imago Dei* has been at the center of major biblical debates, as well as of philosophical ones. In the following I will expand on what I have said earlier about this important biblical doctrine. Does *imago Dei* mean literally in the image, in the likeness, of God? Or, does this mean that we look like God, and consequently, that God is a Charlton Heston look-alike: tall, white, bearded, and full of wrath and contempt for the lawless and lowly. Or, does it mean that human beings were created in the semblance of God, not literally like God, but resembling godself in our ontic-ontological structure. To have been created *imago Dei* meant that we were like God in that we could be, in some respects, like God. The distinctive quality of the Judeo-Christian God is that this is a creator God, a *parthenogenic* and *ex nihilo creatio* God. God is legislator over creation, because it is her creation. To be human means that we can create and cocreate. We are shepherds of God's creation because we contribute to this creation as cocreators. Hannah Arendt gave a distinctive interpretation of this biblical doctrine. In her view, to be created plural and in the image of god meant that we were originators, initiators of new beginnings.

Arendt's concept of natality has its roots in the biblical doctrine of *imago Dei*.[7] This is what it means to be like God, namely that we can inaugurate new beginnings. Erich Fromm, the apostate Frankfurt School critical theorist, added another hermeneutical line to the interpretation of this doctrine. For Fromm, *imago Dei* also meant that the human being was created incomplete, unfinished, and thus essentially undetermined and open to evolution. As he wrote, "Man is seen as being created in God's likeness, with a capacity for an evolution the limits of which are not set. 'God,' a Hasidic master remarked, 'does not say that "It was good" after creating man; this indicates that while the cattle and everything else were finished after being created, man was not finished."[8] Precisely because man is incomplete there is the openness that makes possible history. God's divine plan, *Heilgeschichte*, requires that humans be open to futurity. This futurity is grounded in man's incompleteness. Biological neoteny and philosophical anthropological exocentricity are versions of the biblical doctrine of man's radical openness qua incompleteness.

The way the doctrine of *imago Dei* is interpreted has profound consequences for how we conceive the human being. From our brief discussion it becomes clear that there are at least two ways to understand this doctrine, either negatively or positively. In fact, if the doctrine of *imago Dei* is taken literally, as proscribing a catalog of qualities assigned specifically to the human being by God the legislator, then we have what I like to call here a positive philosophical anthropology, of which Leon Kass's is the most recent version. If, however, we take the doctrine of *imago Dei* as announcing the human as a project and incomplete creation, then we have what I will call a negative philosophical anthropology. The history of Western thought can be read partly as the attempt to mediate between negative and positive philosophical anthropology.[9] While Aristotle, Thomas of Aquinas, Kant, Hobbes, Locke, Mill, Strauss, and more recently Kass, belong to the positive philosophical anthropology tradition, Augustine, Plotinus, Eckhart, Hegel, Marx, Bloch, Adorno, Arendt, and Fromm belong to the negative philosophical anthropology tradition. The debate between these two traditions boils down to the question: is there a way in which doing and being in specific ways is distinctly human, and thus contravening or failing to do them or be them, results in not being human, or ceasing to be human, on the one hand, or, on the other hand, is there a way in which we have not been human precisely because we do not know what it means to be human yet? More succinctly, positive philosophical anthropology tells us how to be human, and thus, how not to be what would challenge our humanity, while negative philosophical anthropology tells us that the question of humanity's essence is not to be answered, not yet so long as history remains an ontological possibility of human Dasein and thus is probably unanswerable, but that it is our ability to ask the question that is indicative of how our humanity is always in question, awaiting further reformulations. One says our humanity is in jeopardy; the other says we have never been human because we still must attain our humanity. Cast in this light, then, the doctrine of *imago Dei* can be read in two mutually exclusive ways: we are created in the image of god and thus are divine in countenance and are therefore commanded to do the utmost not to defile that divine visage; or, we are created like God means we are like God in our complete indeterminability, what Derrida has recently called "incalculability," and are legislators precisely because we are not created but cocreators, and our freedom is prior to any law and any norm. In this chapter, then, I am interested in linking the questions about the basic structure of the human existence, which philosophical anthropology aims to discern, with questions about the political, violence, and the law.

Philosophical Anthropology and Cloning

Up to now I have painted in broad strokes two traditions of philosophical anthropology. In this, I want to argue that Jürgen Habermas and Jacques Derrida's recent interventions and pronouncements on cloning and the human genome should be understood against the background of this debate between negative and positive philosophical anthropology. In fact, I argue that Habermas's arguments in his *The Future of Human Nature* profile the contours of a dangerous, regressive, conservative form of positive philosophical anthropology, dangers and hazards that I think can be countered by Derrida's profiling of a critical, and potentially dialectical, negative philosophical anthropology.[10] I will in the last part of the chapter turn to two other contemporary thinkers that can help us expand on a critical, reflexive, dialectical, negative philosophical anthropology, which I think expands on a historical materialist insight into the accomplishment of our humanity.

Habermas had already broached the issue of cloning in a series of editorials, later published as appendixes to his book *The Postnational Constellation*, masterfully translated by Max Pensky.[11] Each editorial gravitated around a theme: cloning as form of slavery; nature is silent with respect to what is a moral choice; and even if we have the legal, that is civil laws, to deal with clones, the issue is at base a moral-political one. Habermas wrote a lengthier piece entitled "On the Way to a Liberal Eugenics? The

Debate Concerning the Ethical Self-Understanding of the Species"[12] which I analyzed already in the prior two chapters. In this essay, about sixty pages long and the heart of the book, Habermas expands the central intuitions of these earlier editorials. The essay meanders and is probably one of Habermas's least rigorously argued texts.[13] Yet, as I argued in the prior chapter, seven key arguments can be discerned. Let me summarize them: First, genetic screening violates and affronts our bodily integrity. Second, genetic screening, and engineering, contributes to the collapse of the distinction between *being* and *having* a body. This is a distinction that is nicely captured in German with two terms *Leib* and *Körper*. Third, the affronts to our bodily integrity from without and from within undermine our existential freedom. These three arguments are quite surprising in that Habermas is now paying attention to the corporeal dimension of human freedom. Fourth, a form of genetic slavery can develop from genetic screening and intervention that will put in jeopardy the right to an open future that is fundamental to human freedom. Fifth, insofar as our freedom is put in question, and thus undermined, then our own moral identities are undermined and put in question. The morally questionable effects of proceeding with genetic screening and manipulations affect not just present generations that opt in favor of genetic intervention, but also future generations, who would see themselves as products of an asymmetrical choice that has rendered them subordinates to our designs. Sixth, if we step over the Rubicon of genetic screening and positive genetic intervention, we would step over into a moral vacuum in which not even cynicism would have a place, insofar as anything that is within our power would be also executable. Just because we can, does not mean we should or ought. The choices against what we can do, in favor of what we should not do, even if we can, are more indicative of our moral character than the choices to attempt to do everything precisely because we can. In Habermas's view, it is this moral vacuum that is horrible. Seventh, we must assert our moral self-image by opting for a moral-political act that will signal to ourselves and future generations that we did not surrender to the inertia of technological faits accomplis.

In this chapter, however, I want to focus on the phenomenology of bodily existence and the openness to the futurity of human beings. Habermas proceeds from these arguments to propose an ethics of the species (*Gattungs-ethik*), the respect and reverence of which is made possible by a political-moral choice to reject cloning, genetic engineering, and suspect forms of genetic screening and therapeutic genetics. Put bluntly and succinctly, Habermas has used philosophical anthropological arguments to arrive at normative prescriptions. What is distinctive about this Habermasian ethics of the species is that it is enshrined in the achievements of the modern liberal, constitutional, rule-of-law democratic state. It is for this reason that a defense of this ethics is also a defense of the achievements of modernity.[14] A ban on cloning is not just a moral stance; it is also an ethical affirmation of political modernity. This type of argument, however, is very similar to the arguments that Arnold Gehlen made in his books *Moral und Hypermoral* and *Man in the Age of Technology*, albeit with conservative aims.[15] For Gehlen, man's exocentricity demanded that we submit to the rule of institutions and that we let bureaucrats and technocrats direct our fragile and undetermined constitutions. Institutions, especially durable and authoritarian ones, unburden humans from uncertainty and open futurity.

Yet, the young Habermas's position was radically different and extremely original. The phenomenology of the corporeal existence that draws the distinction between *Leib* and *Körper* was developed by Helmut Plessner.[16] In fact Habermas cites him. The key notion of the right to an open future is an idea that we find in the philosophical biology of Jakob Johann von Uexküll, and the philosophical anthropology of Max Scheler, Arnold Gehlen, and in Hans Jonas.[17] Habermas acknowledges Jonas as a source and inspiration.[18] In many ways, then, *The Future of Human Nature* takes us back to Habermas's earliest philosophical stage, one that culminated with *Knowledge and Human Interests*. This needs to be underscored because Habermas abandoned this project, namely, the attempt to ground a theory of knowledge and rationality on anthropologically grounded knowledge interests. *Knowledge and Human Interests* was a philosophical anthropological project, one that sought to ground humanity's domination of nature, the interest in understanding, and the goal of emancipation in the basic structure of human existence.[19] In his 1965 inaugural lecture at the Goethe Universität in Frankfurt, which was later published as an appendix to *Knowledge and Human Interests*, Habermas elaborated five theses that summarized his project. Two theses merit attention. Thesis one declared: "The achievements of the transcendental subject have their basis in the natural history of the human species." And thesis three declared: "Knowledge-constitutive interests take form in the medium of work, language, and power."[20] Then, glossing thesis three, Habermas writes: "What raises us out of nature is the only thing whose nature we can know: *language*."[21] Here we had the seeds of the dissolution of the philosophical anthropological project of a theory of knowledge and rationality. Indeed, and in analogous ways to how Gehlen argues, Habermas came to see that language is grounded in the biological exocentricity and neoteny of the human being, but this same language assumes the role of a protective exoskeleton, a meta-institution of institutions that allows humans to deal with the world in a normed way so as to unburden, *entlasten*, them of their own biological insufficiency. It is language that raises us above our own insufficient, mangled, incomplete biological nature. It is language itself that becomes the medium in which the achievements of the human species are transformed into cognitive, communicative, and ethical-moral faculties and capacities. As Habermas wrote in 1970 in an essay on Arnold Gehlen, "the profound vulnerability that makes an ethical regulation of behavior as a counterpoise is rooted not in the biological weakness of humans, in the newborn infant's lack of organic faculties, and in the risks of a proportionally over-lengthy rearing period, but in the cultural systems that are constructed as compensation." And, "the ethos of reciprocity, which is, as it were, hidden within the fundamental symmetries of possible speech situations, is . . . the unique root of ethics in general, and it is certainly in *no way* a biological root."[22]

Jacques Derrida, on the other hand, has not written extensively on cloning, although he has made some very explicit and incisive comments. Yet, if we understand deconstruction as a critique of presence, as a critique of all ontology in the name of metaphysics, albeit of a negative type, then we can safely aver that deconstruction is also a form of negative philosophical anthropology.[23] There are at least two texts where Derrida has explicitly broached the subject of cloning. The first text is from 1992, when he spoke before an interdisciplinary colloquium organized by the Association Descartes. This text has now appeared in English as "The Aforementioned So-Called Human Genome."[24] The other text is in the lecture from 2002 entitled "The 'World' of the Enlightenment to Come: Exception, Calculation, Sovereignty." This latter text appeared early in 2003 in a short book with the title *Voyous*, along with another lecture entitled "Rogue States."[25] In the 1992 text, really a series of smaller texts written as interventions for different panels and roundtable discussions, Derrida makes the following point, which could be seen as elaborating in different terms the difference between negative and positive philosophical anthropology: "There are two ways of raising the question of man, the essence of man, and the unity of man, of the human species: is man the being that possesses a knowledge about itself? Within the possibilities of self-fashioning . . . is this what man is, essentially? Or is man an I that, given the radical experience of a certain lack of norm, will raise the question of ethics, of freedom, of responsibility"? These two definitions concern the same being, "but on the one side this being is defined as one that knows its *own norms*, that knows itself, that knows its normativity, and that draws the consequences from this knowledge . . . whereas in another way, this being is one that at least asks itself the question of ethics, of freedom, of responsibility, where not only a norm and a knowledge of this kind are lacking, but further, *must be lacking*. I am not saying that they are lacking because of some deficiency, but rather *must be lacking* for a responsible decision to be made."[26] A positive philosophical anthropology is that which projects an image of the human as the type of creature that knows itself and the norms that it must abide by, and that therefore distinguishes it from other creatures. It follows the law of what is already established. A negative philosophical anthropology, on the other hand, departs from this fundamental, incalculable, uncircumventable, absence of the norm knowledge, and the law that is the very condition of the freedom of the human to be moral. In one case, we are moral because we are human, in the other; we become human by being moral.[27]

What Derrida has in mind when he suggests that a "completely different elaboration" is called for, is the "unconditionality of the incalculable," and more specifically, the two figures of rationality that stand on the two sides of the limit of the incalculable that simultaneously call and exceed one another. One may gloss Derrida and suggest that what is at issue in human cloning is not solely the biological nature of the human being, but above all, the unconditionality of the incalculable that makes reason and ethics possible. At issue, thus, is the unconditional incalculability of logos, ratio, reason. The challenge of cloning, of the biotechnological manipulation of the human being, qua biological entity, can be met with an affirmation of the axiomatics of genetic determinism, biologism, and an assured reason that knows its reasonableness. This answer paints a self-assured positive philosophical anthropology that tells us that the human has arrived and must assert its sovereignty. Another answer is that which steps behind the urgency to seek to save the essence of the human in the name of the human, and asks about the excess that allows for the ethical questioning that is at issue itself; it is not an essence that is at issue, but the potentiality to raise the question of the ethical as such. But such a possibility is made possible by a lack, a lack of the norm and the knowledge of what it means to be human, because we have yet to be.

This is a negative philosophical anthropology that affirms that the human is yet to come, *a venir*, as Derrida would say. *Imago Dei*, the God who is absent and yet to come, also announces the human-to-come, and conversely, so long as humans are still to be, can they point in the direction of the God to come.

The reference to a negative theology is not gratuitous. Curiously, there is a theological argument that Habermas developed in his Peace Prize of the German Association of Booksellers speech, entitled "Faith and Knowledge," to reject cloning.[28] We could call this a theological proof of the immorality of cloning. Habermas turns to Genesis, and the doctrine of *imago Dei*, and argues that this God is a "God of freemen." Not even the supreme creator has abrogated for godself this supreme authority, because were God to do this, God would have ceased to be our peer in freedom. And it is here, perhaps, where Habermas's early rejection of positive anthropology meets up with Derrida's elaboration of a negative anthropology.[29]

Retooling the Anthropological Machine

In the Loeb Classical Library edition of Plutarch's *Moralia*, in fifteen volumes, we find in volume 12 two important essays on "animals, humans, and beasts." One of the essays asks whether land animals are nobler than sea animals. The other asks whether beasts are rational or rather whether "irrational animals" do make use of reason. It is this last one that I would like to discuss briefly. In this essay, presented in the form of a dialogue among Odysseus, Circe, and Gryllus, Plutarch articulates a searing critique of what one could call metaphysical anthropocentrism that argues that humans are sui generis and must be differentiated radically from animals, humanity's cousins. Plutarch's playful dialogue rewrites book 10 of Homer's *Odyssey*, but also Aristotle's *Politics*. Whether in the case of Homer or Aristotle, what is at stake is the question of humanity's relationship to *nomos*, that is, the law. We know that Odysseus undergoes a series of adventures, some of them having to do with encounters with marginal humanity and brutal animality. The Cyclops, as was discussed in the introduction and chapter 2, stands in for asocial and marginal existence (see book 9). The Cyclops does not have law, live in isolation, and live off the land without properly tending to it. His existence is mere biological subsistence, and while he has some language, he has no real grasp of it:

for it is through language that Odysseus fools the Cyclops.[30] Plutarch takes issue with Homer's depiction not just of the beastly Cyclops, but also with all animals in the Homeric corpus, and thus, with most of the Greek philosophical tradition that is inspired by Homeric philosophical anthropology. In Plutarch's dialogue, Odysseus asks Circe, the witch that has converted some of his men into animals, namely swine, whether any of his men still remain human. Circe replies positively. Odysseus then demands that they be turned back to proper human form. Circe then brings forward Gryllus, a proper Greek name that literally means, "grunter," to argue the position of those Greeks who would rather remain as animals than become human once again. The extent of the dialogue is Gryllus's refutation of Odysseus's arrogant metaphysical humanism. Gryllus proceeds to demonstrate that animals are more noble and truthful because they are not deceitful and vain; they are more moral, because they never take more than what they need; they are more loving, because they do not conceal their true feelings; and that while animals do use reason, as is evident in their ability to discern what is advantageous to them, they do not use it for beastly and brutal ends, namely the perfection of the tools of the torture of other humans and animals. Only the human makes use of his and her reason for ends that no animal would. At the end, as if trying to grasp for the last possible argument that could be adduced to deride the animal and exalt the human, Odysseus argues against Gryllus that animals do not have an inherent knowledge of God. So, in the end the difference between humans and animals is that the former can know God, while the latter can never even conceive of it. To this Gryllus retorts: "Then shall we deny, Odysseus, that so wise and remarkable a man as you had Sisyphus for a father" (533). Here, Plutarch is making reference to the fact that Sisyphus, rumored to be Odysseus's true father, was condemned to torture in Hades for his cleverness, and more specifically, for having held that the Gods did not exist.

There is another philosophical bestiary that I would like to allude to before we proceed. In the recent science fiction film *Alien vs. Predator*, we find a fascinating continuum among animal, beast, and human. The film articulates a metahistory of humanity, a natural history of enmity and subaltern existence, in which humans are caught between the pincers of beastly technicity and animal bestiality. In fact, speculate the screenwriters of *Alien vs. Predator*, all along we have been bait in a cosmic hunting season ordered for the initiation rites of the beast/animal/hyperhuman Predator—a quasi-humanoid whose face has the claws of a crab-like mouth. On the other hand, we have the Alien, which is pretechnological, prelinguistic, and prehierarchy and lawfulness, and yet is profoundly animal in its maternal tenderness and solicitude toward the unborn. In the film, the Predators return to earth to enact their rite of passage and in the process hapless humans are caught in a war in which, as they trailer announces, "whoever wins, we humans lose." It is this "whoever wins, we lose" that I think is central to the question raised by all philosophical and theological bestiaries. In fact, this affirmation already anticipates our central thesis. The question that is partly answered in this affirmation is the following: where does the beastly lie in the continuum that spreads between the human and the animal? Is the animal between beast and human, with the human closest to the animal, perhaps even standing on the way between beast and human? Or is the human between beast and animal, in such a way that an animal transits to the beastly by way of the human? But what is the beast? Is it not the animal that with the aid of technicity (*techne*) makes war (*polemos*) on other animals, for the sake of its survival, by appropriating the place (*topos*) of the others, and that then makes the claim that those it dispossesses do not have *logos*? The beast is the human/animal on the brink of the abyss carved by *logos*, *nomos*, and *polemos*.

The Pedagogy of Bestiaries and the Logics of Animal Exclusion

During the Middle Ages bestiaries used to perform an extremely important pedagogical role, to recall the running theme of this book. They were used as vehicles to impart the lessons of Christian moral theology,[31] Along with the books of the Bible, bestiaries were extremely popular precisely because they translated, or rather illustrated, the sometimes complex and convoluted moral lessons that were to be derived from the parables of the gospels.[32] Moral proscriptions and admonitions were represented and narrated in pithy, concise, and visual entries in a book that gathered a veritable encyclopedia of demonic and cursed animals with their vices and virtues. Like its Greek precursor the *physiologus*, the goal of the bestiary was didactic and moral.[33] Animals, whether beastly or simply wild, were used to illustrate both what was praised and desirable in terms of moral fortitude, and condemned and excoriated in terms of turpitude and incontinence. The bestiary, however, is able to do its moral work because it maps a complex moral geography that is not at first glance evident. In fact, the bestiary moves along two registers, one that is invisible precisely because its invisibility makes the other register visible. While bestiaries and *physiologi* were putatively about the "immoral morality" of beasts and animals, they were also about, and this was left implicit, what human were supposed to be. Thus, behind every affirmation about what constituted the beastly there was an implicit affirmation about what humans are or are not. Therefore, the more the animal and beast were circumscribed within their animality and bestiality, the more humans were circumscribed within their human exceptionalism and ontological uniqueness. The bestiary thus operates, on one level, on a logic of exclusion and circumscription. What is to be defined is the "human" as such, but by way of a negation, namely, by what we are not, which is represented in terms of the animal and the beast.

At another level, the bestiary and *physiologus* operate on a dialectics of inversions. For in both we also encounter the beast and animal that presages or prefigures the irruption of the horrific, the abominable, the uncanny. The beast, like the animal, is a liminal figure that resides on the borders of the moral geography of human responsibility and iniquity. The beast may incite obedience to a lawful order, to a calculable and discernable sociality, but it may also unleash violence in the human that destroys that sociality. The beast horrifies not just because of the dread it inspires itself, but also because of what it unhinges within our own hearts. This double dread, of the beast qua beast and of the beast in us all, is represented in the beastly God, the god who appears as a savage beast.[34] The bestiary, like the *physiologus*, thus sought to tell moral tales about what God, or the gods, had inscribed in their book of nature. But they also sought to tell us about the horrible powers of the divine and the divine that may erupt as the monstrous, beastly, and animalistic, from within the realm of the natural itself. Thus, the bestiary is both a compendium of divine moral epiphanies and demonic kratophanies, apparitions of the god-devil, God as the devil's nemesis, its destructive and punishing face.[35] The bestiary, in other words, announces in hushed tones that what is circumscribed as the exceptional and is affirmed in the negation of the beast, namely the human, must be ready to turn into what it rejects in order to retain its singular status. This is the dialectical inversion: to be defined as human, as exceptionally human, and thus as neither animal nor beast, humans must be ready to become beastly when confronted by the beast. The beast can be confronted, only and successfully, by the powers of the beastly, the monstrous, the lawless and sacrificial. The bestiary therefore offers us a very unique, legible, and explicit exemplification of two registers: self-definition by negative exclusion and self-exemption by dialectical negation. We are defined by what we are not, but to be and remain what we are, we must be ready to become that which we just excluded as what we are not. In fact, we must be ready to be more than that which we negatively excluded. In this way, the bestiary anticipates the logic of a sovereignty that is both unconditional and sacrificial.

The Beast Within and the Roguish Beast

The Romantics of the eighteenth century spoke of a noble beast, an animal unspoiled by society. Society, in turn, was worse than nature, because in it one found deceit, iniquity, and moral corruption. The fact is that this image already existed in the Western imaginary, at least as early as the sixteenth century.[36] Christopher Columbus had already appealed to the trope of the noble savage when he wrote in his letters to the king and queen of Spain about the natives of the New World. They went about naked, without shame, narrated Columbus. And he went on: they did not have money and seemed to share everything communally. These noble savages were fascinated by the trinkets the Spaniards offered them and did not seem to be concerned with riches, gold or silver, which they used, if they did, for their objects of worship.[37] They were before or beyond guile, calculative self-interests, and perlocutionary instrumentalization, to use the language of postlinguistic turn philosophy. The noble savage is thus linked to the noble beast, an animal pure in its elemental morality and of simple or easy passions, by a juxtaposition with the artificiality, duplicity, and perfidy of social convention and mores. What is often difficult to understand is how this discourse of the noble beast and savage is linked to the exterminating and genocidal logics of conquest, imperialism, and eventually, of total war. Two recent thinkers who have tried to discern the links between the discourse of bestialization and extermination are Mary Midgley and Jacque Derrida. What is noteworthy is that, notwithstanding the differences in approach and style of presentation, they arrive at very similar conclusions.

Mary Midgley began writing about the entwinement of human and beast as early as the late 1970s, when she published her pioneering work *Beast and Man: The Roots of Human Nature*.[38] Early on in this book,

Midgley discusses how the beast, and in particular, the beasts that besieged European man, were both sources of fear and targets of excessive violence. What was particular about beasts was how they exemplified violence beyond measure and order, or what Midgley called "lawless cruelty" (27). The beast, therefore, was the embodiment of an unhinged, measureless, excessive, and thus useless violence; or what we sometimes call wickedness. The beastly is thus linked to evil, the devil, and wickedness. The beast was therefore outside the calculus of measurable and useful violence. In this way, in turn, the violence of the social order was qualified and justified, made to appear both calculable and useful. If there is lawless cruelty outside the social order, there is a lawful violence within the social order that aims at a particular goal. The violence of the order of sociality is useful and contains a measure of utility precisely because it is dispensed through a calculus of pain and force inflicted by a dispassionate arbiter. It is for this reason that at the center of political theory at the dawn of European modernity we find the Hobbesian Leviathan, a beast that is supposed to suppress and domesticate the *homini lupus*, the man wolf, the beast of the war of all against all.

Midgley, however, goes further. She also focuses on the ways in which this discourse of the useless and excessive violence of the beast became the warrant for a superseding violence by the reigning order and the established sovereign. As she narrates, she once read in a journalistic book on wolves that in medieval France wolves used to be flayed alive, partly as punishment, partly as expiation for the wolf's transgressions. At one point the author of this book asked: "Perhaps this was rather cruel," to which the author responds "but then the wolf is itself a cruel beast" (27). Midgley then glosses: "The words sound so natural; it is quite difficult to ask oneself: do wolves in fact flay people alive? Or to take in the fact that the only animal that does this sort of thing is *Homo sapiens*" (27).

What Midgley is laying out for us is the way in which the beast that sits on the pedestal of political authority in modernity is both the protector of the law, of a law that is violent, and the violator of that law. For in the name of the protection of the law, the sovereign must use excessive force, a force that can overcome the violence of the beast outside the law. Thus, the bestiary of modern political sovereignty is conditioned by the syntax of a violence that is threatening, because it is lawless, and a violence that is excessive in order to correct the lawless violence. Midgley articulates this dialectic in terms of the interaction between what she calls the beast without, such as the wolf talked about above, and the beast within. In fact, the beast within is as old as the discourse of bestialization, one that partly replaces the discourse of the lawless gods. In fact, Midgley finds articulations of the beast within in Plato, in *The Republic*, one of the foundational treaties of political theory for the West (37). From Plato, through Boswell, Nietzsche, and up to our own day with Derrida, the beast within is an alibi for a "lawless monster to whom nothing is forbidden" (36). Still, both the beast without and within are creatures of lawlessness, incalculability, unreasonableness, and excess.

Yet, even as the beastly is tracked both outside the walls of the city and in the heart of humans themselves, a fundamental asymmetry remains between the beast and man. The asymmetry exists not only in terms of the measure, force, and quality of the violence exerted by the beast outside and the beast inside, but also in terms of how both are incomparable, incommensurate, and qualitatively different. The violence of the beast is *per* definition beastly, blind, useless, lawless, and excessive. In contrast, the violence of the sovereign is *per* definition, civilized, benign, didactic, pedagogical, and of course, although superlative and disproportionate, still legitimate and sanctioned. It is for this reason that the violence of the established order that is deployed against outsiders and insiders of any given society can easily turn into a genocidal, exterminating, annihilating violence.

For Midgley, the tropes of the beast without and within have served to conceal and disavow humanity's own *ferocity* (31). But there is no beast, neither without nor within, that is lawless in the way we have fabulated. Neither wolves nor lions are unhinged in the ways we imagine them, thus terrorizing ourselves and others, even using that terror as a threat, as a deterrent against infractions and transgressions. But once we start analyzing the myths about beasts to which we cower and tremble, we discover that such beasts in fact obey their own set of laws and conventions. Beasts are neither lawless, nor cruel. They are neither evil nor angelic. They are biological beings with needs and mechanisms to deal with those needs. Midgley notes, "Beasts are neither incarnations of wickedness, nor sets of basic needs, nor crude mechanical toys, nor idiotic children. They are beasts, each with its own very complex nature" (39). There are no beasts without, and for the same reason, there are no beasts within. For Midgley, however, the myth of the beast Within has persisted and survived because it has allowed us to deal with what she calls evil and wickedness, that is, the human ability to be violent beyond any measure, calculus, even compassion and deference. But this coping mechanism has contributed also to a misrepresentation of what it means to be human, the animal who names the "animal" in difference and negative reference to what it deems to be its own exceptionality.³⁹ As Midgley puts it, "Beasts Within solve the problem of evil. This false solution does man credit because it shows the power of his conscience, but all the same it is a dangerous fib. The use of the Beast Within as a scapegoat for human wickedness has led to some bad confusion, not only about beasts (which might not matter) but about Man" (40).

Paradisaic Zoospheres

Just as political theory elaborates some of its most elemental presuppositions in terms of a bestiary, so that we may speak of a political bestiary, as I did above in chapter 2, we can also speak of a philosophical bestiary, of which Friedrich Nietzsche's is the most elaborate and so far the most amply studied, about which we will have more to say later in this book.⁴⁰ Nietzsche's philosophical bestiary, however, has found its most eloquent articulator and practitioner in Jacques Derrida. He has self-confessedly written extensively on animals and the way in which the question of the essence of the human has been answered partly through reference to the animal. In Derrida's view the question of the humanity of the human is entwined with the question of the animal.⁴¹ Derrida, however, has articulated, assuming and transforming Nietzsche's bestiary, his own philosophical bestiary, or what he also calls zoopoetic and zootheologies, in terms of three theses: First, the putative abyss that separates the human and the beast "does not describe two edges, a unilinear and indivisible line having two edges, Man and Animal in general."⁴² Second, "the multiple and heterogeneous border of this abyssal rupture has a history. Both macroscopic and microscopic and far from being closed, that history is now passing through the most unusual phase in which we find ourselves and for which there is no scale. Indeed, one can only speak here of history, of a historic moment or phase" (399) Third, "beyond the edge of the *so-called* human, beyond it but by no means on a single opposing side, rather than 'the Animal' or 'Animal Life,' there is already a heterogeneous multiplicity of the living, or more precisely . . . a multiplicity of organizations of relations between living and dead, relations of organization or lack of organization between living and dead, relations of organization or lack of organization among realms that are more and more difficult to dissociate by means of the figures of the organic and inorganic, of life and/or death" (399). Thus, Derrida's philosophical bestiary is in fact a deconstructive bestiary, one whose goal is not to police the boundary between the human and the animal, the noble and the bestial, the calculable and the excessive. On the contrary, Derrida's bestiary is a "paradisaic bestiary" one whose goal was a project "of constituting everything I [Derrida] have thought or written within a zoosphere, the dream of an absolute hospitality and an infinite appropriation" (405). Thus, against a fabulous bestiary, in the "animalizing imagination"[43] that withdraws and negates communication with the animal, that negates the history of the ways in which human and animals have coexisted and codetermined each other, across different lines of symbiosis and parasitism, Derrida juxtaposes a bestiary of the kingdom of ends, in which beast and man will coexist, or at least speak through each other. Derrida's transformed Nietzschean bestiary turns into a bestiary of unconditional hospitality, and in this way it is a bestiary that refuses and abandons the logics of negative exclusion and dialectical inversion already diagnosed by Midgley's work.[44]

Derrida, however, took the philosopheme of the animal and beast and related them to the issues of sovereignty, war, and law. Thus, for instance, he taught a course at the University of California at Davis in the spring of 2003 entitled "The Beast and the Sovereign."[45] In one of his last public interventions and publications, *Rogues: Two Essays on Reason*, Derrida elaborates the relationships among the beast, the rogue, the sovereign, reason, and law.[46] The two essays that make up this book are certainly vintage Derrida, weaving complex and thick narratives that move back and forth between literature, philosophy, contemporary events, and the turn of phrases in colloquial language that betray both the instability of concepts and their complicity. With a brilliant analysis of the trope of the rogue, Derrida shows the ways in which the projection of the beast from within and without warrants an excessive violence that is the prerogative of the sovereign. The rogue is the one that stands outside the law, but who is also drenched in blood or incited by the smell of blood. The beast is a rogue or roguish. The rogue is lawless, cunning, deceitful, and conniving, but also bellicose and belligerent. The rogue, to use Mary Midgley's expression, is "lawless cruelty" incarnate. The rogue, at least in the French etymology, is linked to *canaille*, someone who is perfidious and treacherous.[47] The *canaille*, in turn, is related to *verminaille*, which means to act as a vermin or to verminate. In French one can actually use the word *vermin* as a verb in such a way that *verminate* is a synonym of *infest*. Although Derrida does not follow to the end this series of correspondences and etymologies, they are nevertheless implied in his analysis.

What Derrida is concerned with showing in *Rogues* is the way in which reason is infested by its own claim to decidability, transparency, calculability. It is infested by this hubristic plenipotency because reason is only reason when it can be reasoned with, when reasons can be given to it, reasons that it cannot expect or foresee. The way in which reason is verminated by the roguish beast of hubristic plenipotency is mirrored in the sovereign's claim to unconditional and identitarian sovereignty. The way in which both reason and sovereignty close off themselves to the critique of their own fictitious stability, coherence, transparency, and calculability is encapsulated in the first line of Jean de la Fontaine's fable "The Wolf and the Lamb": "The strongest are always best at proving they are right." The French version of this first sentence reads, "La raison du plus fort est toujours la meilleure."[48] This first line can be rendered as "the reason of the strongest." In English this expression is often rendered as "might makes right." *Rogues* then is an extended commentary on this line that articulates reason through force or might, law through violence, and violence through the rogue. The reason of the strongest is a roguish reason, a violent reason. The might of the strongest, which imposes its reason, is lawless, *canaille*, cruel, and bloody. The reason of the strongest is the force of might and not the force of reason, a force that does not operate through force, coercion, or violence, but through persuasion, through transformation. But as Derrida points out, whoever invokes the roguishness of the other, whoever calls the other rogue, it is because they themselves are preparing to be rogues. For against the rogue, only force, might, can work. The rogue is not open to reason. The reason of the strongest is imposed upon others. Paralleling the Schmittian move of the sovereign whose very sovereignty is in play in the stepping outside the order of the law, Derrida shows how the rogue is dealt with by the sovereign itself becoming more roguish than the rogue, the rogue that is without any norm or law.

But if this is the reason of the strongest, which imposes its might through its reason, then is there a nonroguish, nonlawless, nonbloody reason? Can there be a sovereignty that is not roguish? Can there be a force that is not rogue? This is what Derrida aims at in *Rogues*, and for the moment, we must cite him in order to begin to approximate what he calls "unconditionality without sovereignty" and "incalculable unconditionality" (149), tropes that point to an enlightenment of reason that is to come and to the democracy that is to come:[49] "Reason reasons, to be sure, it is right [*elle a raison*], and it gives itself reason [*se donner raison*], to do so, so as to protect itself or keep itself [*se garder*], so as to keep within reason [*raison garder*]. It is in this that it is, and thus wants to be *itself*; that it is its sovereign ipseity. But to make its ipseity see reason, it must be reasoned with. A reason must let itself be reasoned with" (159).

Beastly Feasts and Animal Machines

Giorgio Agamben begins his powerful and momentous analysis *Homo Sacer: Sovereign Power and Bare Life* with the observation that the Greeks did not have a single term to refer to life.[50] In fact, they had two, each with very unique connotations. Through a careful exegesis of works by Plato and Aristotle, Agamben shows that *zoe* referred to bare existence, outside a political order or nomos, if we are to use Schmitt's phrase, and *bios* referred to the good life, the life that is only possible within a political order. Indeed, for Agamben, the distinction between *zoe* and *bios* is essential for all of Western political thinking. As Agamben put it: "The fundamental categorial pair of Western politics is not that of friend/enemy but that of bare life/political existence, *zoe/bios*, exclusion/inclusion" (8). The Western political order is founded by the exclusion of bare existence, but this exclusion is an exception, and it is always fragile. For Agamben, bare existence remains liminal, or rather, it is biological existence that can easily slip into expendable animal existence. More properly, bare existence, or *zoe*, is a topos; it is existence that dwells between brute animality and proper humanity. This zoological topos is captured in the trope of the *Homo sacer*, namely he who can be eliminated and extinguished not as sacrifice, but as a killing that is unpunishable: Agamben defined *Homo sacer* more precisely as "the unpunishability of his killing and the ban on his sacrifice" (73). The zoological topos that is the *Homo sacer* furthermore acquires materiality in the death camp. Indeed, the camp is indispensable for the operation of biopolitical power, the power that is based precisely in the exclusion of bare life, at the same time that it includes it by naming it and regimenting it. The camp is the space within which the state of the exception is normalized (170). For Agamben, however, the exception that founds the political order is not that referred to by Schmitt, namely the state of exception that dictates who is friend and who is enemy. Instead, the state of exception is that which distinguishes between who can be killed with impunity and who may not be sacrificed without polluting the political order. Thus, Agamben is trying to think with and against Schmitt, for before there is an enemy, there is a regimentation of life, and life that may be extinguished without punishment and that is also worthless in the process of sacramentalizing the political order. What we must for the moment hold on to is Agamben's insight that *Homo sacer* is a topos and tropos of exception. *Homo sacer* embodies the state of exception that localizes political power, but that also unmasks its limits and might.

In his book *The State of Exception*, Agamben focuses more specifically on the paradoxical character of the state of exception.[51] This paradox is formulated in the following way:

> If exceptional measures are the result of periods of political crisis and, as such, must be understood on political and not juridico-constitutional grounds . . . , then they find themselves in the paradoxical position of being juridical measures that cannot be understood in legal terms, and the state of exception appears as the legal form of what cannot have legal form. On the other hand, if the law employs the exception—that is the suspension of law itself—as its original means of referring to and encompassing life, then a theory of the state of exception is the preliminary condition for any definition of the relation that binds and, at the same time, abandons the living being to law. (1)

Another way of expressing this paradox is through reference to the syntagmas of "necessity does not recognize any law" and "necessity creates its own law" (24). This paradox, however, is again formulated in terms of the topology of the sovereign, who in order to be unconditionally sovereign must step outside his own domain. As Agamben puts it, "The state of exception is an anomic space in which what is at stake is a force of law without law (which should therefore be written: force-of-law [with an x over law])" (39). This anomic space, it turns out, is in fact a threshold, it is troping topos, a space that turns with the force of the law, with the force of its enactment, before law itself is announced and pronounced. "The state of exception marks a threshold at which logic and praxis blur with each other and a pure violence without *logos* claims to realize an enunciation without any real reference" (40). Pure violence without *logos* is what the animal that names itself, to use that turn of phrase by Derrida, attributes to the beast. The beast is lawless violence, violence without *logos*. The beast is lawless cruelty incarnate, to use Mary Midgley's phrase again. The state of exception, then, has two embodiments, both of which dwell in the topos of the threshold. First, there is *Homo sacer*, who turns out to be the Muselmann of the concentration camp, the biological entity that has been excluded from the political realm and sequestered in the camp, the topos of pure exception. Second, there is the beast, whose violence is without measure, without utility, without rhyme or reason, that is to say, illogical, and which dwells in the anomic space of the force of law without law, that is to say pure might and power, without constraint and beyond calculability. Interestingly, Agamben does not make these linkages although he has devoted an extended analysis to the duet man/animal.

Agamben's *The Open: Man and Animal*[52] is a frontal confrontation with Heidegger and the whole philosophical anthropological tradition that sets out to think about human exceptionalism on the basis of the exclusion of the animal from the human.[53] In fact, in an audacious move, Agamben sets out to turn on its head the fundamental question that has guided all forms of humanism. Instead of asking how is it that there can be a conjunction or combination of the animal and the human, the question should be how is it that a caesura, a divide, a line, was drawn that spilt in two what is clearly a continuum. In Agamben's words: "In our culture, man has always been thought of as the articulation and conjunction of a body and a soul, of a living thing and a *logos*, of a natural (or animal) element and a supernatural or social or divine element. We must learn instead to think of man as what results from the incongruity of these two elements, and investigate not the metaphysical mystery of conjunction, but rather the practical and political mystery of separation. What is man, if he is always the place—and, at the same time, the result—of ceaseless divisions and caesurae?" (16) Yet, as generative as this move is, the reason why I bring up *The Open* here, to conclude, is that Agamben opens this book with a commentary on two images from a Hebrew Bible from the thirteenth century. In particular, Agamben focuses on the last two images in the codex. The first, on the upper half of the page, represents the three biblical and primeval "animals" or monsters: the bird Ziz (a winged griffin), the ox Behemoth, and the fish Leviathan. This image is coupled with another image, in the lower part of the page, also indicating the last stage of humanity. This image portrays the messianic banquet at the end of time, when the righteous gather the last day when the Messiah returns and a great feast is to be had. In fact, according to rabbinical tradition, the righteous will feed on the flesh of the biblical monsters, kept by God through time for this express (singular) purpose. Agamben does not focus per se on what the righteous are feeding on, but rather on the images that represent the righteous. Here they are represented not with human faces, but animal heads. Thus the eschatological animals represent the righteous: the eagle, the red head of the ox, the lion, the ass, and the leopard. Agamben wants to conclude from this biblical animal iconography that perhaps the artist of this Ambrosian Bible was in fact suggesting that on the last of days man would reconcile himself to his animal nature (3). Agamben is right to suggest this interpretation. Yet, he misses the glaring caesura in these two images: there are two types of animals here: on the one hand, we have the biblical, primeval monsters or beasts, on which the righteous feed; and, on the other hand, we have the animals, created by God to be named by man, and on which the righteous clearly do not feed. These questions remain, nonetheless: what of the beast in the animal, what of the beast in man, and what of the animal that is not beastly?

The Zoons of NatureCultures

If Midgley broaches the question of the beast and the animal from the standpoint of philosophy, and how the beast was an indispensable point of reference for political theory, and Derrida approached this same question from the standpoint of the philosophical bestiary that makes explicit the parasitism of certain conceptions of reason, law, and sovereignty on the beast, the animal, and the rogue, and Agamben approached the question from the standpoint not of the mystery of the desired conjunction between animal and human, but from the ontological caesura that is ceaselessly drawn between the two, and thus within the human itself, Donna Haraway has broached the issue from the standpoint of technoscience and what she calls NatureCultures. Haraway's work has pioneered a type of thinking that goes beyond the easy dichotomies of artificial and natural, culture and technology, animal and human, biological and mechanical. Haraway's type of analysis also exhibits what we call thick geo-bio-political narratives. In fact, just as we can find Nietzschean and Derridian bestiaries, we can also find a Harawayan bestiary. Haraway's bestiary, however, is made up of organisms that are "worldly embodiments."[54] These worldly embodiments, in turn, are not so much mediated by technosciences, the marriages of science and technology, as instead are allowed in and through technology. Embodiments are for Haraway, infoldings of flesh, machines, social networks, and geohistory. Thus, organisms, HumanAnimal embodiments, are knots of synchronic and diachronic history. For this reason, Haraway's bestiary, a compendium of animals both wild and domesticated, is not so much about the epistemologically constitutive role beasts and animals play in the philosophical imaginary of cultures as it is about the materiality of that co-constitution. Insofar as Haraway's bestiary seeks to trace the geno-pheno-cultural traces of the humanization of beasts and our own domestication by our husbandry of these animals, it contributes to rendering legible more than the epistemic transcendentality of beasts and animals. Her bestiary makes explicit the constitutive interdependence between humans and their "companion species." The narratives that unknot the knots of "worldly embodiments," however are neither benign nor exculpatory. They also bring us up front to, or rather place us at the center of, the geopolitical dimensions of biopolitics, biotechnology, and the production of what Haraway calls "human-animal-technology compounds."[55]

Donna Haraway has been assiduously gathering the most comprehensive post-Human versus Animal, and post-Human exceptionalism, bestiary. Creatures that are neither/nor, and that occupy the in-between zone of and/both populate Haraway's bestiary.[56] These critters, these monsters, are neither nature, that is to say domesticated pure instinct, nor mere animality, that is to say transparent human design and instrumentality. These bio-techno-political "concrescences" are neither mute nature nor vociferous human teleology.[57] They are results of human design and interspecies accommodation. Animals are their own semiotic agents, and humans transform themselves in the process of domesticating animals. While all of these claims can be illustrated by practically every piece of writing that Haraway has done, perhaps even beginning with her essay "The Promises of Monsters: A Regenerative Politics for Inappropriate/d Others,"[58] for the purposes here of illustrating the bio-geo-techno-political dimensions of the Harawayan bestiary I will focus on her short essay "Chicken." I want to focus on "Chicken" for two reasons: first, because the essay is part of a book entitled *Shock and Awe: War on Words*, which was conceived and organized by the research cluster Feminisms and Global War Project of the Institute for Advanced Feminist Research at the University of California Santa Cruz.[59] The book is structured as a dictionary, with entries ranging from "accident," "coronation," through "we'll all be dead," and "words." The avowed aim of this radical lexicon is to offer "alternative etymologies, genealogies, fragments of everyday life, and glimpses of social history as a form of defense and defiance in an escalating war on words" (1). Haraway's contribution to this lexicon of "defense and defiance" is an entry on *chicken*, which begins with the words "Chicken is no coward" (23). The entry is narrated from the perspective of Chicken Little, the trope of the animal who is always announcing the end of the world. Chicken Little is the messiah of the end of the world, either through natural disaster or human induced apocalypse. We get to read about the chicken feeding the slaves that built the Egyptian pyramids and the role the chicken has played in the imperial pageantry and imagery of the US, as well as the poultry industry that feeds the world. Chicken Little has reason to be apocalyptic. "For, at the end of a millennium, in 2000, 10 billion chickens were slaughtered in the U.S. alone. Worldwide, 5 billion hens—75 percent in cramped, multi-occupancy, quarters called battery cages—were laying eggs, with Chinese flocks leading the way, followed by those in the United States and Europe" (25). Haraway's bestiary entry "chicken" is split in two by the subtitle "sick." So, chicken's story is complicated by disease and interspecies virus transit. The story of Chicken Little is also a story about "prototypes for techno-scientific, export-oriented, epidemic-friendly chicken industries" (28). In the end, chickens worldwide are not strangers to biodiversity and bioterror. "Chicken Little is, of course, no virgin to debates about political orders" (28). *Chicken*, then, as an entry into a posthumanist versus nature bestiary is about following the threads that knot into the infoldings of biomateriality that leads us through the traces of bio-geo-history and HumanAnimal co-constitution. "Follow the chicken and find the world" (29).

The world that we find, however, is one structured by what Haraway calls somewhere else "four-part" composition. This composition is complicated in and through: "co-constitution, finitude, impurity, and complexity."[60] What is woven in and through this four-part composition are the following: NatureCultures, ManAnimals, BioPolitics, TechnoSciences, CyBorgs, Co-Evolution, in which it is not the case of an ontology of neither-nor, but of "ontological choreographies"[61] of the both-and, always with and not only. The animals and beasts that perform their own "hermeneutic labor (and play)" through their own specific "material-semiotic requirements,"[62] in Haraway's bestiary, can be taken to be pointing in the direction of what she calls "livable politics."[63] There were never beasts, nor animals, nor monsters per se. But there have always been "companion species." A politics of enmity based on an ontology of the other as the nonhuman that is the animal, or what can also be called *divinimality* to use that felicitous neologism by Derrida,[64] is no longer acceptable. A politics of coexistence, a livable politics becomes both possible and necessary—a politics beyond monsters, beasts, roguish animals, and infesting vermin that must be domesticated, at best, or exterminated, at worst.

"Whoever wins, we lose," says the human before the beastly sovereign and the beast outside sovereignty. "If we win, they lose," ponders the panda bear. But who wins, really, wonders the posthumanist humanoid? The plenipotentiary *Homo sapiens*, whose other closest of kin has been *Homo martialis*—man the creature for and of war—answers the humanoid, who yearns to be a good animal. Conjoined by means of Midgley and Agamben, Derrida and Haraway point us in the direction of a new logos, nomos, and topos in which humans are not the "fattest squealer pig" at the top of the pecking order, and Chicken Little leads us with her gentle feathers to the edge of a livable geo-bio-politics, or zoosphere of peaceful and just coexistence.

III
Toward a Companion Species Ethics

Chapter 7

Animal Is to Kantianism As Jew Is to Fascism

Adorno's Bestiary[1]

> By referring to a number of little noticed outlines or suggestions of Adorno's in the book he wrote in the United States with Horkheimer, *Dialektik der Auflklärung*, or in *Beethoven: Philosophie der Musik*, I would try to show (I have already tried to do this elsewhere), that here there are premises that need to be deployed with great prudence, the gleams at least of a revolution in thought and action that we need, a revolution in our dwelling together with these other living things that we call the animals. Adorno understood that this new critical—I would rather say "deconstructive"—ecology had to set itself against two formidable forces, often opposed to one another, sometimes allied.
>
> —Jacques Derrida, "Fichus"[2]

Deconstructive Zoontology

In 2001 Jacques Derrida was awarded the Theodor W. Adorno Prize, which the city of Frankfurt am Main confers upon those who in the spirit of the Frankfurt-based Institute for Social Research pursue interdisciplinary work that cuts across the sciences, humanities, and arts.[3] Derrida's speech, entitled "Fichus," is surely one of the most important essays in the Derridean corpus, for in it he lays out in rather unequivocal terms the ways in which his work stands within the tradition of the Frankfurt School.[4] At the source of much of his thinking and preoccupations stands the towering figure of Walter Benjamin. Derrida in fact asks why there

160 | The Philosophical Animal

is no Benjamin prize, when so much of Adorno's work is dependent on Benjamin and when so much of contemporary thinking is so enduringly nurtured by his mangled intellectual corpus. After fascinating discussions of Hegel, Freud, the question of language and national identity, of what it means to be a German Jew, Derrida offers the abstracts, "in the style of a TV guide," of seven chapters that would make up the contents of a book that would "interpret the history, the possibility, and the honor of this prize."[5] It is chapter 7 of this hypothetical book that I want to briefly discuss as a way to introduce my concerns in this chapter. Derrida notes that this last chapter would be the one that he would most enjoy writing, "because it would take the least trodden but in my view of the most crucial paths in the future reading of Adorno."[6] This chapter would deal with Adorno's animals, or what I have here called in the subtitle "Adorno's Bestiary." To give us a TV guide–style abstract of the question of the animal in Adorno, Derrida focuses on two texts in Adorno. The first is a fragment that is now in his posthumously published book on Beethoven. The passage reads, and I quote Adorno now:

> Ethical dignity in Kant is a demarcation of differences. It is directed against animals. Implicitly it excludes man from nature, so that its humanity threatens incessantly to revert to the inhuman. It leaves no room for pity. Nothing is more abhorrent to the Kantian than a reminder of man's resemblance to animals. This taboo is always at work when the idealist berates the materialist. *Animals play for the idealist system virtually the same role as the Jews for fascism.* To revile man as an animal—that is genuine idealism. To deny the possibility of salvation for animals absolutely and at any price is the inviolable boundary of its metaphysics.[7]

Derrida closely follows this passage, remarking on the German terms used and highlighting in particular the uses of "taboo" and "insult." But then Derrida glosses the text, introducing a turn of phrase that he finds extremely important: "Fascism begins when you insult an animal, including the animal in man. Authentic idealism (*echter Idealismus*) consists in *insulting* the animal in man or in treating a man like an animal."[8] Derrida immediately evokes the "but on the other hand" and turns our attention to another set of fragments in Adorno's work. The fragment in question is now part of *Dialectic of the Enlightenment*, and it is entitled

"Man and Beast." Derrida is making reference in this fragment to a sentence in which Adorno and Horkheimer call into question the opposite attitudes to "insulting" and "reviling." Derrida paraphrases the following sentence, "The precondition of the fascist's pious love of animals, nature, and children is the lust of the hunter. The idle stroking of the children's hair and animal pelts signifies: this hand can destroy. It tenderly fondles one victim before felling the other, and its choice has nothing to do with the victim's guilt."[9] Derrida notes that these passages urge us to "fight against the ideology" that is concealed in the Nazis' "troubled interest" in animals and nature, to the point of vegetarianism.[10] Derrida is in fact drawing our attention to the dialectical tension between the insult against the animal in the human that is the foundation of fascist genocide, and the fascist's pseudo-zoophilia, which is concealed in the Fuhrer's love of his dogs and his supposedly obsessive vegetarianism.

I want to remark on three aspects of Derrida's concluding chapter on "animals" in his hypothetical book and in particular on his not-so-subterranean relationship to Critical Theory. First, there is the highly charged and potentially polemical character of Derrida's comments, in which he links Kant to Fascism, and putatively to the ecological and animal questions of the twentieth and twenty-first centuries, by way of a Jew who survived the Holocaust. What is also noteworthy is that Habermas was present at this speech and that both were during the fall and winter of 2001 beginning a sort of collaboration and intellectual friendship. It is around this time that both Derrida and Habermas are being interviewed by Giovanna Borradori for what later became *Philosophy in a Time of Terror*.[11] Here one may suggest that Derrida is making a point about the Kantian turn of second generation Critical Theory, one that both forgets and occludes the animal in man. The second remark concerns Derrida's proclaimed happiness were he to write this chapter. The fact is that he did write such a chapter, or in fact, he wrote several versions of this chapter. As is well known, Derrida was lecturing on the animal, the beast, sovereignty and reason toward the end of his life. In fact, as Adorno developed a bestiary, Derrida also developed his own bestiary, but one that he wanted to call with the dual names of zoopoetics and zootheologies.[12] (Here I must make reference to Cary Wolfe and David Wood's indispensable works on the question of the animal in Derrida's work, in lieu of even a synoptic overview.[13]) This brings me to the third remark, and that is that Derrida, as the faithful and tireless reader that he was, had discovered a vast and unexplored dimension of Adorno's work when he noted that the question of the animal (which should not be written or thought in the singular according to Derrida) is, to repeat, the "least trodden" and the most significant in the future appropriation of Adorno's work. In the following, therefore, I want to focus on the trope of the animal in Adorno's work, one that acts as a hinge between Adorno's negative anthropology, on the one hand, and his critique of totalitarian reason, on the other. I will also discuss the way in which Adorno's notion that "nothing is more abhorrent to Kantianism" than to be reminded of the animal semblance of humans is related to a cognate though hardly explored notion in Adorno's work, namely his notion of "natural history." I will conclude by returning to Derrida in order to raise the question of the historicity of the animal-human question, and the role that a historical materialist philosophical anthropology can play in the context of an age of in which animal extermination and extinction converge.

Adorno's Animal Ethics:
To Live As If One Had Been a Good Animal

There is a picture of Adorno that has become iconic not just of Adorno's relationship to the world, but also of the ethereality and obscurity of his writing. The picture, which is now on the cover of the dust jacket of the recently released massive biography of Adorno by Stefan Müller-Doohm, indeed portrays a man lost in thought, his gaze fixed in the distance, but aimed inwardly. His lips are slightly open, but downcast, as if about to say something or anticipating an expression of horror or regret. Martin Jay described this picture well, which also was on the cover of his book on Adorno: "The cumulative effect produced by the photo is powerful, showing us a man brooding in subdued sadness about the untold horrors of his life time."[14] Yet, there is another photograph that is as telling of Adorno. The photograph was taken around 1943, when Adorno lived in California. It portrays him at his desk, turned backward looking at the photographer. His desk is cleared, though to the right there is a table with trays filled with papers. The desk, an ungainly contraption towering over him, is decorated with animal figurines. There are two giraffes, a gazelle, and a horse. To his left there is a large sculpture of what appear to be two peacocks rubbing heads, bowing to each other. Perched on one of the levels of the cabinet that rises over the desk is a little stuffed teddy bear. Adorno is wearing his glasses, and there is a smile on his lips.

Adorno in fact had a great fondness for animals. We now know that he used to visit quite frequently the Frankfurt Zoo with his mother and his aunt, whom he called a second mother. He had a great affection for large, slow, and patient herbivores, such as hippopotamuses, rhinoceroses, and wombats. This sentiment he avowed without subterfuge or shame. In a letter to Bernhard Grzimek, the director of the Frankfurt Zoo, dated April 23, 1965, Adorno wrote:

> Would it not be wonderful if Frankfurt Zoo could acquire a pair of wombats? I have fond memories of these friendly and cuddly animals from my childhood and would love to be able to see them again . . . And may I also remind you of the existence of the babirusa, or the horned dog as I suppose it is called in English, which was also one of my favorite animals during my childhood; a delightful bizarre pachyderm. I hope it hasn't become extinct in the Malaysian archipelago? And lastly, what is the situation with the dwarf hippos they used to have in Berlin?[15]

Early in his life he imagined himself as Archibald the rhinoceros, and referred to Gretel, his wife, as the modern giraffe. Horkheimer was identified with the mammoth, and there is a drawing by him paying tribute to his animal soul, in which the mammoth is shown trying to shave and carries the note: "Mammoth self[-]shaving must be difficult." There is a very telling, though playful letter from the late 1930s from Adorno to Horkheimer, written while Adorno was in England:

> The rhinoceros king Archibald has a golden crown with a fat pear and golden layers of skin over his eyes, but stands aloof from active government. He is having an affair with the giraffe "Gazelle," occasionally wears a silk-grey pair of pajama trousers, and has published a pamphlet, the pan-humanist manifesto. It has appeared in the publishing house of the united jackals and hyenas. For years he has been working on his magnum opus. It is called "The Rhinoceros Whip," and is the theoretical groundwork of a society that includes the animals.[16]

As Detlev Claussen notes in his biography of Adorno, Adorno and Horkheimer refer to each other as pachyderms not only because of their thick skins, but also because of their placid temperaments and ability to digest mountains of literature as though it were grass.[17] It would be inappropriate and entirely contrary to the entwinement between the private and public in Adorno's work to dismiss these musings and playful assimilation into the animal. There is an unmistakable continuity between Adorno's lifelong fascination and identification with animals and what he wrote and argued in his philosophical writings. We ought to take seriously what Adorno wrote in his letter to Horkheimer quoted above, namely that he aimed to develop a "theoretical groundwork of a society that includes the animals." This groundwork would entail developing a new anthropology and a new metaphysics in which the animality of humans would be acknowledged, and space would be made for a "natural history" that would point us in the direction of a future progress that is truly mindful of the incompleteness of our humanity. Here we cannot fail to remark on the similarities between Adorno's concern with the animal in the human and Herbert Marcuse's rescue of the Orphic and narcissistic eros that counter the violence and brutality of the Promethean myth. These similarities are not only at the level of the content of images, allegories, and metaphors, but also at the level of methodology: that is to say, both Adorno and Marcuse seek to use myth against reified and ossified rationality.[18]

In a discussion from 1956 between Horkheimer and Adorno, the latter affirms: "Philosophy is truly there to redeem what lies in the gaze of an animal [Die Philosophie ist eigentlich dazu da, das einsulösen, was im Blick eines Tieres liegt]."[19] In a letter of congratulations to Horkheimer on his seventieth birthday from 1965, Adorno wrote, "You [Du] once told me that I treat animals like humans, and you humans like men. There is something there."[20] What is "there" is a dialectical move to see in animals humans and in humans animals, precisely what the project of a natural history aims to keep in the foreground. A passage in *Minima Moralia* expresses explicitly this movement. In paragraph 68 Adorno considers the way in which the gaze of the animal and what looks like an animal are related: "The possibility of pogroms is decided in the moment when the gaze of a fatally-wounded animal falls on a human being. The defiance with which he repels this gaze—'after all, it's only an animal'—reappears irresistibly in cruelties done to human beings, the perpetrators having again and again to reassure themselves that it is 'only an animal' because they could never fully believe this even of animals." Here, the license, and even perhaps the imperative to exterminate another human being appears when the animal gaze peers through the eyes of the human—the human that gazes back like a wounded animal. We need to read paragraph 68 in conjunction with paragraph 33, entitled "Out of the Firing Line":

> Cinema newsreel: the invasion of the Marianas, including Guam. The impression is not of battles, but of civil engineering and blasting operations undertaken with immeasurably intensified vehemence, also of "fumigation," insect-extermination on a terrestrial scale. Works are put in hand, until no grass grows. The enemy acts as patient and corpse. Like the Jews under Fascism, he features now as merely the object of technical and administrative measures, and should he defend himself, his own action immediately takes on the same character . . . Consummate inhumanity is the realization of Edward Grey's human dream, war without hatred.

War without hatred means war that has become a cleansing operation, an operation to fumigate and exterminate a vermin, a plague. The enemy is no longer human, but a vermin. The pivot, though, is the formulation, "like Jews under Fascism," recalls the other equivalence: "animal is to Kantianism as Jews are to Fascism." If we inure ourselves to the animal gaze, which is a gaze that addresses our unaccomplished humanity, we already have extinguished our subjectivity and have eviscerated it of anything that would give worth to its preservation.

What kind of subjectivity is worth preserving, and how could it be preserved in such a way that it allows itself to be addressed by the gaze of the animal other? Part of the answer is to be found in the first excursus of the *Dialectic of Enlightenment*, which deals with Odysseus. Here, Odysseus is read as a prototype of bourgeois subjectivity, but also as a cipher for the struggle against nature, on the one side, and myth, on the other. Odysseus's misfortunes and adventures are a travail against the irrational forces of nature, but also against the irrational force of rationality bent on self-preservation. Odysseus epitomizes the way in which "the history of civilization is the history of the introversion of sacrifice—in other words, the history of renunciation."[21] Homer's Odysseus captured the tragedy to which humans are condemned by civilization, namely to destroy in themselves that for which they surrender themselves to society. Odysseus, at the same time, personifies the promise of that for which we submit ourselves to so much privation and self-denial: a return home against the will of the gods, the overcoming of fate. Between this tragedy and promise is profiled a way out, namely not to reject in us what is nature, but also not to succumb to its mimetic violence. "At the moment when human beings cut themselves off from the consciousness of themselves as nature, all the purpose for which they keep themselves alive—social progress, the heightening of material and intellectual forces, indeed, consciousness itself—become void, and the enthronement of the means as ends, which in late capitalism is taking on the character of overt madness, is already detectable in the earliest history of subjectivity."[22] The birth of subjectivity in fact is inaugurated by the instrumentalization of what is nature in us and of external nature itself into means for our survival. The task, thus, is to dethrone the reversal of means into ends and to establish properly the correctly lived life, a life or form of living that looks to the other, as other, and sees in it a challenge to our hitherto narrowly conceived humanity. If our humanity is not yet accomplished, it is because our proper relation to our animal others is not yet established. The task of humanization is not the rejection of nature in us, but its proper recognition in us. To paraphrase Marx's comments in his 1844 *Economic and Philosophic Manuscripts*, via Adorno, then, the humanization of nature is also the naturalization of humanity.[23]

The last sentence of paragraph 68 in *Minima Moralia* speaks to this task: "The mechanism of 'pathic projection' determines that those in power perceive as human only their own reflected image, instead of reflecting back the human as precisely what is different. Murder is thus the repeated attempt, by yet greater madness, to distort the madness of such false perception into reason: what was not seen as human and yet is human, is made a thing, so that its stirrings can no longer refute the manic gaze."[24] This manic gaze is the gaze of that subjectivity born of the sacrifice of nature in us that refuses to be gazed back at by that which it claims it has vanquished and prevailed over. This nature must be insulted, because it was the source of our torment and reminds us of our own weakness and dependence on it.

Yet, there is something that is between nature and socialized society that forces us to look at, and be looked at by, nature in such a way that our being nature is ever present and recollected. This is the work of art. Philosophy redeems what lies in the gaze of the animal by rescuing what is preserved in the expression of works of arts. It is through art that humans are able to neutralize instrumental reason bent on dominating nature. Indeed, the work of art is dialectics at a standstill in that it exemplifies what it seeks to overcome by precisely highlighting what it is: always mimesis, always remembrance, always the self-confessing avowal that is an anti-commodity commodity that never renounces its announcement of the *promesse du bonheur* by renouncing utopia in the now. In his last book, *Aesthetic Theory*, Adorno talks about the relationship between semblance and expression in artworks. It is through semblance that artworks communicate, but they communicate neither what they portray nor the subjectivity of the artist that imprints them with life. Artworks communicate the non-identical through their semblance of the object. But just as importantly, works of art communicate or express not a formed and fully autonomous subjectivity, but rather what Adorno called "the protohistory of subjectivity." As he wrote in *Aesthetic Theory*, "Artworks bear expression not where they communicate the subject, but rather where they reverberate with the protohistory of subjectivity, of ensoulment, for which tremolo of any sort is a miserable surrogate. . . . The expression of artworks is the nonsubjective in the subject: not so much the subject's expression as its copy: there is nothing so expressive as the eyes of animals—especially apes—which seem objectively to mourn that they are not human."[25] Through artworks, nature peers back at humans, but also the yearning for a rightly lived humanity gazes mournfully at us, who see in artworks also the stigmata of historical suffering, but also a primordial joy of living. Artworks are also above all about useless passions, the end without ends, the disinterested interest, and the pleasure for the sake of pleasure itself. The work of art is a playful charade. In this, it is also mimesis, and there we are harkened back to our species protohistory, as well as to our ontogenesis: once we were children and as children we were innocent animals. Adorno writes:

> In its clownishness, art consolingly recollects prehistory in the primordial world of animals. Apes in the zoo together perform what resembles clown routines. The collusion of children with clowns is a collusion with art, which adults drive out of them just as they drive out their collusion with animals. Human beings have not succeeded in so thoroughly repressing their likeness to animals that they are unable in an instant to capture it and be flooded with joy. . . . In the similarity of clowns to animals the likeness of humans to apes flashes up; the constellation animal/fool/clown is a fundamental layer of art.[26]

This constellation is what makes of artworks the site for the expression of what is not human, albeit using human means.[27] Here art is indispensable to ethics; in fact, it is the groundwork for a moral philosophy.

If we read the statement Adorno made in 1956, "philosophy is truly there to redeem what lies in the gaze of an animal," in tandem with the last section (153) in his *Minima Moralia*—a book dedicated to Horkheimer—where he claims that "the only philosophy which can be responsibly practiced in face of despair is the attempt to contemplate all things as they would present themselves from the standpoint of redemption," then we can safely infer that Adorno would have been comfortable with the following statement: the only philosophy that we can practice responsibly today is one that would seek to redeem without prevarications the ethical appellation in the animal gaze. Such a philosophy would in fact combine two categorical imperatives, one imposed upon humanity by Hitler and the metonym of fascism, the other by Kantian derision and idealistic abhorrence of the animal in humanity. One categorical imperative would command: "to arrange their thought and actions so that Auschwitz will not repeat itself, so that nothing similar will happen."[28] The other would command: "to try to live so that one may believe oneself to have been a good animal [ein gutes Tier gewesen zu sein]."[29] One of the most astute analysts of Adorno's work, Gerhard Schweppenhäuser, notes with respect to this claim that if we are to take it seriously we have to ask not just why we should be moral, but two further questions: why is morality immoral and immorality moral?[30] Schweppenhäuser holds that these two questions are implicit in all of Adorno's work on morality, especially in part three of the *Negative Dialectics*, as well as in his lecture course from 1963 entitled *Problems of Moral Philosophy*.[31] But as I have been suggesting, the imperative to "live so that one may believe oneself to have been a good animal" is related to Adorno's critique of metaphysics and its implicit positive anthropology that delimits the human and reason by invidiously excluding the animal and that which is not at the service of instrumental reason. Schweppenhäuser calls Adorno's ethics a negative moral philosophy, which rejects extant moral philosophy, as much Kant's as Hegel's, not only because of the way both are at the service of socialized society and the totalized totality, but also because bourgeois morality enshrines the autonomous free subject that is an empty shell, one immolated at the altar of subjectivity. There is no morality proper to human freedom, because humans as such have yet to realize their humanity in accord with their animal nature. Morality is negative, yet to be achieved, precisely because our humanity is yet to be achieved. Thus,

Adorno's negative anthropology, an anthropology without *anthropos*,[32] is matched by a negative moral philosophy that denounces the immorality of what we take to be moral and discovers in the immoral the guide to what is moral. In *Negative Dialectics*, Adorno writes: "That man is 'open' is an empty thesis, advanced—rarely without an invidious side glance at the animal—by an anthropology that has arrived. . . . That we cannot tell what man is does not establish a peculiarly majestic anthropology; it vetoes any anthropology."[33] If we cannot tell what the human is, precisely because it has yet to be achieved, we also cannot tell what the animal is. Just as Adorno develops a negative anthropology, he also traces the lineaments of a zoology without the animal—or rather and to be more precise, a philosophical animalistics without the animal. It would not be incorrect to refer here to Derrida's own project of a zoopoetics, a creation through and vis-à-vis the drawing of the lines within the continuum of the animal. Still, to speak of an anthropology without *anthropos*, a zoology without an animal, and a bestiary without the beast, is to speak of a historical materialism that thinks the natural as part of the historical and the historical as partly natural. In order to clarify Adorno's stand on his historical materialist philosophical anthropology and bestiary, we must take recourse to his views on what he called already in 1932 "the idea of natural history." As has been noted by Max Pensky, the concept of *Naturgeschichte* is "candidate for the most troubling and most resistant" concepts in Adorno's thinking.[34] It is clear that it was originally formulated in terms of a critique of Heidegger's fundamental ontology and existential analytics, but later it was retained and transformed into a critique of all attempts to assimilate nature into history and subjectivity into complete socialization. As the essay's translator has astutely noted, the closest conceptual analogue to *Naturgeschichte* is Horkheimer and Adorno's genealogy of primal subjectivity in the allegory of the *Odyssey*, as developed in the first excursus in the *Dialectic of Enlightenment*.[35] Natural history is neither *historia naturalis*, as was practiced by scholastic philosophers and theologians, who sought to read in nature the designs of some divine will and plan, nor is it nature as would be studied by the natural science, in which the changes in nature would be told in the form of a narrative. The key passage from the 1932 lecture is the following:

> If the question of the relation of nature and history is to be seriously posed, then it only offers any chance of solution if it is possible to comprehend historical being in its most extreme historical determinacy, where it is not historical, as

natural being, or if it were possible to comprehend nature as an historical being where it seems to be most deeply itself as nature . . . The retransformation of concrete history into dialectical nature is the task of the ontological reorientation of the philosophy of history: the idea of natural history.[36]

Natural history, contrary to the seeming oxymoronic ring of the expression, seeks to naturalize history and historicize nature in order to break through the reification of both: nature is not solely the repetition of the same, nor is history the ceaseless emergence of the new. The idea of natural history, in fact, turns out to be no more than a reconstruction of dialectical materialism. Nothing makes this more evident than Adorno's explicit claims in *Negative Dialectics*, where he inserts the above quoted passage from the 1932 lecture and then proceeds to conclude the section entitled "Natural History" by quoting Marx from the *German Ideology*: "We can only know a single science, the science of history. History can be considered from two sides, divided into the history of nature and the history of mankind. Yet there is no separating the two sides; as long as man exists, natural and human history will qualify each other." This passage is then followed by Adorno's oblique gloss on it: "The traditional antitheses of nature and history is both true and false—true insofar as it expresses what happened to the natural element; false insofar as, by means of conceptual reconstruction, it apologetically repeats the concealment of history's natural growth by history itself."[37] The category of natural history, therefore, can contribute to the dialectical cracking of a historical totality that sets up a sacrificial stage on which our humanity is immolated through its appearing as the supposed savage logic of nature.

"Natural History": What Follows after the Animal

In July of 1997 Derrida gave a ten-hour address at the Cerisy-la-Salle conference devoted to his work. The title of the conference was "The Autobiographical Animal."[38] Responding to a question afterward by Elisabeth Roudinesco concerning "animals rights," Derrida summarized how the key philosophers dealt with in his presentation—Descartes, Kant, Heidegger, Levinas, and Lacan—had broached the question of the animal:

> Now, when it comes to the relation to "the Animal," this Cartesian legacy determines all of modernity. The Carte-

sian theory assumes, for animal language, a system of signs without response: *reactions* but no *response*. Kant, Levinas, Lacan, Heidegger (much like the cognitivists [I would add to Derrida's list, Habermas and Honneth] hold a position in this regard identical to Descartes'. They distinguish *reaction* from *response*, with everything that depends on this distinction, which is almost limitless. With regard to the essential and to what counts on a practical level, this legacy, whatever the differences may be, governs modern thought concerning the relation of humans to animals.[39]

Derrida proceeds to argue that the discourse of animal rights, which is predicated on human rights, replicates the logic and principles that have in the first place necessitated that we extend such protection to animals. The solution in fact turns out to be part of the problem, the medicine, the very source of the ailment: "Consequently, to want absolutely to grant, not to animals but to a certain category of animals, rights equivalent to human rights would be a disastrous contradiction. It would reproduce the philosophical and juridical machine thanks to which the exploitation of animal material for food, work, experimentation, etc., has been practiced (and tyrannically so, that is, through an abuse of power)."[40] It is this contradiction that Adorno confronts squarely, but without flinching from it and deeming it a "disastrous" one. I want to conclude by arguing that Derrida is absolutely right to refocus our attention on this hitherto little explored aspect of Adorno's work, not just because it foregrounds a series of profound reflections that have immediate relevance for us today, as we face an unprecedented and irreversible ecological crisis, but also because it allows us to shed light on a methodological dimension of Adorno's work that seems to have lost some of its appeal and luster due to the linguist turn of Frankfurt School Critical Theory.

Derrida's "The Animal That Therefore I Am (More to Follow)," which I dealt with in chapter 6, raises a series of extremely evocative questions, of which I will focus only on two.[41] The title, a play on French grammar that links the verb *to be* to *follow*—as David Will notes, "[a]n obvious play on Descartes's definition of consciousness (of the thinking animal as human)" which "also takes advantage of the shared first-person singular present form of *être* (to be) and *suivre* (to follow) in order to suggest a displacement of that priority, also reading as 'the animal that therefore I follow after.' "[42] Indeed, Derrida evokes the many valences of *to follow*: to be after, to seek, to come after, to be next to, to be with, to be in a temporal chronology that is ambiguous as to whether the after is before or after, in the sense that the human is what comes after the animal, or that the human is in search of his or her animality. One of the things Derrida is alluding to, evidently, is the Darwinian notion that *Homo sapiens* comes after prior evolutionary extinctions or failures. We are thus in the grip of that realization that we are after all descendants of apes, and so we are also in the grip of the obsessive quest after our missing link. We are part of "natural history," and humans cannot be explained without reference to that logic of evolution.

The temporal after, of the human that is after the animal in herself, is related to another important reflection in Derrida's lecture. Derrida in fact will formulate two hypotheses. The first hypothesis formulates that for over two centuries human beings have been "involved in an unprecedented transformation." And this "mutation" has affected what we call "imperturbably" the "animal or animals." Here Derrida notes the asymmetry between what has been happening to "the human" and what has not happened to the animal. On one side we have ceaseless change and transformation, on the other, immutability and stasis. Derrida wants to arrest and truncate the assumed historicality of the human and imputed ahistoricality of the animal. The transformation of humanity as is reflected in this putatively new consciousness about the animal is not and will not be described by Derrida as a "historical turning point."[43] To describe it in such terms would be to reinscribe in the very attempt to think the human and the animal jointly the very line that has kept them separated from and alien to each other. That one has history, and the other does not. That one dwells properly in the historical, while the other dwells in timeless nature.

The second hypothesis is announced after Derrida has pronounced that "the animal looks at us, and we are naked before it. Thinking perhaps begins there."[44] We must not overlook the striking similarity between Derrida's formulation and Adorno's formulation quoted above that "philosophy is truly there to redeem what lies in the gaze of an animal" [Die Philosophie ist eigentlich dazu da, das einsulösen, was im Blick eines Tieres liegt]."[45] The second hypothesis, nonetheless, is formulated in three paragraphs, which I will abbreviate for the sake of space in the following way: (1) that the abyss between the human and the animal does not have two edges; (2) that this rupture has a history; (3) that beyond this line that challenges its very tracing and legibility is the multiplicity of the living.[46] Together, these three paragraphs formulate the hypothesis that Derrida's work has been properly about limits, about their logics, their violences, and their transgressions. The subject of this second hypothesis is what Derrida calls *limitrophy*: the turning of limits, the forms of limits, the turning of limits, among which, of course, is the limits of the human.[47] In Adorno's language, then, Derrida's project has been "about transcending the concept by way of the concept"[48] by exploding and exposing the concept's historicity that is negated by being assumed to be a timeless category that is independent of both history and nature.

The Anthropocene: The Age of the Sixth Extinction

We have not ceased to be animals, and will never cease to be, for whatever is part of our evolution is still part of our natural evolution, just as numerous animals have not ceased to be animals even if they have coevolved with humans. To refute and insult the animal in the human is to exile humans to an impossible pedestal, one from which it can fulminate and rain violence against that which it deems its inferior. Both Adorno and Derrida are resolute in their philosophical commitment to recognizing that we are inextricably woven into the natural history of all animals, and all that is living in general, even as we have sought to define ourselves by distinguishing ourselves from it. We're in the midst of crossing three important thresholds that will surely alter not just the meaning of what it means to be human, but also of what it may mean to be a nonhuman animal. The first has to do with the correlated processes of population explosion and mega-urbanization of humanity.[49] Together, they mean the exacerbated stress on the planet, as well as the inevitability of having to think of large sectors of humanity as surplus, redundant, even burdensome, humanity. We are at the point at which we are having to think of humanity as a plague on the planet and humanity itself. The population growth of humanity is exponentially and inversely related to the habitats of other animal species. In fact, scientist have coined a name for this planetary age in which humans essentially have taken over the entire planet, transforming it in unprecedented ways: the Anthropocene.[50] The more humans and the more space they take up to live and to consume, the less space for other animals, the less other species can survive in macro- and micro-habitats. For this reason, we are facing what paleontologists have been calling the "sixth extinction." In 1993, biologist E. O. Wilson projected that about thirty thousand animal and plant species were becoming extinct yearly. More recently scientist have begun to argue that this estimate is actually higher.[51] In his 2002 book *The Future of Life* Wilson offers a bleaker prospect when he affirmed that "at least a fifth of the species of plants and animals would be gone or committed to early extinction by 2030, and half by the end of the century."[52] The Anthropocene is also the age of the animal extinction. What will become of the earth after such a massive extinction, on a scale larger than that occasioned by earlier earthly catastrophes? Humans may become extinct, and the earth will have become a "planet of weeds," as David Quammen put it.[53] The third threshold has to do with the genetic manipulation of genomes, both animal and plant alike. It is not only that we have been genetically modifying plants and animals, the so-called GMOs, sometimes even mixing animal and plant genomes. It is difficult not to expect that some scientist has not already engaged in some sort of genetic manipulation, whether therapeutic or enhancing, of the human genome. It is here where Adorno's concept and dialectical method of "natural history," becomes relevant. Neither a supererogatory ethics that grants to animals unique or elevated moral status, nor a mere utilitarian ethics of the preservation of animals, a kind of moral considerability of animals by proxy, will do. Adorno's historical materialism and negative philosophical anthropology remits us to an uneasy responsibility that is both simultaneously a responsibility for what is human and animal in us, and for the animal, without which we cannot be, both morally and materially. The animal in us gave rise to reason in us, but also to the affect that makes us vulnerable to the suffering in animal others and that our guides moral solicitude toward others. There is an aphorism by Leo Tolstoy that expresses beautifully what I take to be Derrida's and Adorno's inchoate, if not explicitly avowed, positive response to the gaze of the animal: "When a man does not live as man, he is beneath the animal."[54] When man lives like a parasite and a plague, he is both less than human and less than animal. Let us learn to live like good animals, as Adorno put it when he reformulated the Kantian categorical imperative.

Chapter 8

Interspecies Cosmopolitanism

Introduction

Cosmopolitanism is at the very least three things: an ethical stance, a political agenda, and a philosophical methodology.[1] As the synergetic synthesis of these three elements, then, cosmopolitanism is a way of seeking an orientation and trying to find a proper place in the world with others, and for others. It is a world-making, a worlding, a practice. Cosmopolitanism, therefore, challenges cartographies of exclusion based on teleologies, theodicies, and ontologies that support exceptionalisms and invidious hierarchies. We can think of cosmopolitanism as a practice of mapping cartographies of cohabitation, rather than of binding through boundary-making and mapping topologies of exception. Yet, as transgressive and "cosmopolitan" as recent debates and rearticulations of cosmopolitanism have been, very few thinkers have acknowledged the elephant in the room: can, should, must cosmopolitanism take up the question of animal others, of what Haraway has called "companion species"?[2] It can be said that this imperative is already implied in the etymology of the word itself: cosmo-politics. The word means, literally, to be a citizen of the world, to be in the world, to cohabit the world, to be with, in companionship with others in and of the cosmos.[3] Yet, the polis in cosmopolitics refers to a distinct set of human practices: political practices through which humans as members of self-determining and artificial units recognize each other. Politics is an eminently human practice that entails drawing distinctions that bound and bind by excluding while including and include while excluding. There is indeed something oxymoronic about cosmopolitics, for how can other beings in the cosmos enter into the political contract that is entailed by a cosmopolitical stance and agenda? Cosmopolitics, however, is more than a political agenda, or a political imperative. It is an ethical stance and a philosophical methodology that places in question the ground on which the political itself is drawn. Cosmopolitics is a metapolitical reflection; it is the name for questioning of the political as such. In fact, as it will be argued here, cosmopolitics is to a politics of cohabitation of "becoming-with-companions,"[4] what political theology was to a politics of the exception, that is, its overcoming and dialectical sublation. As a politics of "becoming-with-companions" that entails also a distinct form of worlding, of making worlds, this form of cosmopolitanism requires the enlightenment of cosmopolitics itself—cosmopolitanism has to become cosmopolitan. This means, above all, its becoming not simply a cosmopolitanism of the being-alone of humans, the egocentric, Cartesian, Leibnizian, Kantian cosmopolitanism of human exceptionalism, but an interspecies cosmopolitanism that acknowledges from the outset that, to quote Anna Tsing, "human nature is an interspecies relationship."[5] If cosmopolitanism in general challenges the cartographies that exclude other human beings from the community of humanity, the interspecies cosmopolitanism challenges the most fundamental of cartographies, namely that which draws a boundary between human animals and nonhuman animals.

In fact, interspecies cosmopolitanism commands us to rethink not simply the political as such, but also the ethical. Here, we follow the tracks left by Kelly Oliver, who herself was tracking the pedagogical traces of nonhuman animals. In her book, *Animal Lessons: How They Teach Us to Be Human*, Oliver argues that "either kinship with animals is possible or kinship between humans is impossible (and perhaps both). Either way, we must rethink the very notion of kinship, making it strange rather than familiar."[6] Indeed, unless we are able to conceive of a humanity that is not predicated on the ritual elimination and ontological exclusion of animal others, then the humanity we have hitherto conceived of will continue to result in concomitant acts of dehumanization and genocide. This leads to the second major argument in Oliver's book, and I quote, since she has put it so succinctly and clearly: "We need to move from an ethics of sameness, through an ethics of difference, towards an ethics of *relationality* and *responsivity*. Animal ethics requires rethinking identity and difference, by focusing on relationships and response-ability."[7] This is the ethics that Haraway names a cosmopolitics of "interspecies contact" in which being with different others entails worlding differently. Oliver and Haraway urge us to consider how most moral philosophy has failed to think of the question of the animality of the animal in relationship to the humanity of the human, and more specifically, how the entwinement of the sovereignty of one—human—with the exclusion of the other—the animal—requires that we rethink ethics *tout court*. It should not go unnoted that the exclusionary trope of the animal/human is entwined also with the dyad of animal/woman, and animal/race. Rethinking the ethics of provincial human exceptionalism that is so urgently required in view of the challenge of animal philosophy, and the planetary ecological crisis, will thus also lead us to rethink the relationship among ethical responsibility, gendering, and racing. Such rethinking of the ground of ethics in terms of "strangeness" and "responsiveness to difference," leads us to rethink the gendering and racing of embodied vulnerability. The ethics of corporeal vulnerability and codependence requires an ethics of limits, of conservation, of generosity that makes us perpetually vigilant, or as Haraway puts it, "subject to the unsettling obligation of curiosity,"[8] to the ways in which modes of embodiment render us mutually—if not always symmetrically—injurable and thus vulnerable. Interspecies cosmopolitics is an *autre-mondialisation*, a worlding of entangled vulnerabilities, caring touching, codependences, acknowledged having become-with as companions.

The Exceptional Animal

The project of interspecies cosmopolitanism requires that we think beyond either anthropocentrism or zoocentrism.[9] This entails, however, that we educate ourselves to think beyond the metaphysical chauvinism that centuries of anthropocentrism have instigated. At the center of the philosophical, religious, theological, and ethical legitimation of this anthropocentrism is the Judeo-Christian tradition, and at the heart of this tradition are two related ideas. On the one hand, there is the idea that humans were created in the image of God, the *imago Dei* doctrine; on the other, we have God's delegation of creation to the sovereignty of humanity, that is, the doctrine of human dominion over the earth. It could be said that humans are sovereign over creation precisely because they are God's creation that most resemble Godself. Regardless of whether human dominion is grounded in *imago Dei*, or whether we inherit the earth directly from God, it can be seen that human control over nature is predicated on our assumed distinctness, our having been singled out by God. It should be pointed out that Judeo-Christian monotheism became the basis for a form of universalism that established a horizontal relationship among humans. So long as humans were creatures of God, we were expected to treat all of them in similar, if not equal ways. Being children of God was a form of cosmopolitanism inasmuch as it leveled the horizontal plane of human moral considerability. Although such inchoate moral universalism got cashed out in de facto exclusion and exceptions, the de jure injunction to consider all human beings as equal by virtue of their divine lineage continues to fuel certain critical cosmopolitanism. Most importantly, however, the Judeo-Christian tradition established the ground on which human exceptionalism would be built.

Since we began to accept the notion that humans were created in God's image and delegated to rule over creation, humanity has been educated to see itself as metaphysically alone. An abyss separates us not simply from other animals, but even from God. This religiously and theologically justified human exceptionalism has also been the source of human solitude. We dwell alone in a world in which we only resemble God. In Kelly Oliver's terms, our exceptionalism has meant disavowing our kinship with other animals. Exiled from heaven, and masters over nonhuman animals, we think ourselves entirely alone. The blessing of our divine kinship turns into the curse of our worldly solitude.

As a visceral reaction, zoomorphism challenges the hubris of anthropocentric exceptionalism. We are not the lonely animals sundered from both God and the animal kingdom by our divine lineage. Instead, humans are taken just as another animal, and all animals are like us. Behaviorism and neurobiochemistry are just the most recent iterations of the reactive belief that wants to think of humans as just another animal, no more and no less sophisticated than other animals. Biological reductive views of humans and animals aim to erase the differences among human and nonhuman animals. In the end we are all, as animals, a bundle of hormones, pheromones, and instinctual drives that have to do with chemical reactions. In a more recent iteration of this perspective, human and nonhuman animals are no more than bundles of DNA resulting in different phenotypes. Notwithstanding its attempt to reject the religious-theological worldview of human exceptionalism, zoomorphism still reenacts its hierarchies and divisions. If we take evolutionary biology as an umbrella term for all attempts to bridge the rift between human and beast, to speak in hyperbolic language, we can see how evolutionary biology reinscribes the divine *scala naturae* into the incremental and dynamic phylogenetic stages. As Joseph and Barrie Klaits put it: "For the fixed Chain that according to the Christian view ascended from animal through man to angels and God, eighteenth-century biologists were on the verge of substituting the dynamic concept of evolutionary development."[10] The abyss between humans and other animals is no longer ontological, but remains unbridgeable and inscrutable, as the infinitesimal differences between genome and genome are now the cause of distinctness.

The abyss between human and animal is as depthless as that between the anthropocentric and zoomorphic view that erases this distinction. Interspecies cosmopolitanism requires, then, that we think past this metaphysical extortion. We must accept neither anthropocentrism nor zoomorphism because the rejection of one or the other inevitably means the affirmation of human exceptionalism. In Haraway's words, what we require is a "robust nonanthropomorphic sensibility that is accountable to irreducible differences,"[11] which at the same time, it needs to be underscored, accounts for these irreducible differences as resulting from a process of worlding together. In other words, circumventing human exceptionalism requires that we acknowledge the becoming-with of human and animal others. Or more precisely, becoming human is partly an anthropo-zoo-genetic practice, to use the language of Vinciane Despret.[12] I will return to this trope in the last chapter of this book, acknowledging, in this context perhaps in too Aesopian terms, the coming to terms with the vertigo of being in a world in which we are no longer exceptional, in which living-with means worlding-with, which means having to respond, and respect, beyond the metaphysical injunctions and ontological verities of a fictitious supremacy. The ethics of cohabitation entailed by an interspecies cosmopolitanism requires that we descend down the *scala naturae* of both Christianity and evolutionary biology into the messy world of companion species.[13]

Tracking Jacques Derrida, who is tracking Freud and Lacan, we can talk about three major ethical-metaphysical panics, panics occasioned by three great historical traumas that have left distinct psychic wounds, which continue to force us to reenact anthropocentric exceptionalism.[14] The first trauma was occasioned by the Copernican decentering of the earth. This meant that the earth no longer occupied a unique place among the celestial bodies. Our home was just another rock caught in the grip of celestial forces that all they intimated of the divine was their precision and beauty. Copernicus exiled us to an immense cosmos in which we would trek without sense of uniqueness or purpose. The second trauma was occasioned by Darwin's theory of evolution. Human, as well as all life, was a product of a nonteleological process of evolution. The death of species, and individuals, could not be translated into a theodicy of salvation. Contingency was introduced into the very fabric of our organic being. Like every other living being, we were caught in the same logic of extinction and survival, without guarantee that our next evolutionary gain would secure our perpetuation. Finitude was simply an ontogenetic factor, and it became also a phylogenetic factum: species are fated to transform into something else that may no longer be kin. We may become something that we will no longer recognize as being our progeny. The third trauma was caused by Freud, who exiled us from the mansion of an allegedly unassailable castle of rational self-legislation. Freud, like Darwin, showed how we are deluded animals: animals who disavowed their kinship with other animals, animals who refused to recognize that their autarky is figurative and not real. Haraway suggests that a fourth trauma has been inflicted on human narcissistic exceptionalism: "the informatic or cyborgian, which infolds organic and technological flesh and so melds that Great Divide as well."[15] This fourth trauma has rubbed in our faces the fact that we are our technologies, that our bodies are biotechnological *dispositifs*, which we have manipulated in the process of domesticating animal others. We have become who we have become by inventing/developing biotechnologies of domesticating others. We are our own domesticated animals.

We should see these four traumas and their corresponding wounds not as precipitous plunges from the heights of achieved ascents, but the slow dismantling of fictitious steps on a ladder that has allowed us to delude ourselves that we live above the world of other living beings. These four traumas have been awakening us to the fact that we live on a fragile planet with other living beings who are vulnerable with us. We are no longer too far from God and too close to animals. We have ceased to be exceptional, but we also have ceased to be alone. Instead of ontological solitude, we have recognized that we dwell in a community of living others, of animal others. We are part of a community of living beings, with whom we are entangled in irreducible and uncircumventable relationships of codependence. An ethics of cohabitation requires a politics of life, not in the sense of a biopolitics of biocapitalist exploitation, but a politics of companion species flourishing.[16]

Building the Peaceful Kingdom[17]

Earlier I intimated that there seems to be a fundamental contradiction at the core of the notion of cosmopolitanism. On the one hand, there is a reference to the whole wide world, to the universe, to the boundless expanse of nature, the known and unknown "cosmos." On the other hand, there is a reference to an all-too human notion, to a circumscribed, limited, fragile, and at times unacknowledged institution, namely the polis as a realm in which humans rise above nature inasmuch as they live in a world made according to laws they dictate. Thomas Hobbes captured this tension wonderfully in his *Leviathan*. In the state of nature we are like rapacious and unhinged wolves, while it is only in a contingently constructed commonwealth that we acquire rights. In the state of nature there is no right. We are all equal, but only because we are all equally capable of killing each other, either by strength, cunning, or machination. We have risen above the state of nature and created an artificial automaton that wields the sword of war in order to impose a peace. Peace, which is unnatural, is the foundation of the polity within which we acknowledge each other as equals under the watchful eye of the sovereign. Even for Immanuel Kant, we remained irrevocably citizens of two worlds: the phenomenal world of nature and the noumenal world of the moral law. Kant also captured the contradiction at the heart of the "cosmopolitan" ideal in one of the most provocative versions of the categorical imperative: "Act as though the maxim of your action can become a universal law of nature." Lucretius and Marcus Aurelius already understood this dual "citizenship" of the human. Kant's philosophical anthropology, which can be argued inverted Jean-Jacques Rousseau's on philosophical anthropology, as well as his cosmopolitan project, are ultimately based in the Stoic notion that it is precisely as creatures of nature that we all belong to the same *nomos*. Kant went so far as to argue that it is "nature" that compels us to rise to the level of the self-legislating creature that we have become. The cunning of nature itself has forced us to become cosmopolitan. In this sense, then the contradiction that Hobbes, Rousseau, and Kant noted at the heart of cosmopolitanism dissolves, but not without giving rise to a different contradiction. From Hobbes, through Locke and Rousseau, to Kant, the juxtaposition between nature and the polis is resolved into the realization that the artificial creature that is the commonwealth, to use Hobbes's language, is but a natural response of the human. For, as Margaret

Macdonald put it curtly, "Even Hobbes' unpleasant savages have sufficient sense, or reason, to enable them to escape their 'natural' predicament."[18]

Indeed, it is by the "law of nature" that humans are compelled to seek their preservation by entering into the contract that establishes the commonwealth. Politics is not contrary to human nature, but rather an extension of it. But already in chapter 14 of part 1, "On Man," Hobbes reveals a new contradiction: If the state is an artificial creation, to what extent does it supersede or remain tethered to the natural condition of the human? Locke will make explicit this contradiction when he argued that the aim of government is the preservation of fundamental natural rights, the most fundamental of these being the right to one's life and the fruit of one's labor, which is undertaken for the sake of one's preservation. For Locke, then, the fundamental end of political society is the preservation of private property, a legal fiction if there ever was one, but which is grounded in the right granted by the state of nature. The contradiction, or paradox, is now between the authority the sovereign has to create and enforce the law and the "natural" rights individuals have which that sovereign must either aim to protect or use as guides for its own legislating. The opposition between nature and state now becomes the opposition between some natural rights and some artificial rights. Jeremy Bentham would attempt to dissolve this contradiction in the corrosive acid of his legal positivism and utilitarianism. Law is always and only the law enacted by extant authority. Law can only aim at the general welfare of the commonwealth, and there is no other gauge or standard by which to adjudicate on the legitimacy of the law. In his line-by-line critique of the French *Declaration of the Rights of Man and of the Citizen*, Bentham claims: "There are no such things as natural rights—no such things as rights anterior to the establishment of government—no such things as natural rights opposed to, in contradistinction to, legal: that the expression is merely figurative; that when used, in the moment you attempt to give it a literal meaning it leads to error, and to that sort of error that leads to mischief—to the extremity of mischief." This claim will be rearticulated most succinctly and quotably in the following way: "*Natural rights* is simple nonsense: natural and imprescriptible rights, rhetorical nonsense,—nonsense upon stilts."[19] If "natural rights" can no longer guide the production of law by the sovereign, is then the sovereign a blind and absolute legislator? For Bentham, however, there is notwithstanding his rejection of natural right, a reference to nature. He begins his *Introduction to the Principles of Morals and Legislation* with the booming affirmation: "Nature has placed mankind under the governance of two sovereign masters, *pain* and *pleasure*. It is for them alone to point out what we ought to do, as well as to determine what we shall do . . . The *principle of utility* recognizes this subjection, and assumes it for the foundation of that system, the object of which is to rear the fabric of felicity by the hands of reason and law."[20]

All of post-Kantian moral and political philosophy is but an attempt to resolve what we can call the Hobbes-Bentham problem, which has two horns. On the one hand, we have the problem of either the deference, nay subordination, of the artificial automaton that is the commonwealth to something that remains "imprescriptible," or, on the other hand, the utter subordination of all rights to the fiat of the sovereign. The dilemma here is that we either subordinate the commonwealth to something that is itself not part of the general contract, but the reason the commonwealth is itself created, namely the preservation of the life of each individual, or we subordinate to the sovereign, even if this demands we surrender our life for the alleged preservation of the life of the commonwealth. We could say, following Michel Foucault, that biopolitics is already inchoate in Hobbes's *Leviathan*.[21] On the other, we have the problem of having to give primacy to reason over happiness, or, on the other side, having to acknowledge the force of an authority that is either guided by rationally discernable principles or that is simply the expression of a principle that is subordinate to feeling (pain and pleasure).

Bentham sought to dissolve the paradox of the origin of the commonwealth, but he fell back upon a different conception of human beings, one that conceives them as natural creatures of feeling and of passion. Bentham trades Hobbes's philosophical anthropology that grounds reason in nature for a philosophical anthropology that grounds reason in feeling, which is grounded in nature, nonetheless. At play here, however, is always a metaphysical conception of the political association, law and government. So long as political philosophy remained ensnared in the tangles of a philosophical anthropologies grounded in the metaphysics of nature, cosmopolitanism remained caged in the provincialism of an anthropocentric metaphysics.

Cosmopolitanism, however, has been stripped of this metaphysical baggage and has been developed in much more abstemious philosophemes. A stronger claim can be made, in fact, namely that the moral and political promise implicit in cosmopolitanism is cashed out in proportion to the way in which moral and political philosophies that raise its banner disavow and dispossess themselves of strong metaphysical commitments to either humans and nature. Cosmopolitanism calls for a postmetaphysical stance, and postmetaphysics finds its lingua franca in cosmopolitanism.[22] Thus, a quick survey of the contributions to the clarification of cosmopolitanism as a desirable and possible ideal in the twenty-first century—that is to say, a survey of the works by Martha Nussbaum, Kwame Anthony Appiah, Judith Butler, and Walter Mignolo, to mention the ones that have influenced me the most—reveals that we can analyze cosmopolitanism as both an "epistemic" and a "moral/ethical" principle. As an epistemic attitude it challenges the monopoly of one worldview and advocates epistemic humility and fallibilism. As an ethical/moral principle or guiding norm, it commands the mutual respect of humans and the solicitous moral regard for those who are our others. Cosmopolitism, in short, implies a dual relationship that urges that we remain cognitively open to the other and that we be morally accountable for and to the other. Cosmopolitanism is not at all like what we can call "elite" knowingness or Davos man internationalism. Cosmopolitism is not simply an insouciant tolerance that blithely looks on with amusement at others. To put it in terms of Habermas's language, cosmopolitanism brings together the first-person with the third-person perspective. To put it in pedestrian terms: this person, life form, cultural configuration, etc., matters to me and I have an uncircumventable moral relationship to it, but I also can see myself as someone who is challenged to know it and to see how in knowing it, it transforms my view of the world. As an ethical/moral relationship, cosmopolitanism is thus about coexistence and cohabitation—to use Judith Butler's language.[23] To act and to know the world from a cosmopolitan standpoint is to ask oneself about the conditions and duties of coexisting and cohabitating. Indeed, Kant already noted that it was the fact of the planet's finitude that forces us to seek to occupy every corner of the planet with equal claim as every other human being. The physical fact of the geography of the planet forces us to be cosmopolitan, namely to aim to coexist and cohabit. Kant, as well as most Kantians after him, did not consider to what extent this cosmopolitan ideal of coexistence and cohabitation included nonhumans. We know that in his ethics lectures Kant talked about subsidiary duties to animals; that is, we do have duties to animals but only as a proxy for duties toward other humans.

Arguably one of the greatest challenges we face as humans, in general, and as philosophers, in particular, is the ecological crisis. This crisis has several components, or rather, victims. First and foremost, there is the moral and political challenge entailed by the fact that the poorest of the poor will suffer once again disproportionably the disastrous consequences of the warming up of the atmosphere. Second, there is the moral and political challenge of how to distribute the burdens of halting and hopefully reversing the ecological effects of too much consumption, which again is unevenly distributed throughout the planet. Third, there is the moral and political challenge of the depletion of biodiversity throughout the planet. This extinction of life, due to human agency, has been so massive that biologists and ecologists call it the "Sixth Extinction," to compare it with other similar extinctions that have taken place in the natural history of life on earth.[24] Of course, this is not one but several moral and political challenges, for the massive planetary extermination of countless species is not just of consequence to the overall status of life on the planet, but also to the unforeseen consequences for future generations. Indeed, the future of life on the planet is not simply an issue about future human life, but also of both plant and animal life *tout court*. It is this particular cluster of problems that I want to consider, namely to what extent the already two-millennia-old ideal of cosmopolitanism must be rethought in terms of not just a legal/political order of rights, of mutual rights and duties, that is extended to only human subjects, but now of rights and duties that must be extended to the entire space of nature, of the cosmos, of that physical horizon in which we live, to which we belong, along with every other living being on the planet. We are truly on the threshold of a cosmopolitan order that captures the earliest intuitions of the Stoics, namely that by nature we all, as living beings, live under a legal umbrella that grants us all rights, that is, equal protections. In the following I will argue that the combined resources of discourse ethics, deliberative democracy, and dialogic or communicative cosmopolitanism can provide us with the kind of critical resources that would allow us to face some of the challenges that we face due to the ecological crisis. Most concretely, I want to argue that the universalization, discourse, and democratic principles Habermas has elaborated by linguistifying Kant's moral philosophy allow us to develop a nonmetaphysical and nonanthropocentric grounding of the rights of nature. It is precisely Habermas's postmetaphysical turn that has allowed Frankfurt School–inspired Critical Theory to be able to offer some theoretical tools that can help in the discussion of what rights not just other humans and cultures have, but also what other nonhuman being may or should have. Postmetaphysical Critical Theory has matured not simply to a postsecular stance, but also to a postanthropocentric moral and legal consideration of life. In this way, then, postmetaphysical thought is the foundation for an interspecies cosmopolitanism that offers a decentered universalism that thinks from the standpoint of the future of life on the planet. We are now in the position to recognize that the moral and political promise of cosmopolitanism can be actualized if we transform intraspecies cosmopolitanism into an interspecies cosmopolitanism, lest we betray cosmopolitanism's inner logic of dissolving no longer tenable and extremely costly anthropocentric "ontological luxury."[25]

Postmetaphysical Law

Habermas's most extensive treatment of the question of animal others is to be found in his long essay entitled "Remarks on Discourse Ethics," which is included in *Justification and Application: Remarks on Discourse Ethics*.[26] In section 13 of the main essay, "Remarks on Discourse Ethics," Habermas is addressing Günther Patzig's critique of discourse ethics' anthropocentrism and its putative deficit with respect to ecological moral and ethical challenges. Habermas acknowledges that the anthropocentric profile of Kantian deontological moral theories, of which discourse ethics is a variant, do seem to blind them to "questions of the moral responsibility of human beings for their nonhuman environment" (105). Even within a Kantian framework it would be possible to recognize that there are duties toward animals and nature precisely as derivative or secondary duties, which are always referred to human beings, existing or future ones. But Patzig pushes past this recognition. He asks: Does nature have a claim on our duty to respect it independently of our duties to humans? Does nature have a moral status that commands our respect independent and irrespective of other human beings? Habermas acknowledges that we do have the moral intuition that animals do make moral claims on us precisely in their bodily integrity, which is revealed to us when they suffer some cruelty. Habermas writes: "We have an unmistakable sense that the avoidance of cruelty towards all creatures capable of suffering is a moral duty and is not simply recommended on prudential considerations or even considerations of the good life" (106). In fact, Habermas is here rejecting Kant's subordination of our duties toward animals to duties toward other human beings. "Animals confront us as vulnerable creatures whose physical integrity we must protect *for its own sake*" (106). This *for its own sake*, is what in humans we call personal dignity. Thus, animals may be said to have a unique form of dignity that commands our moral consideration. The moral considerability of nonhuman suffering is based on their vulnerable physical integrity. Animals are irreducibly alive and thus also vulnerable in their own way. But, taking distance from Patzig, Habermas notes that these moral claims remain of a different character and order than the claims humans make on us. There is no way in which our moral considerability of animal suffering can be part and parcel of the deontological structure of the moral point of view. Why? Habermas makes the following distinction. When we address the physical vulnerability of an animal we are addressing the bodily integrity of a nonhuman animal. When we address the physical vulnerability, or injurability, of a human being, we address it in terms of personal integrity (of which physical integrity is only a part, even if it is only a large and important part). Habermas notes, and I quote at length because it is so crucial:

> The person develops an inner life and achieves a stable identity only to the extent that he also externalizes himself in communicatively generated interpersonal relations and implicates himself in an ever denser and more differentiated network of reciprocal vulnerabilities, thereby rendering himself in need of protection. From this anthropological point of view, morality can be conceived as the protective institution that compensates for a constitutional precariousness implicit in the socialcultural form of life itself. Moral institutions tell us how we should behave towards one another to counteract the extreme vulnerability of the individual through protection and considerateness. Nobody can preserve his integrity by himself alone. . . . Morality is aimed at the chronic susceptibility of personal integrity implicit in the structure of linguistically mediated interactions, which is more deep-seated than the tangible vulnerability of bodily integrity, though connected with it. (109)

Evidently, our moral duties toward the personal integrity of other human beings do not carry over into animals, because we cannot attribute personality to them, since they are not part of our communicative world, although they are part of our lifeworld. What is meant here is that they do not enter into the world of giving and taking reasons, of providing justifications that call for the redeemability of our speech acts. We don't come to an understanding with them about something in the world, even if we are in nonverbal forms of symbolic interaction with them. Habermas concludes: "Like moral obligations generally, our quasi-moral responsibility towards animals is related to and grounded in the potential harm inherent in all social relations" (109). Thus, not only does the suffering of animals command our moral considerability, on the grounds that the physical integrity of animals is an issue for their own lives—it is their suffering that commands my moral response to them—they also command our moral considerability because even if we are not able to reach "understandings" with them, they are embedded within social relations within which they are vulnerable to the potential harm that is part and parcel of every social interaction.

Still, how are these moral claims embodied in our social interactions? How do our moral intuitions take shape in social institutions and direct our social interactions? This is what Habermas set out to answer in his *Between Facts and Norms*.[27] At the heart of this treatise on law and democracy are two key ideas, which are directly relevant to the aims of the present chapter. First, that "law is the medium through which communicative power is translated into administrative power."[28] This is to say that the power that is generated when humans come together to act in accord guided by an opinion generated through public discussion and publicly held gets transformed into administrative action. Law is the medium that transforms this communicative power into administrative wherewithal. Second, "law is the only medium in which it is possible reliably to establish morally obligated relationships of mutual respect even among strangers."[29] Rights, which is the way we experience law, embody moral intuitions while also guiding our everyday interactions in a noncoercive way that nonetheless regularizes our mutual expectations. Rights stabilize our mutual behavioral expectations and serve as either disburdening or unburdening mechanisms insofar as they transfer the weight of moral oughts to the positive sanction of enforceable law. In this way, law is Janus-faced. One face is directed toward enforceable sanction, while the other points in the direction of moral duties. In fact, in a paper entitled "Human Dignity and the Realistic Utopia of Human Rights" Habermas put it this way:

> Because the *moral promise* is supposed to be cashed out in *legal currency*, human rights exhibit a Janus face turned simultaneously to morality and to law. Notwithstanding their exclusively moral *content*, they have the *form* of enforceable subjective rights that grant specific liberties and claims. They are designed to

be *spelled out in concrete terms* through democratic legislation, to be *specified* from case to case in adjudication, and to be *enforced* in cases of violation. Thus human rights circumscribe precisely that part of morality which *can* be translated into the medium of coercive law and become political reality in the robust shape of effective civil rights.[30]

Evidently, this way of thinking about law assumes that law is not just the fiat of the sovereign but instead that positive law is the materialization of rational decisions that either have or would have the assent of all those affected by those laws. Rights result from the crystallization of the abstract character of the "legal form"; that is, rights are the instantiation of the general form of law. To use Rousseau's language, we could say that "right" or "*droit*" is only that which treats the general body politic in the form of generality. The form and content of law is always general, that is, it applies to all, and establishes a general relation among the individual members of the polity. Habermas takes this key Rousseauian idea of the general form of law, and links it with what he calls the democratic principle, namely: "Only those statues may claim legitimacy that can meet with the assent (*Zustimmung*) of all citizens in a discursive process of legislation that in turn has been legally constituted."[31] The interpenetration of the legal form with and by the democratic principle is the site of the genesis of rights. A polity must always deliberate on what "statues" it is willing to submit so as to deal with the contingencies of economics and politics. Rights are always being generated to deal with those contingencies, but at the basis of the legislative edifice is a set of basic rights that allows for the further specification of rights. At the same time that rights are meant to "stabilize" our behavioral expectations, they are also, and perhaps most importantly, meant to give voice to our moral intuitions, those intuitions that could be the basis for an agreement about how we should treat each other and all kinds of members of the polity, even if we don't acknowledge them directly as our equals and merely treat them as strangers or "others."

This overview of how we can justify granting animal rights on a non-metaphysical, nonanthropocentric, nonhuman exceptionalism assumption on a discourse ethical, deliberative democracy understanding of the genesis of rights also allows to note the following: interspecies cosmopolitanism is a hybrid ethical-political-legal stance. It aims to bring about a transformation in our moral sensibilities and expand the horizon of those beings that command our moral considerability. Consequently, it is also making claims about what moral intuitions ought to be translated into rights, that is, enforceable legal sanctions and claims. And, thus, it is also about the philosophy of law. In this sense, interspecies cosmopolitanism stands at the borders of political theory and moral philosophy. It calls for a radical enlightenment in those fields, in fact. Interspecies cosmopolitanism is a form of "Animal Politics,"[32] or what has been called by Donaldson and Kymlicka a form of "Zoopolitics,"[33] or what Ivano Dionigi has called a *Res publica naturalis*.[34] Following Ahlhaus and Niesen, we can identify at least five distinctive features of this form of animal politics.[35] First, it brings to the forefront the question of the political and legal subjection of both humans and animals, and thus, second, it raises the question of coercion of animals and animal-human relations. Third, and following from the antecedent, it demands that we explicitly discuss the forms of the inclusion of animals into human polities, on the one hand, and on the other, that we deal with the "sovereign" claims on animals collectivities (such as for instance the populations of wild animals in the many nature preserves in Africa, or the numerous wild horses roaming the plains of the Midwest in the United States). Fourth, this zoopolitics thus must articulate normative standards that ought to aim at their realistic and practical implementation. In this sense then animal politics is also jurisgenerative. Fifth, in so far as animal politics challenges the boundaries of political inclusion and exclusion, it is also part of democratic theory. Animal politics, qua interspecies cosmopolitanism, is a contribution to democratic theory in general and deliberative democracy in particular. Animal politics qua interspecies cosmopolitanism remits us to the recognition of the moral imperative of democracy, that is, that there are moral justifications for democracy over other forms of political organization. In other words, interspecies cosmopolitanism puts the spotlight on the moral foundations of democracy and the entwinement of morality and law.

Conclusion: To Live under the Categorical Imperative of Being a Good Moral Companion Species

Comte de Buffon wrote in his massive *Histoire naturelle* (1753), "If there were no animals human nature would be far more incomprehensible."[36] After Darwin, Freud, Nietzsche, and Haraway, we should say: "If there were no animals, we humans would have never become," not simply because we would not have evolved the way we evolved, but simply because our entire biological makeup is suffused with the mingling of biota and DNA soup of entangled evolution of companion species. The *scala naturae* through which we ascended to a deluded cosmic solitude has been dismantled. As traumatic as this dismantling may have been, we should joyfully embrace the sobriety that it has allowed us to gain by plunging us into the world in which we have to assume a different ethics, an ethics without moral absolutes, and metaphysical certitudes. Cosmopolitics, when seriously pursued, decenters us, uproots us from our provincialisms and chauvinisms. It commands an obsequious questioning and curiosity about how we have become with, how we have worlded with, companion species. As Haraway put it: "Cosmopolitical questions arise when people respond to seriously different, felt and known, finite truths and must cohabit well without a final peace. If one knows hunting is theologically right or wrong, or that animal rights positions as dogmatically correct or incorrect, then there is no cosmopolitical engagement."[37] Interspecies cosmopolitanism is a way of responding to these finite truths by means of which we must cohabit without a final peace, bereft of any metaphysical or ontological guarantees for our abiding by the force of our own laws. I have offered a postmetaphysical reading of rights that allows us to dispense with anthropocentric exceptionalism when drawing up the right to impose on us duties and responsibilities for different others. Isabelle Stengers has captured well the epistemic and metaphysical parsimony of interspecies cosmopolitanism when she writes: "No unifying body of knowledge will ever demonstrate that the neutrino of physics can coexist with the multiple worlds mobilized by ethnopsychiatry. Nonetheless, such coexistence has a meaning, and it has nothing to do with tolerance or disenchanted skepticism. Such beings can be collectively affirmed in a 'cosmopolitical' space where the hopes and doubts and fears and dreams they engender collide and cause them to exist. That is why, through the exploration of knowledge, what I would like to convey to the reader is also a form of ethical experimentation."[38] Interspecies cosmopolitanism is born from the new matrix of knowledge that has emerged after the four traumas we discussed above, which have led us to land on our feet in a world of entangled relations, but also from what Stengers here calls ethical experimentation. Interspecies cosmopolitanism is the response to a new categorical imperative: "to try to live so that one may believe oneself to have been a good animal [ein gutes Tier gewesen zu sein]."[39]

Chapter 9

Bestiaries of Extinction

Anthropodicy or Anthropohippology

Introduction

Writing, and reading, a final chapter should feel like going on a horse ride. It may begin like an easy walk, then, as the horizon opens, your horse takes off on a trot, as you bounce up and down to keep with the rhythm. Then there is a burst, and the horse takes off, and you gallop into the open expanse. You are now one with your horse. You feel the strength, the sheer sense of velocity, and how there is a symbiosis, a speechless communication. You have become a centaur. You surrender to your horse, even as you hold on to your reins, and you tighten your legs around the waist and stomach, but not too tightly, just enough so that you can keep your balance. You touch your horse, softly on its front, with your whole hand, at the bottom of its long neck, and maybe hold on to its mane. It seems like she is happy. She is a mare. Then, she slows down. You have come to the end of the valley and now there is a rocky, steep mountain to climb. She knows how to go up these rocky hills. You lean forward into her long neck and whisper something, "da'a girl"—or maybe "it's okay, take it easy." A final chapter is also a load, a lot of baggage, heavy, full of miscellanea and old knowledge. So, instead of a saddle, you have hoisted on her several pounds of stuff (maybe corn, beans, plantains, coffee sacks, crates with bullets, a heavy machine gun, a rifle, surely a machete, who knows what you must carry. In our case lots of books, off-prints, old manuscripts, and heavy, but beautiful, bestiaries and copies of rare *Physiologia*, because we refuse to use digital copies), and you begin your trek up the mountain pass. Many horses, mules, and donkeys have come this way. Their hoofs have literally carved the mountain into a trail. These are not trails that fade in the forest, like those of that man who seems never to have been with a horse, Heidegger, but trails that will always be found, as they are now part of the physiognomy of the mountain. And then, all you can do is hold on to the tail of your horse, which will carry your baggage and pull you up the steep hill. Hold on to this tail. A chapter in a book is like a horse's tail, especially when it comes at the end.

Bestiaries: From Theodicy to Anthropodicy

When my daughter was a young child we embarked on a project: to produce her own bestiary. I had given her for one of her birthdays a huge collection of sparkling pens. I think it had fifty or more pens. I got her an artist sketchbook with thick paper, which then I bound with a fake snakeskin to give it an ancient and uncanny feeling. Then they (that is their pronoun now) would draw fantastic creatures, monsters, animals; then they proceeded to color with their glittering ink pens. Then I would use my black ink fountain pen to do accents and write the legend of the animals. They would say: these are these animal's powers, weaknesses, how they reproduce, how long their offspring must be nursed, and so on. I would then ask them: What do they eat? When do they rest? Who or what are its predators? Then, I would write all of this in pseudo-Gothic letters, in black ink, with red ink accents. We had fun making up gentle and horrifying creatures. They kept their bestiary, and now it is safely preserved at their maternal home. Why a bestiary? I am not sure. It is possible that they saw me read them, and I have some copies in my library.

Before bestiaries, there were *Physiologia*, or *Physiologus*, and before that Aristotle, and before that, there was the whole fauna of mystical, sacred, and domestic creatures from Egypt, Babylonia, and Macedonia. For the West, however, our most immediate source is, without question, Aristotle, who can be considered the first naturalist, or scientist, in the strict sense. He wrote several volumes: *History of Animals, Parts of Animals, Movement of Animals, Progression of Animals, Generation of Animals,* and even *Plants* and *Clouds,* as I mentioned in the first chapters of this book.[1] Aristotle was not only a keen observer of animals, as is evident from his *History of Animals*, but he also was one of the first philosophers to systematically differentiate between empirical observation and theoretical systematization. Notwithstanding his own extensive empirical observations, he aimed to get behind the evidence of things seen, to those unseen things that give coherence to the observable world. In book 1 of the *Metaphysics*, for instance, Aristotle offers a genealogy of the origins of abstract speculation, and of course, he begins with what we know as the Ionian or Pre-Socratic philosophers (Heraclitus, Parmenides, Democritus, etc.).[2] What is interesting is that he calls them, in the *Metaphysics*, φυσιόλογος (physiologus), and what they do φυσιολογέω (physiologia), that is, "natural theorists," or what we today call either a naturalist or scientist (à la Charles Darwin, Henry David Thoreau, Rachel Carson, or Edward O. Wilson), and natural science, or physics, or biology, or what in the late Middle Ages was called natural philosophy (what Galileo, Kepler, Laplace, and Newton, practiced), respectively.[3] Some translators of Aristotle have translated φυσιόλογος as either "natural philosopher" or "physicist." Both of these translations are misleading; the first because Aristotle is precisely distinguishing those that attempt to arrive at the first causes and principles of the world from what is evident in nature from those that do so by reason alone, and because what the pre-Socratics studied was not just matter, but all living beings, fauna and flora. The word *physiologus* is a composite word: *phusis* and *logos*, that is, on the reason of the natural world, or the science of the natural world.

While the *Physiologus* was Greek in origin, most of the few copies we have inherited come from the Latin translations. They are eminently Christian texts, and their authorships are shrouded in mystery. They became one of the most popular, widely read, copied, and translated texts of the early Middle Ages. The *Physiologus* also became the source of medieval animal imagery and imaginary mingled with sacred iconography, as well as the source for homiletic and religious texts of the later Middle Ages. In English we have an outstanding translation by Michael J. Curley with his extensive introduction.[4] The *Physiologus* is made up of fifty-one chapters, each devoted to a creature; each chapter is no longer than two or three pages. Each chapter describes the creature, where it may be found, what it interacts with, what is its behavior, and then offers biblical references to explain what it means from the standpoint of theology and the Christian religion. The chapters are not arranged alphabetically, but rather in terms of what appears to be a hierarchy of nobility. The Curley translation begins with the Lion, and closes with Sun-lizard and the Sun-eel. There are entries of fantastic and fabulous creatures: the Phoenix, the Dragon, the Echinemon, and of course, the Unicorn. The text as a whole offers an allegorical interpretation of the natural world. It meant to decipher God's divine plan in the book of creation. To this extent, the *Physiologus* was not meant to be a treatise of natural history, like the books of Aristotle or the pre-Socratics. Rather it offered a mystical and theological hermeneutics that would enable humans to discern God's moral plan through deciphering physical creation. As Curley notes: "By the beginning of the Christian century, however, φυσιολογέω had acquired a range of meaning extending from early Greek speculative zoology and physics to the occult practices of exotic peoples."[5] In parallel, the word φυσιόλογος acquired a different meaning than "natural theorist." It now connoted one who "interpreted metaphysically, morally, and, finally, mystically the transcendent significance of the natural world."[6] In short, the *Physiologus* was a protean and generative archetypal text that absorbed ancient knowledge and assimilated it into Christian moral theology and sacred iconography while serving as both a didactic and pedagogical text. At the very least, it left us with a sacred iconography and a moral semiotics that aimed to read God's creation as a moral plan.

By the end of the twelfth century, however, the *Physiologus* was absorbed into what became during the late Middle Ages another of the most popular forms of moral instruction through the reading of God's revelation as a moral plan, namely the bestiary, or book of beasts. It can be argued that the bestiary assimilated the *Physiologus* and expanded it to include new or newer etymologies, such as those of Isidore of Seville.[7] While the *Physiologus* was made up of fifty-one chapters, bestiaries could be made up of as many as one hundred and fifty chapters, expanding not only descriptions of both real and fantastic creatures, but also adding new descriptions to these creatures.[8] Arguably, the bestiary became even more important because of its visual power. There are more extant bestiaries than there are copies of the *Physiologus*, partly because bestiaries became both works of sacred art and the objects of patronage. Bestiaries were objects that made evident the wealth of kings, princes, or feudal lords, who underwrote their production. They were also supremely versatile pedagogical tools that took religious iconography to new levels of beauty, as well as semiotic systematization.

The word *bestiary*, however, has different meanings. For instance, bestiary could refer to all those texts that derived from the *Physiologus*, or to a particular text with several copies not all of them identical, although presenting themselves under one name, such as the bestiary of Philippe de Thaon or the *Physiologus of Theobaldus*, of which 150 copies survive; it could refer to an individual copy bound with other books, or as part of a larger book that could include other texts, such as the etymologies of Isidore of Seville; it could also mean any compilation of symbolic creatures that emulated the *Physiologus*, such as Guillaume Apollinaire's cycle of poems or Ted Hughes's own animal poems; finally, it could also refer to any collection of animal images or descriptions that no longer have any moral, theological, or symbolic meaning, as in Japanese anime, although even here you can discern something like a moral pedagogy at work.[9] To this list of meanings, I would add another one, the bestiaries of empire, by which I mean that list of photographs and profiles compiled by colonizing powers to bestialize and animalize enemies that must be exterminated and eradicated.[10] Eventually, the bestiary gave birth to another genre that became very popular during the Italian Renaissance, namely the *Fiore di Virtú*, or Flower of Virtue.[11] This later version can be read as the secular moral version of the earlier moral, theological *Physiologus*.[12] As we try to live through the Anthropocene, yet another meaning to bestiaries has sedimented: a catalog of the creatures we have exterminated and made extinct.[13] We thus need to speak of the bestiaries of extinction.

Stephen M. Meyer, a political scientist and philosopher at MIT, speaks more emphatically of biotic extermination and depletion.[14] He gathers the anthropogenic factors that have given rise to the Anthropocene under three types of factors.

First, there is the massive transformation of the planetary landscape, by the industrialization of agriculture, the cutting down of forests and jungles to give way to grass fields for our livestock, today brutally made evident by deforestation in the Amazon. Without question, part of the transformation of the planetary landscape is the mega-urbanization of the planet that require metals, stone, and sand in order to build its skyscrapers that reach ever higher into the sky. The Anthropocene is the age of manufactured landscapes.

Second, there is the geochemical transformation not only of the atmosphere but also the oceans and rivers of the planet. This is what we call pollution. We have changed the chemistry of the planet to the extent that we have changed the chemistry of our own bodies. The earth is now part of a metabolic process in which we have implicated the atmosphere, the earth, and every living being.

Third, there is the anthropogenic biotic consumption and manipulation over millennia, which has transformed the planet into a farm in which animals and plants are grown for the provision of humans and their needs. Human beings and their animals constitute 90 percent of the mammalian biomass of the planet. The planet is our zoo and our buffet. This biotic consumption means that we lose between 17,000 and 100,000 species of plants and animals annually.[15] It is projected that in the next century, we will lose more than half of all the species, which is equivalent to a fourth of the total genetic material of the planet.[16] This biotic extermination has been called the "sixth extinction," one of the most massive extinctions of life that the planet has seen in the history of life on planet earth.[17]

Meyer believes that such massive extinction of life on the planet entails the end of the wild, and for this reason he also believes that a new "chain of being," a new "ladder of life" has emerged. This new ladder is now composed of three types of species.

Weedy species are species that can only flourish in the environments created by human beings. These species are genetically homogeneous and have emerged because of the direct or indirect intervention of human beings. These species contribute little to genetic diversity and, at the same time, these are species that may not be able to survive outside the environments constructed by human beings. Here one only needs to think of the cows, cats, and dogs we have bred to such degrees that they could never survive on their own in the "wild."

Relic species are species that do not flourish in the environments created by human beings. These come in two forms: natural species and artificial species. These survive only in the preserves and protected areas or sanctuaries cordoned off by humans. These species only have a symbolic character for the human being and for this reason are relics of what we humans destroyed and exterminated. Here the horse is paradigmatic, as I will argue below.

Ghost species are species that cannot survive in the Anthropocene, in the new environment we created, and that with the growing humanization of the planet see themselves fated to their extinction. These species will only survive in urban zoos and as genetic specimens preserved in genetic banks. As Diane Ackerman put it, in the Anthropocene, "nature" is what humans cordoned off as "not artificial."[18] The extinction of so many species means the impoverishment and dummying down of life on the planet. Meyer put it succinctly and dramatically: "The web of life will become the strand of life."[19] Here, we only need to think of all those species we have exterminated within our own time, such as the great auks and the passenger pigeon that were hunted into extinction.

The extinction bestiaries of the Anthropocene may be organized not simply along the lines of the medieval bestiary, namely animals, plants, rocks, insects, biblical and mythical creatures, but perhaps along the lines Meyer suggests, with an additional list: bioengineered species, one that should contain the illustration, works, images, and sculptures of artists such as Patricia Piccinini, Jane Alexander, and and Guillermo Gómez-Peña.[20] In her introduction to the majestic and exquisite *Book of Beasts: The Bestiary of the Medieval World*, Elizabeth Morrison writes: "Perhaps the bestiary's notion that the animal world provides a mirror reflection of human relations could prove as salutary for us as it was for the medieval readers. In ascribing human emotions, hopes, fears, and prejudices to our animal familiars, we have the opportunity to learn something valuable about ourselves."[21] If the medieval bestiary was a way to decipher a moral theology that could guide humans to an ethical life, the extinction bestiaries of the Anthropocene now offer us a moral evaluation of our own impact not just on human animals but on the whole life of the planet. If medieval bestiaries were theodicies, our extermination bestiaries are anthropodicies. If the former offered moral lessons of God's beneficence and guidance, the latter would offer us an indictment of the goodness of humans.

Anthropohippology or *Homo equestriens*

Recently, due to some intense health issues, I have been keeping track of what I am able to keep of my body and what I must give up to stay alive. This sounds absurd and macabre: to give up part of your body to stay alive! But I am alive because of my body. So, how is giving up parts of my body a way to stay alive? Redundancies are the mother of survival. The most important redundancy, I would hazard, is that we have bodies, but we are not entirely our bodies. We can chip away, vivisect, amputate, remove, . . . -dectomy galore, and most of our "I" would remain, perhaps even be enhanced and revised, but we would have become surely a more strengthened determined "I." We are not one, but at the very least two, but more likely, multiple, for our sense of our selves is multiple and lives off our bodies only to degrees. We are not all bone, muscle, blood, and flesh. Surely, we are also more our memories, dreams, yearning, the stuff of our relations, both physical and not, which formed and sustain us, which are not physical parts, but mental projections. We are our imagined and ideal bodies.

I guess I started to keep an unconscious inventory of my body because of where and when I grew up. I grew up in the 1970s in Colombia, before I migrated to the US when I was a very young adolescent and no longer a virgin one. I lost part of my innocence in a whorehouse in some unnamed town in the wilds of Colombia. I spent a lot of my youth in the mountains and valleys of southwest Colombia, in the flood plains of the Cauca River, between the western and central cordilleras. I grew up riding horses, walking up steep hills crowned in fog to get the cows, clearing the undergrowth of coffee trees, picking their beans, hiking down to the creek to bathe in a water hole, chasing pigs, and learning how to kill chickens by pulling their necks and twisting. Everyone around me had multiple scars. From when they fell from a horse, or when they cut off a finger cutting something, or when they got in a fight in town, or something as innocuous as falling off the makeshift bridges we made to pick coffee beans on the steep mountains. I got some scars from those years, when a pig slammed me against some barbwire that cut into my legs and then, because I was falling, it ripped across my young flesh. No stitches were required. But, if I had needed them, I would not have gotten them. I was hours away from town. There was no 911 in my area at the time. The flesh wounds of youth! They are so faded but are deep burrows in my body and my memory. They are no longer tender, and yet they are the trace of what made strong, not a man, but a human.

One important formative memory of what I now realize were rewards was being brought along for the monthly visit to town, to bring in coffee, plantains, whatever we were growing that was in season, to sell it and then to buy the month's provisions for home. These were great adventures, full of a sense of accomplishment, but also hard work, exhaustion, and thirst. We would prepare everything days in advance. Then on a Saturday morning, we get up before dawn and get the horses and mules, and load them with everything we could. We aimed to cross the top of the next mountain range before the midday sun. We wanted to spare our horses and mules the strain of that merciless and shadowless sun. Funny, how we never thought of lugging water bottles—such things did not exist in those times and parts. I would hold onto the tail of a horse as we walked. I don't recommend you do that, unless your horse knows you or the horse is going up a steep hill, with half a ton of stuff on its back. But our horses knew us. They knew me. I don't want to project, but I think they also got a sense of safety knowing someone was covering their back. The tail is the blind spot of a horse, which has almost 360-degree eyesight. They pulled us along, and we edged them on, while we had their back.

Coming into town was glorious. We had been trekking for five, six, seven hours, depending on whether it was all sun or some rain. But once in town, the goal was to unload and move our stuff quickly into the marketplace. My uncle would have gone ahead, while we found a spot to tie up the horses and take a break. Many times, I remember dozing off under one of our horses as they got water and ate their meal, as we waited. Then, once we knew where to deliver the load, we could go into the market—we called it *la galleria*. Imagine a Mexican, or Italian, or Spanish market, full of farmers selling everything, meat, spices, potatoes, chickens, fresh produce, everything and anything—the smells were intense, glorious, and I remember feeling alive and rejuvenated just smelling and hearing so much human and animal activity. Still, I so indelibly remember the smells, the colors, the people's toothless smiles, and I remember the *carniceros*, the people cutting and selling the meat. I remember how the cows I helped raised were dismembered and put on wooden tables or hanged from hooks to be bought by the restaurants or regular people. My doctor didn't understand my wry humor when I told him that he had marked me like a pig at a Chinese market—I didn't say Colombian, because I didn't think there were any in New York. I guess my doctor had never been to a meat market, or a Chinese market for that matter. This is not morbid. When you go in for a serious operation, your doctors use markers to trace where they are going to cut you and what they will take. That has happened to me, many times, and every time it happens I remember my cows, horses, and pigs. The difference is I get to keep some of my body and live on.

Sifting through my memories, most importantly, I remember the sounds, the yells—abbreviated words into syllables, for there is this art of yelling in a *galleria* that is not language but pure communication—but also the weathered skins, the missing fingers, the broken limbs, the wobbling and hobbling men, the stooped men. All my cousins were my age or slightly older, but not by much. I just remember everyone being old and hurt and wrinkled and wounded in some way or another. I guess we lived under the sovereignty of an unspoken rule: life is violent and you will get hurt. You will heal unless you don't. Living is hurting and getting over it.

But one important part of that time in my very extended youth was falling asleep, if only briefly, from exhaustion. I remember falling asleep under our horses, which reminds me of how regal horses are. Have you seen a horse pee? They gush; they are Niagara Falls. And you wonder, where did they get all that water from? They do this graceful four-leg spread out, as if they don't want their shoes to get wet. Unless, of course, if they are mares. And the mares are even more graceful. I remember seeing them pee and the steam rising from the ground. Compared to cows, horses are so polite, civilized, and clean. Many a human should be ashamed they don't pee like a horse or a mare.

Horses have four legs, and four arms. They talk with their heads, eyes, whole body, including tails, and, of course, their legs. When horses are anxious, they stump. When they are excited, they hoof with their front legs, which they also do when they are tired or bored. When they are angry, they stump down with their back legs, which is like being pummeled by a sixteen wheeler. When they are upset and really angry, they raise their hind leg and kick you as hard as they can, which is very, very hard. When they are tranquil and happy, they hoof with their front legs, as if they want to put their hoof on your hand. There is more to horse hoof language than I can reveal now, but sleeping under a horse is a gift. It is a hoofed tent, too.

Riding a horse is one of the most incredible experiences, especially when they start perspiring. I had a girlfriend that when she got excited, she would smell like a horse. I swear. It is an intoxicating smell: I associate it with strength, sun, salt, pure flesh, physicality, honesty and trust. Horses don't sweat like we sweat—their skins get damp but not wet. They don't trickle with wetness. They don't sweat when they are nervous. The heat rises from them. If it is cold, you can see the steam rise from them. They are physical engines, exuding their power. They will swing their tails and head back and forth, as if fanning themselves. And yet they don't shudder in the cold, as we do. I never saw a horse refuse to continue because it was too hot or too cold. But I have seen donkeys refuse to go on. I want to sweat like a horse. It is so civilized. And steam in the winter and not shudder.

All of this reminds me that cows don't have the manners of horses. They don't clean themselves well, or rather they are not as clean as horses. Yes, of course, being clean is a matter of degree. But, I don't remember falling asleep under a cow, whereas I have under horses. I am thinking of all of this, because I also remember how vulnerable horses are, even as they are so majestic, powerful, regal, beautiful, self-aware of their grace and prowess. Have you seen a horse or a cow with a crutch? I have seen dogs with no hind legs, pulling themselves along with their front legs. I have seen little dogs with no front legs jumping, like a kangaroo. I've seen horses get worms in their skin, and they can be removed, but I have not seen a horse hobble. If they hobble, something is already gone way too bad. I have seen horses limp because the horse's shoe—by something or someone—was not placed properly on the hoof, or has pierced their skin, muscle, or bone when nailing the horseshoe onto their hoofs. They then have to be healed and that takes time. Have you seen a horse get their horseshoe nailed to their hoof? An amazing proposition. You better exude confidence and smell like a horse before you attempt to nail a horseshoe onto a horse's hoof. I am thinking of this because I have not seen a horse on three legs, whereas I have seen many a human on one and even none.

I have seen a dead man, encased in the coagulated pool of his blood. This happened when I was very young, living in a small city in Colombia. We woke up and someone going off to work in the morning found the body. He must have been knifed and not shot. There was a huge pool of blood. He drowned in his own blood. Or his blood was drained out of his body. Both statements are probably right. That is when I got a sense of how much we are just blood, liquid flowing through our veins. I have seen cows lifted up from their legs and their necks knifed and their blood drained—I did not know a cow could hold that much blood. Being dead is the extreme of woundedness. Death is the ultimate wound. Or, is it that there is a wound from which we can't recover, but what is that wound?

Perhaps that was too long a preamble to begin to discuss the horse, which interestingly does not appear in the *Physiologus* but does in most medieval bestiaries.[22] The horse belongs to the family of the Equidae, of which only the genus of the *Equus* is today the most prevalent. The earliest members of the Equidae were the *Sifrippus* and *Hyracotherium* (both from the early Eocene, which is 56 to 33.9 million years ago, more or less on the heels of the fifth extinction at the end of the Cretaceous-Tertiary, when dinosaurs became extinct and mammals emerged). These early specimens were polydactyl, that is, they had at least three toes. These gave way to the *Mesohippus*, which lived in North America 37 million years ago. During the Miocene, that is, 20 million years ago, when the planet warmed up, forests retreated, and plains developed, primitive horses moved from the forest to the plains. The earliest known specimen that gave rise to the modern horse is the *Merychippus*, which lived around 17 to 11 million years ago. *Hipparion* evolved around the beginning of the Miocene period, but they were hunted into extinction by early hominids and did not survive the warming of the planet.[23] Around 12 million years ago the *Dinohippus* evolved, having developed a single hoof. This also lived in North America. During the Ice Age (approximately 2.5 million years ago) they migrated to Europe and Asia, in particular the Eurasian steppes, while becoming extinct in their place of origin.[24] About 6,000 years ago, human and horse evolution began to merge when they began to be domesticated and not simply hunted for their meat.[25] By 2600 BC, there is archaeological evidence that a hybrid breed of horses was already in use in the Sumerian civilization of the Middle East.[26] As anthropologist and historian Pita Kelekna put it: "While equids had evolved over a period of 60 million years, bipedal hominids first appeared a little over 6 million years ago to gradually develop the cerebral capabilities that today characterized modern *homo sapiens* . . . only about 6,000 years ago did the world brainiest biped team up with the world's fastest quadruped."[27] It is for this reason that Kelekna suggests that we ought to think of *Homo sapiens* as also a *Homo equestriens*. We became *sapiens* by domesticating *equus* for, unlike the other animals humans domesticated, the horse was the most versatile of mammals, allowing humans to travel long distances, engage in war, till the land, and be a companion.

In 2003, just over a decade after he was my teacher in graduate school, the German philosopher of history Reinhart Koselleck, famous for his contribution to what he called "historical semantics" and for editing the massive *Geschichtliche Grundbegriffe: Historisches Lexikon zur Politisch-sozialen Sprache in Deutschland* (*Historical Basic Concepts: Historical Lexicon to the Political and Social Language in Germany*),[28] received the historians prize awarded by the German city of Münster. For the occasion, he delivered a moving and fascinating speech titled "Der Aufbruch in die Moderne oder das Ende des Pferdezeitalters" ("The Start into Modernity or the End of the Age of the Horse").[29] What should also be noted, and I did not know this when he was my teacher, is that Koselleck had served during World War II on the Eastern Front as a member of the horse-drawn artillery.[30] In this lecture Koselleck offers the novel idea that world history ought to be divided into three periods: prehorse, horse, and posthorse ages.[31] He also talked about what he called the "hippological turn," which in more than one way augured humanity's entry into history, and thus had tremendous world-historical consequences.[32] While horses do not, strictly speaking, make history, they have enabled humans to make it not just by transforming our natural world, but also by allowing us to wage war and create expansive empires that forcefully brought humans, religions, and languages together. The horse was not only one of the most versatile domesticated animals that humans had at their disposal. Horses transformed the horizon, speed, and lethality of war. The horse was a vector of power, information, and violence. The horse itself was a weapon.[33] The horse, before television and mass media, was a catalyst for colonization, imperialism, and globalization. The innumerable monuments across every major city in the world, in which world historical figures appear immortalized always riding a horse, testify to the role of horses in human history. One of the most striking examples of the historical significance of the horse is without question the Terracotta Army of the first Emperor of China, Quin Shi Huang (259–210 BC), with its six hundred life-size horses and the estimated seven thousand infantry soldiers.

I got to see some of these terracotta horses, chariots, and warriors sometime in 2018, when there was an exhibition at the Franklin Institute in Philadelphia. I went there with another girlfriend, who never smelled like a horse, but all odiferous qualifications aside, the exhibition was spectacular. The museum showcased the terracotta warriors with a wonderful installation that projected onto the terracotta figure, in slow and transforming motion, the supposed colors that they originally wore. What was remarkable, to me, was the level of individual and unique detail each warrior had. There are several thousand such warriors in Emperor's Quin Shi Huang's necropolis, and each one is singular. And so were the horses. There were also all kinds of other animals, which had been also replicated in what today we would call the canteen or kitchen areas of an army barracks. In the exhibit, they had either replicated or brought from China a full-scale carriage drawn by four horses astride. Each horse was also unique. Emperor Quin Shi Huang must have understood how important the horse was to China, but also to the entire empire he had unified against the horse-riding nomads of the Mongolian steppe.

In his 2003 Münster speech, Koselleck is less interested in defining what the "Moderne" may be, and more in marking what he calls the end of the age of the horse. He is not a chronologist but a historian of historical semantics, that is, how words shift meaning across time, registering how our concepts thus also change. Today we talk about the "horsepower" of an engine. The power of the steam engine and then the gasoline-burning engine is modeled after the power that a horse or horses together could exert. My Mini Cooper has up to 208 horsepower. Allegedly, when I drive at 90 miles per hour, and my Mini can do that without my noticing, I am riding a chariot with 208 horses hauling me and my bestiaries. Minis and non-odiferous girlfriends aside, hippology is all around us. For Koselleck, the end of the age of the horse came slowly but dramatically and fatefully. First, we had the invention of the steam engine, then came the train, and then the city tram, which used to be hauled by horses. And yet, even as late as World War II, horses played a key role, a kind of "farewell to the horse." Koselleck writes that during World War I the Germans brought to the war 1.8 million horses, while in World War II they brought 2.7 million, of which only about 9,000 survived.[34] One only has to look at pictures of both wars to get a sense of the slaughter of both humans and horses (which one can find in Raulff's book[35]), or watch the incredibly moving 2011 movie *War Horse* (produced and directed by Steven Spielberg, which in turn was based on Michael Morpurgo's 1982 novel of the same title). Then, laconically, Koselleck notes that "the Russian landscape, because of its structural conditions, still belongs to the horse-age. The war could not be won with the horse, and yet it could not be waged without it."[36]

Raulff, in his exquisite and fascinating book *Farewell to the Horse*, quotes historian Ann Hyland, describing the moment when humans first mounted a horse: "It was a small step, albeit a brave one, for man to mount a horse." Then, Raulff notes: "The comparison with the moon landing is certainly not exaggerated. The moment when man began, by domesticating and breeding, to connect his fate with the horse—not with a *nutritional* intention, but with a *vectorial* aim—may have been, before the invention of writing, the narrow gate through which man entered the realm of history."[37] This is why the natural history of *Homo sapiens* cannot be uncoupled from that of the horse, and thus we should talk in the same breath of *anthropohippology*, or as Kelekna put it, *Homo equestriens*, as we speak of *Homo necans*, *Homo faber*, and *Homo laborans*.[38] In fact, the human as the *zoon politikon* is unthinkable without *Homo equestriens*. Where humans went, so went the horses carrying them, loaded with their provisions, weapons, books, bibles, and sacred objects. Like humans, horses have made the entire planet their habitat.

Why was the horse so essential and indispensable to both our own anthropogenesis and entry into the "realm of history"? Raulff argues persuasively that there are three possible answers. First, there is the answer provided by physics. The horse is a vector of energy. The horse, as a grass eater, can transform rough prairie grasses into incredible amounts of energy. Second, there is the answer related to knowledge and experience. The horse is a vector of knowledge. As Raulff put it: "The horse was part of a complex economy of various knowledge areas (medical, agrarian, military, artistic) and types of knowledge (empirical, experiential, scientific), as well as a long literary tradition founded in antiquity."[39] Here it would be important to note that one of our sources for the origins of Western philosophy, Xenophon, who was a soldier along with Socrates, as well as his student, wrote a treatise titled *On Horsemanship*. Third, there is the answer provided by affect or the economy of emotions. Horses are objects of and inspire admiration, pride, and hubris, and they are metonyms for freedom and subordination. The horse is, as Raulff notes, a *semiophore* or semaphore, that is, a vector of human emotions, moods, passions, and affect. According to Raulff, then, the symbiosis between humans and horse, symbolized in the centaur, is best captured in three economies: the economies of *energy, knowledge*, and *pathos*. "Besides its functions as converter of energy and object of knowledge, the horse is also a converter of pathos."[40]

Extinction as Anthropodicy

Charles Darwin's 1859 paradigm shifting book *On the Origin of Species by Means of Natural Selection or The Preservation of Favoured Races in the Struggle for Life*, now referred to in an abbreviated way as *On the Origin of Species*, could also have been titled *On the Origin and Extinction of Species by Means of Natural Selection and Human Extermination*. It is clear that for Darwin there is no evolution without extinction. In the introduction to his 1859 book, he writes: "I am fully convinced that species are not immutable; but that those belonging to what are called the same genera are lineal descendants of some other and generally extinct species, in the same manner as the acknowledged varieties of any one species are the descendants of that species. Furthermore, I am convinced that Natural Selection has been the main but not exclusive means of modification."[41] If natural selection is the main but not exclusive means of the extinction and modification of species, what are the other means? For one, natural catastrophes, such as a giant meteor colliding with our planet, but also anthropogenetic factors, such as deforestation, salination of the seas, pollution, hunting into extinction, and the selection of both animal and plant breeds leading to monocultures and thus the depletion of biotic diversity. Humans are also a "means" of natural selection. In fact, Darwin comes quite close to admitting this. In chapter 14, "Recapitulation and Conclusion," he writes: "Man does not actually produce variability; he only unintentionally exposes organic beings to new conditions of life, and then nature acts on the organisation, and causes variability. But man can and does select the variations given to him by nature, and thus accumulate them in any desired manner. He thus adapts animals and plants for his own benefit or pleasure."[42] But humans not only created, intentionally and unwittingly, new environmental conditions, they have also deliberately and in full consciousness exterminated species. Elizabeth Kolbert rightly notes: "Darwin's theory about how species originated doubled as a theory of how they vanished. Extinction and evolution were to each other the warp and weft of life's fabric, or, if you prefer, two sides of the same coin."[43]

Extinction is where natural and human history intersect most violently, like tectonic plates colliding or tearing apart, creating seas and oceans. This point of intersection, collision and crash, or sundering, rending apart, and tearing, is what we now name the Anthropocene.[44] Human history has become an agent of natural history. Since the beginning of the Pleistocene humans have become a geological and natural selection force, a vector of extinction and evolution. To this extent, humans have taken on the role of a demiurge, a demigod. And where there is a God, the question of justice comes into play. Monotheism, namely the invention of an omnipotent, omniscient, and absolutely benign God, logically gave us the problem of theodicy: If the one God is all-powerful, benign, and just, why is there evil in the world? Why do we suffer so unjustly? Why do natural catastrophes happen? Why is there so much unmerited pain, hunger, and death? *Theodicy*, a term invented by Gottfried Wilhelm Leibniz, by combining *theo* (god) and *dyke* (justice), means literally "God's justice." However, with Augustine in the fourth century CE and Boethius in the sixth, the question had already arisen: Why is there evil in the world? Augustine, I would argue, gave us the most sophisticated and consequential answer, which I would describe as: the *voluntaristic*, namely that evil is produced by the human's free will when it turns against God's law and will (perhaps an unfortunate consequence of having been created by God with a free will); and the *ontological*—evil is nothing, the nothing that yawns when God withdraws from creation and the world. Evil is the absence of God and the *epistemological* or *gnoseological*. This means that evil is ignorance or the absence of knowledge of God's providence, or God's plan for humanity and the world. What appears as evil may in fact be a lesson. Here is where Augustine and Boethius converge on the question of theodicy. Humans have tunnel vision. God is omniscient. We can never decipher God's designs. Salvation is dispensed with brutal lessons.[45]

In general, theodicy is a defense of God, a justification of God's inscrutable soteriological plan. The Anthropocene, with its extinctions and yet more to come human and animal suffering, raises the question of anthropodicy, that is, a defense and justification of the existence of humans as a force of nature. Is it better or worse that humans evolved to conquer and transform the earth, and subordinated it to their evil will? Should we think of humans as the worst disaster to have visited the planet, not unlike the asteroid that killed the dinosaurs? This is not a Jonathan Swiftian misanthropic question, but a Kantian question about the "sociability" of humans: Are humans a force of good and lawfulness or not? None can answer that question but other humans, just as we are the only ones that can answer the question of theodicy.

In her wonderful book, *The Age of the Horse: An Equine Journey through Human History*, Susanna Forrest writes: "Humans have a lamentable habit of loving too late—so it was with the wild horse."[46] She wrote this as a way to introduce the saga of the Tarpan and Takhi horses, which had been exterminated in their original habitats, survived in zoos, and then were re-wilded, that is, reintroduced into their original habitats. Horses are not about to become extinct, although some of their predecessors are, by natural and anthropogenic factors. Today, there are over 150 breeds of horses, all bred to do their unique tasks. Horses, like national heroes, have become national brands.[47] If you have never seen a Lipizzan, or a Garrano, the most elegant and regal of horses, all you have seen are but pale copies of a horse.

Again, while horses are not about to become extinct, our accelerating Anthropocene age has come about in part through the "dehorsification" of our world.[48] In his illuminating book, *The Story of the World in 100 Species*, Lloyd assigned to the horse the rank of 58, lower than the dog, elephant, tick, pig, and deer, but higher than that of the sperm whale, chicken, tobacco, and grape. The way Lloyd arrived as this rank was by tabulating these scores: evolutionary impact, impact on human society, environmental impact, global reach, and longevity. There must have been something wrong in Lloyd's tabulation, for as Koselleck, Raulff, Williams, and Forrest have argued and shown, the horse catapulted humans into global and planetary history.

I want to close by underscoring that we became *Homo sapiens* mostly by becoming *Homo equestriens*. Anthropogenesis is deeply entangled with anthropohippology. As Raulff put it beautifully: "The horse's capacity to be tamed and bred turned the swift horse into a domestic animal that could be steered by man. In a word, as a *vector in animal form*, the horse became *a political animal* and the most important companion of *Homo sapiens*."[49] When my children were young, and we traveled by car across the US, from East Coast to West Coast, and back, we would listen to and read, relisten to and reread, James Herriot's books. There is one story that still haunts me. It is in chapter 14 of his *It Shouldn't Happen to a Vet*, when he narrates the story of being called to take care of some horses. I should let Herriot tell the story, and let him have the last word:

> "Get by, leave off!" he shouted. "Daft awd beggars." But he tugged absently at the mare's forelock and ran his hand briefly along the neck of the gelding.
> "When did they last do any work?" I asked.
> "Oh, about twelve years ago, I reckon."
> I stared at John. "Twelve years! And have they been down here all that time?"
> "Aye, just lakin' about down here, retired like. They've earned it an' all." For a few moments he stood silent, shoulder hunched, hands deep in the pockets of his coat, then he spoke quietly as if to himself. "They were two slaves when I was a slave." He turned and looked at me and for a revealing moment I read in the pale blue eyes something of the agony and struggle he had shared with the animals.[50]

Notes

Introduction

1. Richard Rorty, "Contemporary Philosophy of Mind," *Synthese* 53, no. 2 (November 1982): 323–348.

2. See the wonderful collection Lorraine Daston and Gregg Mitmann, eds., *Thinking with Animals: New Perspectives on Anthropomorphism* (New York: Columbia University Press, 2004).

3. Anat Pick, *Creaturely Poetics: Animality and Vulnerability in Literature and Film* (New York: Columbia University Press, 2011), 6. See also Amanda Rees and Charlotte Sleigh, *Human* (London: Reaktion Books, 2020), especially the introduction and the conclusion, "Imhumanism."

4. Cary Wolfe, ed., *Zoontologies: The Question of the Animal* (Minneapolis and London: University of Minnesota Press, 2003).

5. Jacques Derrida, *The Animal That Therefore I Am*, ed. Marie-Louise Mallet, trans. David Wills (New York: Fordham University Press, 2008).

6. Elisabeth de Fontenay, *Le silence des bêtes: La philosophie à l'épreuve de l'animalité* (Paris: Fayard, 1998).

7. Paul Waldau and Kimberly Patton, eds., *A Communion of Subjects: Animals in Religion, Science, and Ethics* (New York: Columbia University Press, 2006).

8. Armelle Le Bras-Chopard, *El zoo de los filósofos: De la bestialización a la exclusión*, trans. María Cordón (Madrid: Taurus, 2003), 25.

9. Edward O. Wilson, *Biophilia: The Human Bond with Other Species* (Cambridge, MA: Harvard University Press, 1984), 58.

10. Matthew Calarco, *Zoographies: The Question of the Animal from Heidegger to Derrida* (New York: Columbia University Press, 2008).

11. See Calarco, *Zoographies*, 103–8; See also Wolfe, *Zoontologies*, 20 and Heather Keenleyside, "The First-Person Form of Life: Locke, Sterne, and the Autobiographical Animal," *Critical Inquiry* 39, no. 1 (Autumn 2012): 116–41.

12. Cora Diamond, "The Difficulty of Reality," in *Philosophy and Animal Life*, ed. Stanely Cavell et al. (New York: Columbia University Press, 2008), 47.

13. Max Horkheimer and Theodor W. Adorno, *Dialectic of Enlightenment: Philosophical Fragments*, trans. Edmund Jephcott (Stanford, CA: Stanford University Press, 2002), 206.

14. Ralph R. Acampora, *Corporal Compassion: Animal Ethics and Philosophy of Body* (Pittsburgh: University of Pittsburgh Press, 2006).

15. Sue Donaldson and Will Kymlicka, *Zoopolis: A Political Theory of Animal Rights* (Oxford: Oxford University Press, 2011).

16. Ivano Dionigi, ed., *Animalia* (Milano: BUR saggi, Rizzoli, 2010).

17. See the brilliant analysis of this discussion in Plato's *Protagoras* by Hans Blumenberg in *Work on Myth*, trans. Robert M. Wallace (Cambridge, MA: MIT Press, 1985), 328–49.

18. I explore this more extensively in "A Letter on *Überhumanismus*: Beyond Posthumanism and Transhumanism," in *Sloterdijk Today*, ed. Stuart Elden, 58–76 (Cambridge: Polity, 2012).

19. See my essay "Appendix-Religion in Habermas' Work," in *Habermas and Religion*, ed. Craig Calhoun, Eduardo Mendieta, and Jonathan VanAntwerpen, 391–407 (Cambridge: Polity, 2013).

20. Jürgen Habermas, *Knowledge and Human Interests*, trans. Jeremy J. Shapiro (Boston: Beacon Press, 1971), 312. Henceforth page numbers are in the body of the text.

21. Humberto Maturana and Francisco Varela, *The Tree of Knowledge: The Biological Roots of Human Understanding*, trans. Robert Paoulucci, rev. ed. (Boston: Shambala Press, 1992), 193. Quoted in Cary Wolfe, *Before the Law: Humans and Other Animals in a Biopolitical Frame* (Minneapolis: University of Minnesota Press, 2013), 70.

22. Donna Haraway, "Species Matters, Humane Advocacy: In the Promising Grip of Earthly Oxymorons," in *Species Matters: Human Advocacy and Cultural Theory*, ed. Marianne DeKoven and Michael Lundbland (New York: Columbia University Press, 2012), 18.

23. Acampora, *Corporal Compassion*, 5.

24. Ibid., 19.

25. Élisabeth de Fontenay, *Without Offending Humans: A Critique of Animals Rights*, trans. Will Bishop (Minneapolis: University of Minnesota Press, 2012), 50.

26. Ibid., 50.

27. Ian Hacking, "Conclusion: Deflections," in *Philosophy and Animal Life*, 163–64.

28. Eduardo Mendieta, "The Biotechnological *Scala Naturae* and Interspecies Cosmopolitanism: Patricia Piccinini, Jane Alexander, and Guillermo Gómez-Peña," in *Biopower: Foucault and Beyond*, ed. Vernon Cisney and Nicolae Morar, 158–79 (Chicago: University of Chicago Press, 2015).

29. de Fontenay, *Without Offending Humans*, 3.

30. Jorge Luis Borges, with Margarita Guerrero, *The Book of Imaginary Beings*, revised, enlarged and translated by Norman Thomas di Giovanni in collaboration with the author (New York: E. P. Dutton, 1978), 21–22.

31. Homer, *The Odyssey*, trans. Robert Fagles, introduction and notes by Bernard Knox (New York: Penguin Books, 1996).

32. Ulrich von Wilamowitz-Moellendorff, *Glaube der Hellenen*, Vol. 1 (Berlin: Weidmannschen Buchhandlung, 1931), 14, quote in Horkheimer and Adorno *Dialectic of Enlightenment*, 263. Henceforth when I quote from this book, the page numbers will be in the body of the text.

33. See Richard B. Rutherford, "The Philosophy of the *Odyssey*," in *Oxford Readings in Classical Studies: Homer's Odyssey*, ed. Lillian E. Doherty, 155–88 (Oxford: Oxford University Press, 2009).

34. Gary Steiner, *Anthropocentrism and Its Discontents: The Moral Status of Animals in the History of Western Philosophy* (Pittsburgh: University of Pittsburgh Press, 2005), 42.

35. Steiner, *Anthropocentrism and Its Discontents*, 42.

36. Emmanuel Levinas, "The Name of a Dog, or Natural Rights," in *Animal Philosophy: Ethics and Identitiy*, ed. Peter Atterton and Matthew Calarco (London and New York: Continuum, 2004), 49.

37. Hermann Broch, "The Style of the Mythical Age: On Rachel Bespaloff," in *War and the Iliad*, ed. Simone Weil and Rachel Bespaloff (New York: New York Review of Books, 2005), 108.

38. David K. O'Conner, "Rewriting the Poets in Plato's Characters," in *Cambridge Companion to Plato's Republic*, ed. G. R. F. Ferrari (Cambridge: Cambridge University Press, 2007), 56.

39. See Luce Irigaray, *Speculum of the Other Woman*, trans. Gillian C. Gill (Ithaca, NY: Cornell University Press, 1985), 244.

40. Hans Blumenberg, *Höhlenausgänge* (Frankfurt am Main: Suhrkamp Verlag, 1989).

41. Irigaray, *Speculum of the Other Woman*, 243.

42. O'Connor, "Rewriting the Poets in Plato's Characters," 71.

43. Ibid., 72.

44. Irigaray, *Speculum of the Other Woman*, 321.

45. From a footnote in the translation of the *Symposium* by A. Nehamas and P. Woodruff, included in John M. Cooper's edition of Plato's *Complete Works* (Indianapolis/Cambridge: Hackett Publishing Company, 1997), 497. See also Paul Johnson, *Socrates: A Man for Our Times* (New York: Viking, 2011), 29–31.

46. For representations of Socrates, see Gernot Böhme, *Der Typ Sokrates, Erwiterte Neuausgabe* (Frankfurt am Main: Suhrkamp Verlag, 2002), especially the section in part VI titled "On the Physiognomy of Socrates and Physiognomy in General." See also Kenneth Lapatin, "Picturing Socrates," in *A Companion to*

Socrates, ed. Sarah Ahbel-Rappe and Rachana Kamtekar, 110–55 (Malden, MA: Wiley-Blackwell, 2006).

47. Franz Kafka, *Parables and Paradoxes*, bilingual ed. (New York: Schocken Books, 1961), 89–93.

48. There is a wonderful essay by Barbara Engh that unfortunately I cannot engage here, but that nonetheless is food for further thought on the question of sound, crying, song, voice, and mimesis. See "Adorno and the Sirens: Tele-pho-no-graphic bodies," in *Embodied Voices: Representing Female Vocality in Western Culture*, ed. Leslie C. Dunn and Nancy A. Jones, 120–35 (Cambridge: Cambridge University Press, 1994).

Chapter 1

1. J. M. Coetzee, *Doubling the Point: Essays and Interviews* (Cambridge, MA: Harvard University Press, 1992), 248. Italics in original.

2. John Berger, *About Looking* (New York: Vintage International, 1991), 4–5. Italics added.

3. The list of Coetzee's work is lengthy, but I will be referring to the following. In the body of the text I will refer to the year and page number of the book.

> *Dusklands* (New York: Penguin Books, [1974] 1985).
> *From the Heart of the Country* (New York: Harper, 1997). The Penguin edition is from 1982, with slightly changed title of *In the Heart of the Country*.
> *Waiting for the Barbarians* (New York: Penguin, [1980] 1982).
> *Life and Times of Michael K.* (New York: Viking, 1984).
> *Foe* (New York: Penguin, 1987).
> *Age of Iron* (New York: Random House, 1990).
> *Doubling the Point: Essays and Interviews* (Cambridge, MA: Harvard University Press, 1992).
> *The Master of Petersburg* (New York: Viking, 1994).
> "Meat Country," *Granta* 52 (Winter 1995): 41–52.
> *Giving Offense: Essays on Censorship* (Chicago: University of Chicago Press, 1996).
> *Boyhood: Scenes from Provincial Life I* (New York: Penguin, 1998).
> *The Lives of Animals* (Princeton, NJ: Princeton University Press, 1999).
> *Disgrace* (New York: Viking, [1999] 2000).
> *Stranger Shores: Literary Essays, 1986–1999* (New York: Penguin, 2002).
> *Youth: Scenes from Provincial Life II* (New York: Penguin, 2002).
> *Elizabeth Costello* (New York: Viking Penguin, 2003).
> *Slow Man* (New York: Viking Penguin, 2005).
> *Inner Workings: Literary Essays, 2000–2005* (New York: Viking Penguin, 2007).

4. Coetzee, "Meat Country," 49.
5. Derek Attridge, *J. M. Coetzee and the Ethics of Reading: Literature in the Event* (Chicago: Chicago University Press, 2004).
6. Coetzee, *Doubling the Point*
7. Ibid., 367.
8. Ibid.
9. Ibid., 368.
10. I attempted an analysis of this economy of bestiality in "The Imperial Bestiary of the U.S.: Alien, Enemy Combatant, Terrorist," in *Radical Philosophy Today IV*, ed. Harry van der Linden and Tony Smith, 155–79 (Charlottesville, VA: Philosophy Documentation Center, 2006).
11. Berger, *About Looking*.
12. Coetzee, *Boyhood: Scenes from Provincial Life I*, 1–2.
13. Ibid., 102.
14. Coetzee, *Dusklands*, 80.
15. Martin Heidegger, *The Fundamental Concepts of Metaphysics: World, Finitude, Solitude*, trans. William McNeill and Nicholas Walker (Bloomington and Indianapolis: Indiana University Press, [1929–1930] 1995).
16. Coetzee, *Waiting for the Barbarians*, 60.
17. Coetzee, *Age of Iron*, 190.
18. Attridge, *J. M. Coetzee and the Ethics of Reading*, 104.
19. Coetzee, *Age of Iron*, 198.
20. Coetzee, *The Master of Petersburg*, 80.
21. Ibid., 80–81.
22. Ibid., 83.
23. Coetzee, *Disgrace*, 143.
24. Ibid., 124.
25. Ibid., 146.
26. Ibid., 143.
27. Coetzee, *The Lives of Animals*.
28. See Ian Hacking, "Our Fellow Animals," *New York Review of Books*, June 29, 2000, https://www.nybooks.com/articles/2000/06/29/our-fellow-animals/.
29. Coetzee *Elizabeth Costello*, 102.
30. Ibid., 65.
31. Ibid.
32. Ibid., 64.
33. Ibid., 63–64.
34. Ibid., 64.
35. Ibid., 79.
36. Ibid.
37. Ibid., 80.
38. Ibid.
39. Ibid., 96.

40. Donna Haraway, *The Companion Species Manifesto: Dogs, People, and Significant Otherness* (Chicago: Prickly Paradigm Press, 2003).
41. Coetzee, "Meat Country," 46.
42. Coetzee, *Lives of Animals*, 34.
43. Martin Woessner, "Coetzee's Critique of Reason," in *J. M. Coetzee and Ethics: Philosophical Perspectives on Literature*, ed. Anton Leist and Peter Singer, 223–47 (New York: Columbia University Press, 2010).
44. Cynthia Willett, "Ground Zero for a Post-moral Ethics in J. M. Coetzee's *Disgrace* and Julia Kristeva's Melancholic," *Continental Philosophy Review* 45 (2012): 1–22. My text is based on an earlier version of Willett's text, but my stance toward it is unaffected by the expanded text.
45. Ibid., 6.
46. Ibid., 20.
47. Kelly Oliver, *Animal Lessons: How They Teach Us to Be Human* (New York: Columbia University Press, 2009).
48. The review can be found in J. M. Coetzee, *Inner Workings: Literary Essays 2000–2005* (New York: Penguin Books, 2008).
49. In Lewis Gordon, *Fanon and the Crisis of European Man: An Essay on Philosophy and the Human Sciences* (New York: Routledge, 1995).

Chapter 2

1. Dedicated to Chris Gollon, who sees more because he makes what we see.
2. Alan of Lille, *De Incarnatione Christi*, PL CCX, 579A. Quoted in *Animals in the Middle Ages*, ed. N. Flores (New York: Routledge, 2000), ix.
3. I have found extremely informative and useful the chapter "The Bestiary" in Lisa Verner, *The Epistemology of the Monstrous in the Middle Ages* (New York & London: Routledge, 2005), 91–122, as well as the introduction to *Beast and Birds of the Middle Ages: The Bestiary and Its Legacy*, ed. W. Clark and M. McMunn (Philadelphia: University of Pennsylvania Press, 1989), which has an extensive bibliography on bestiaries.
4. *Summa de Arte Predicandi*, viii, quoted in *Book of Beasts*, facsimile of MS Bodley 764, Christopher de Hamel, p. 15.
5. T. H. White, *The Book of Beasts* (New York: G. P. Putnam's Sons, 1954), 231–32.
6. Homer, *The Odyssey*, trans. Walter Shewring (Oxford: Oxford University Press, 1980), 101.
7. Ibid., 105.
8. M. Horkheimer and T. W. Adorno, *Dialectic of Enlightenment*, trans. Edmund Jephcott (Stanford, CA: Stanford University Press, 2002), 43–80. See Excursus I: "Odysseus or Myth and Enlightenment." 43–80.

9. See Walter Burket's discussion of this chapter in *Homo Necans: The Anthropology of Ancient Greek Sacrificial Ritual and Myth* (Berkeley: University of California Press, 1983), 130–34.

10. *Sophist*, 230d–231a. Italics added.

11. *Lysis*, 212.

12. *Republic*, 376 a–b.

13. *Republic*, 565d–566b. See Burket's discussion of this myth in *Homo Necans*, 84–93.

14. *Historia Animalium*, Book IX, paragraphs XXXVIII to L.

15. See the entry on "Elephants" under "Animals in the Bible" in the *Catholic Encyclopedia*, http://www.newadvent.org/cathen/01517a.htm.

16. Pliny, *Natural History*, vol. 3, books 8–11, trans. H. Rackham (Cambridge, MA: Harvard University Press, 1938-1963), sections 3–111, pages 11–13.

17. Plutarch, *Moralia: Volume XII*, trans. Harold Cherniss and W. C. Helmbold (Cambridge, MA: Harvard University Press, 1957), 501–5.

18. Ibid., 531–32.

19. Debra Hassig, *Medieval Bestiaries: Text, Image, Ideology* (Cambridge: Cambridge University Press, 1995), 129.

20. White, *The Book of Beasts*, 56.

21. Ibid., 56.

22. Ibid., 59.

23. Ibid., 59.

24. Ibid., 59.

25. Ibid., 62.

26. Ibid., 64. Here T. H. White has introduced a very telling footnote that begins: "Jews did not like dogs, and the attitude of the Bible to these charming creatures is uniformly revolting." Footnote 1, page 64.

27. Ibid., 66–67.

28. Ibid., 67.

29. Ibid., 24.

30. Ibid., 27.

31. Ibid., 28.

32. Ibid., 27.

33. Alixe Bovey, *Monsters and Grotesques in Medieval Manuscripts* (London: British Library, 2002), 32.

34. Johan Tralau, "Leviathan, the Beast and the Myth: Medusa, Dionysos, and the Riddle of Hobbes's Sovereign Monster," in *Cambridge Companion to Hobbes's Leviathan*, ed. Patricia Springborg (Cambridge: Cambridge University Press, 2007), 61–62.

35. Patricia Springborg, "Hobbes's Biblical Beasts: Leviathan and Behemoth," *Political Theory* 23, no. 2.: 362.

36. Carl Schmitt, *Land und Meer: eine weltgeschichtliche Betrachtung* (Leipzig: Philipp Reclam, 1942).

37. Carl Schmitt does not mention the Sphinx, but given the context and what is explicitly said, we can safely conclude that this is what he would have said. What Schmitt does write is the following: "The invention of the airplane marked the conquest of the third element, after those of land and sea. Man was lifting himself high above the plains and the waves, and in the process, acquired a new means of transportation, as well as a new weapon. Standards and criteria undertook further changes. Hence, man's possibilities to dominate nature and his fellow man were given the widest scope. It is easy to understand why the air force was called the 'space weapon.' The spatial revolution which it is carrying out is especially direct, forceful and obvious. Aware as one is that airplanes criss-cross the air space above seas and continents, and the waves broadcast by transmitters in every country cross the atmosphere and circle the globe in a matter of seconds, the temptation sets into conclude that man has conquered not only a third dimension, but also the third element, air, the new elemental space of human existence. To the two mythical creatures, leviathan and behemoth, a third would be added, quite likely in the shape of a big bird. Notwithstanding, caution is recommended when making such affirmations, the implications of which are not all at the tips of our fingers. As a matter of fact, if one thinks of the technology necessary for human prowess to manifest itself in the air space, and of the engines that propulsate the air fortress, it seems that the new element of human activity is fire." Carl Schmitt, *Land and Sea* (Washington, DC: Plutarch Press, 1997), 57–58. There is now another translation published by Telos Press in 2015.

The bird that is fire and spits fire would be either a dragon or a sphinx. See my essay on Schmitt's text "Land and See" in *Sovereignty, Spatiality and Carl Schmitt: Geographies of Nomos,* ed. Stephen Legg, 260–67 (New York and London: Routledge, 2011).

38. Carl Schmitt was a keen analyst of Hobbes, thus it is not arbitrarily that I refer to him. See Carl Schmitt, *The Leviathan in the State Theory of Thomas Hobbes: Meaning and Failure of a Political Symbol* (Chicago: University of Chicago Press, 2008).

Chapter 3

1. Jacques Derrida, *The Animal That Therefore I Am,* trans. David Wills (New York: Fordham University Press, 2008), 79–80.

2. Peter Sloterdijk, *Nicht gerettet: Versuche Nach Heidgger* (Frankfurt am Main: Suhrkamp Verlag, 2001).

3. Jeffrey Herf, *The Jewish Enemy: Nazi Propaganda during World War II and the Holocaust* (Cambridge, MA: The Belknap Press of Harvard University Press, 2006).

4. I explore these ideas in my essay "The Imperial Bestiary of the U.S.: Alien, Enemy Combatant, Terrorist," in *Radical Philosophy Today IV*, ed. Harry van der Linden and Tony Smith, 155–79 (Charlottesville, VA: Philosophy Documentation Center, 2006).

5. Stuart Elden, "Heidegger's Animals," *Continental Philosophy Review* 39 (2006): 273–91, quote at 274–75.

6. Martin Heidegger, *Being and Time* (Albany: State University of New York Press, 1996), 70, 246, 346.

7. Martin Heidegger, *The Fundamental Concepts of Metaphysics: World, Finitude, Solitude*, trans. William McNeill and Nicholas Walker (Bloomington and Indianapolis: Indiana University Press, 1995), 176.

8. Ibid., 177.

9. Ibid., 285.

10. Martin Heidegger, *Being and Truth*, trans. Gregory Fried and Richard Polt (Bloomington and Indianapolis: Indiana University Press, 2010), 3.

11. Ibid., 4.

12. Ibid.

13. Ibid., 9.

14. Ibid., 84.

15. Ibid., 84.

16. Ibid., italics in original. See also paragraph 34 of *Being and Time*.

17. Ibid., 85.

18. Ibid.

19. Ibid., 87, italics in original.

20. Ibid., italics in original.

21. Ibid., 100, italics in original.

22. Ibid., 80, italics in original.

23. Martin Heidegger, *Logic as the Question Concerning the Essence of Language*, trans. Wanda Torres Gregory and Yvonne Unna (Albany: State University of New York Press, 2009). I will refer to both this edition and the GA (this is the Gesamtausgabe, or complete edition of Heidegger's works) edition.

24. See Richard Wolin, ed., *The Heidegger Controversy: A Critical Reader* (Cambridge, MA: MIT Press, 1993), which contains the Rector's Speech, as well as many other political texts from the same period as these courses.

25. See Heidegger, *Logic as the Question Concerning the Essence of Language* [German], GA 38, 172.

26. Ibid. [English], 9.

27. Ibid., GA 38, 46, [English], 41; I corrected the English translation.

28. Ibid. [English], 50.

29. Ibid. [English], 52; compare 97.

30. Ibid. [German], GA 38, 60.

31. Ibid. [English], 69; (GA 38, 81).

32. Ibid.

33. See ibid. GA 38, 89.
34. Ibid. [German], GA 38, 83.
35. Ibid. [German], GA 38, 97.
36. Martin Heidegger, *Logik als die Frage nach dem Wesen der Sprache* (GA 38A) (Frankfurt am Main: Vittorio Klostermann, 2020), see page 177.
37. Ibid. [English], 136, bold added for emphasis (GA 38, 165).
38. Ibid. [German], GA 39, 169, paragraph 29.
39. Cited by Thomas Sheehan in "Heidegger and the Nazis," *New York Review of Books* 35, no. 10 (June 16, 1988): 38–47, quotes are at page 42, notes 20 and 21, respectively. These passages are now in GA 79, *Bremer und Freiburger Vorträge* (Frankfurt am Main: Vittorio Klostermann, 1994), pages 27 and 56 respectively.
40. Martin Heidegger, *On the Way to Language*, trans. Peter Hertz (New York: HarperCollins, 1982), 107.

Chapter 4

1. Leon Kass, "The Wisdom of Repugnance," in *Flesh of My Flesh: The Ethics of Cloning Humans: A Reader*, ed. Gregory E. Pence (Lanham, MD: Rowman & Littlefield, 1998), 21.
2. Jürgen Habermas, *Die Zukunft der menschlichen Natur: Auf dem Weg zur einer liberalen Eugenik?*(Frankfurt am Main: Suhrkamp, 2001), 124–25.
3. Ibid. I have benefited from having access to a preliminary translation of this text that Max Pensky generously allowed me to consult. I cite, however, from the German text.
4. This book of Habermas has received a lot of attention and generated a vast literature. I found very informative Stephan Kampowski, *A Greater Freedom: Biotechnology, Love and Human Destiny (In Dialogue with Hans Jonas and Jürgen Habermas)* (Eugene, OR: Pickwick Publications, 2013), especially because Kampowski shows the implicit and explicit links between Jonas's and Habermas's approach to biotechnological modifications of humanity. See also Bernard G. Prusak, "Rethinking 'Liberal Eugenics': Reflections and Questions on Habermas on Biotechnology," *Hastings Center Report* 35, no. 6 (Nov.–Dec. 2005), 31–42.
5. See my essay "A Letter on *Überhumanismus*: Beyond Posthumanism and Transhumanism," in *Sloterdijk Today*, ed. Stuart Elden, 58–76 (Cambridge: Polity, 2012).
6. Ibid., 43.
7. See the excellent article by Bonnie Steinbock, "Preimplantation Genetic Diagnosis and Embryo Selection," in *A Companion to Genetics*, ed. Justine Burley and John Harris, 175–90 (Malden, MA: Blackwell, 2002).
8. This topic was actually broached by Habermas in a series of editorials, now printed in Jürgen Habermas, *The Postnational Constellations: Political Essays*,

ed., trans., and with an introduction by Max Pensky (Cambridge, MA: MIT Press, 2001), 163–72. In these brief editorials Habermas makes use of Hans Jonas's argument about the right to an open future to reject cloning.

9. See Elizabeth Fenton, "Liberal Eugenics and Human Nature: Against Habermas," *Hastings Center Report* 36, no. 6 (Nov.–Dec. 2006), 35–42.

10. Habermas, *Die Zukunft der menschlichen Natur*, 62.

11. Habermas had already expressed similar views in his long essay "Remarks on Discourse Ethics," where he writes: "The person develops an inner life and achieves a stable identity only to the extent that he also externalizes himself in communicatively generated interpersonal relations and implicates himself in an ever denser and more differentiated network of reciprocal vulnerabilities, thereby rendering himself in need of protection. From this anthropological point of view, morality can be conceived as the protective institution that compensates for a constitutional precariousness implicit in the sociocultural form of life itself. Moral institutions tell us how we should behave toward one another to counteract the extreme vulnerability of the individual through protection and considerateness. Nobody can preserve his integrity by himself alone. The integrity of individual persons requires the stabilization of a network of symmetrical relations of recognition in which nonreplaceable individuals can secure their fragile identities in a *reciprocal* fashion only as a members of a community." See Jürgen Habermas, *Justification and Application: Remarks on Discourse Ethics*, trans. Ciaran P. Cronin (Cambridge, MA: MIT Press, 1993), 109.

12. Habermas, *Die Zukunft der menschlichen Natur*, 62–63.

13. Ibid., 63.

14. Ibid., 63.

15. Ibid., 73–74.

16. Richard C. Lewontin, *The Triple Helix: Gene, Organism, and Environment* (Cambridge, MA: Harvard University Press, 2000).

17. The study of the genome is called genomics. The study of the proteotype is called proteomics. In the wake of the mapping of the human genome and the unexpected discovery that the human genome has as many genes as a mustard seed, proteomics has to be explored as the next genetic frontier. See the following articles in *Scientific American*: Karen Hopkin, "Proteomics: The Post-Genome Project," *Scientific American* 265, no. 2 (August, 2001): 16; Carol Ezzell, "Proteins Rule," *Scientific American* 286, no. 4 (April 2002): 40–47.

18. Barry Commoner, "Unraveling the DNA Myth: The Spurious Foundation of Genetic Engineering," *Harper's Magazine* (February 2002): 39–47; quotation from 47.

19. Cows, pigs, and horses are very similar to dogs, in fact, and as Donna Haraway points out, these creatures occupy a unique place in the ontology of living organisms because they are neither/not, not both/and. As Haraway remarked in an interview: "Dogs [and here I would interject cows, horses, and pigs] have this

large array of possible ontologies, that are all about relationship and very heavily about relationships with humans in different historical forms . . . I am interested in the fact that dogs are not us. So they figure not-us. They are not just cute projections. Dogs do not figure mirror-of-me. Dogs figure another species, but another species living in very close relationship; another species in relation to which the nature/culture divide is more of a problem, than a help, when we try to understand it. Because dogs are neither nature, nor culture, not both/and, not neither/nor, but something else" (interview with Donna Haraway, forthcoming).

A lot of Haraway's work is about thinking about this "something else" for which she sometimes uses the term of "cyborg." See the brief but excellent overview of her work by George Myerson, *Donna Haraway and GM Foods* (Cambridge: Icon Books, 2000).

20. There is a very moving and profoundly unsettling message in Steven Spielberg's *AI* movie from 2001. The little android engineered as an ersatz son, who then is abandoned by his mother, is revived after millennia of lying dormant at the bottom of the frozen seas of earth by a future alien race. In the memories of the android's positronic brain, humanity lives on. We are remembered by our creations. Our inventions become our passport to immortality.

21. See Gerhart B. Ladner, *The Idea of Reform: Its Impact on Christian Thought and Action in the Age of the Fathers* (New York: Harper Torchbooks, 1967).

22. Giovanni Pico della Mirandola, *Oration on the Dignity of Man* (Chicago: Gateway, 1856).

23. See in Hannah Arendt, *The Life of the Mind* (San Diego, New York, London: Harvest/HBJ, 1981), the discussion (from the second volume) on *Willing* (pp. 109–10), where Arendt explicitly links the discussion of *imago Dei* to natality. See also her dissertation *Love and Saint Augustine* (Chicago: University of Chicago Press, 1996). The discussion of natality in *The Human Condition* (Garden City, NY: Doubleday Anchor Books, 1959) links up the Genesis story, from where the doctrine of *imago Dei* stems, to the discussion of the plurality, as well as the issue of beginnings and natality.

24. See the wonderful essay by Carol Rovane, "Genetics and Personal Identity," in *A Companion to Genethics,* ed. Justine Burley and John Harris, 245–52 (Malden, MA: Blackwell, 2002). On the technofantasies about downloading minds into computers, see Ray Kurzweil, *The Age of Spiritual Machines* (New York: Viking, 1999). See also the short stories by Greg Egan, especially "Closer," collected in his book *Axiomatic* (New York: Harperprism, 1997), 261–76, for one of the most philosophically sophisticated sci-fi explorations on the implications of genetic engineering and computer simulations for personal identity.

25. See Bernhard Schlink, *Flights of Love* (New York: Pantheon, 2001), and Bernhard Schlink, *The Reader* (New York: Vintage Books, 1995).

26. Habermas, *Die Zukunft der menschlichen Natur,* 49–50.

27. Peter Singer, "Shopping at the Genetic Supermarket" (lecture presented at Stanford University, Fall 2001). I am quoting from the manuscript, pp. 6–7.

28. Jürgen Habermas, *Justification and Application: Remarks on Discourse Ethics*, trans. Ciaran P. Cronin (Cambridge, MA: MIT Press, 1993), 65.
29. Ibid., 66.
30. Ibid.
31. Ibid., 66–67.
32. John Rawls, *A Theory of Justice* (Cambridge, MA: Harvard University Press, 1971), ¶11, 60.
33. Ibid., ¶17, 107–8.
34. Gregory E. Pence, *Who's Afraid of Human Cloning?* (Lanham, MD: Rowman & Littlefield, 1997), 113.
35. Jeremy Rifkin, *The Biotech Century: Harnessing the Gene and Remaking the World* (New York: Jeremy P. Tarcher/Putnam, 1998).
36. See Jennifer Ackerman, "Food: How Safe? How Altered?," *National Geographic* 201, no. 5 (May 2002): 2–50; citation from p. 35, statistics from p. 37.
37. See Kristin Dawkins, *The Gene Wars: The Politics of Biotechnology* (New York: Seven Stories Press, 1997), 25–26.
38. See Marc Lappé and Britt Bailey, *Against the Grain: Biotechnology and the Corporate Takeover of Your Food* (Monroe, ME: Common Courage Press, 1998), 1–18. See also the special issue on "Biopiracy and Biotechnology" of the *Peace Review* 12, no. 4 (December 2000). See also Vandana Shiva, *Stolen Harvest: The Hijacking of the Global Food Supply* (Boston: South End Press, 1999), and Vandana Shiva, *Biopiracy: The Plunder of Nature and Knowledge* (Boston: South End Press, 1997).
39. See David Shenk, "Biocapitalism: What Price the Genetic Revolution?," *Harper's Magazine* (December 1997): 37–45; quotation from p. 44.

Chapter 5

1. Axel Honneth and Hans Joas, *Social Action and Human Nature* (Cambridge, UK: Cambridge University Press, 1988), 9–10.
2. For my reading of political modernity see Albrecht Wellmer, "Models of Freedom in the Modern World (1989)," in *Endgames: The Irreconcilable Nature of Modernity. Essays and Lectures*, 3–38 (Cambridge, MA: MIT Press, 1998).
3. See Hans Jonas, "Biological Engineering—A Preview," in *Philosophical Essays: From Ancient Creed to Technological Man* (Chicago and London: University of Chicago Press, 1974), 141–67; for Jonas's contrast between general engineering and biological engineering, see pages 142–46.
4. Leon R. Kass, who was named director of the Council on Bioethics by US President George W. Bush, argues that genetic engineering is qualitatively different from other forms of engineering because, first, it alters the germ line; and second, it creates new capacities and norms of health and fitness. The first concern, as I will argue, is perhaps the strongest aspect of this line of argumen-

tation. The second concern is the weakest, for from generation to generation the capacities and norms of humans have changed. Prolonged life expectancy, fertility drugs, socialized healthcare, and new reproductive technologies are unhinging our expectations about when and what humans can do. At the same time, new diseases have begun to proliferate: breast cancer, heart disease, STDs, HIV, obesity, and diabetes. See Leon R. Kass, "The Moral Meaning of Genetic Technology," *Commentary*, September 1999, 32–38.

    5. Hans Jonas, "Evolution and Freedom: On the Continuity among Life-Forms," in *Mortality and Morality: A Search for the Good after Auschwitz* (Evanston, IL: Northwestern University Press, 1996), 59–74, quote on 66.

    6. Habermas relies on Helmut Plessner's distinction between *Leib* and *Körper*, and in general in his phenomenological philosophical anthropology. See the discussion of Plessner, and Habermas's debts to his works, particularly in his precommunicative turn, in Axel Honneth and Hans Joas, *Social Action and Human Nature* (Cambridge: Cambridge University Press, 1988).

    7. See Edith Kurzweil, *The Age of Spiritual Machines* (New York: Viking, 1999). According to Kurzweil, this new evolutionary step will be taken by the year 2099, a mere seventy-seven years from now; see page 280 in the book. This might sound overly optimistic, but then again, a mere seventy-seven years ago we did not have computers, had not landed on the moon, nor had the notion that organic life could be understood in terms of chains of information.

    8. See my essay "The Legal Orthopedia of Human Dignity: Thinking with Axel Honneth," *Philosophy and Social Criticism* 40, no. 8 (2014), 799–815.

    9. Hannah Arendt, *The Human Condition* (Garden City, NY: Doubleday Anchor Books, 1959).

    10. See the wonderful essay by P. S. Greenspan, "Free Will and the Genome Project," *Philosophy and Public Affairs* 22, no. 1 (Winter 1993): 31–43. Greenspan, however, thinks that genetic engineering does present a challenge to our notion of freedom as self-control, virtue as an attainment, and consequently to the idea of moral character as an achievement: "What it [genetic engineering] may seem to threaten is the value we place on freedom as self-control, insofar as it makes out the exercise of self-control as indirect in the sense of being mediated by something other than the agent's thought processes and their natural behavioral consequences" (42). On the grounds of Greenspan's own discussion about free will, however, I fail to see how successful self-control does not remain a challenge, a hurdle, a leap of faith even for the most genetically optimized beings.

    11. Jürgen Habermas, "Historical Consciousness and Post-Traditional Identity: The Federal Republic's Orientation to the West," in *The New Conservatism: Cultural Criticism and the Historian's Debate* (Cambridge, MA: MIT Press, 1989), 249–67, quote on 251.

    12. Eric Lander quoted in Ralph Brave, "Governing the Genome," *The Nation*, December 10, 2001, p. 3.

13. See Jürgen Habermas, *Postmetaphysical Thinking: Philosophical Essays* (Cambridge, MA: MIT Press, 1992), 28–53. Habermas has now given us a more expansive elaboration of what he means by "postmetaphysical" in his latest magnum opus, *Also a History of Philosophy, Volume 1: The Project of a Genealogy of Postmetaphysical Thinking* (Cambridge: Polity Press, 2023). See also my essay: "Postmetaphysics and Postsecularism," *Review of Politics* 84, no. 2 (2022), 257–62.

14. See J. H. Elliott, *Spain and Its World 1500–1700* (New Haven, CT, and London: Yale University Press, 1989), especially chapter 3: "The Discovery of America and the Discovery of Man."

15. See Enrique Dussel, *Ética de la Liberación en la epoca de la globalización y la exclusion* (Madrid and Mexico: Trotta, 1998), especially the introduction.

16. See my essay "From Imperial to Dialogical Cosmopolitanism," *Ethics & Global Politics* 2, no. 3 (2009): 241–58.

17. Walter Mignolo, "The Many Faces of Cosmo-polis: Border Thinking and Critical Cosmopolitanism," *Public Culture* 12, no. 3 (Fall 2000): 721–48.

18. See Eva Feder Kittay, *Love's Labour: Essays on Women, Equality, and Dependency* (New York: Routledge, 1999).

19. As Habermas has written, "The person develops an inner life and achieves a stable identity only to the extent that he also externalizes himself in communicatively generated interpersonal relations and implicates himself in an ever denser and more differentiated network of reciprocal vulnerabilities, thereby rendering himself in need of protection. From this anthropological point of view, morality can be conceived as the protective institution that compensates for a constitutional precariousness implicit in the sociocultural form of life itself. Moral institutions tell us how we should behave toward one another to counteract the extreme vulnerability of the individual through protection and considerateness. Nobody can preserve his integrity by himself alone. The integrity of individual persons requires the stabilization of a network of symmetrical relations of recognition in which nonreplaceable individuals can secure their fragile identities in a reciprocal fashion only as a members of a community."

See Jürgen Habermas, *Justification and Application: Remarks on Discourse Ethics*, trans. Ciaran P. Cronin (Cambridge, MA: MIT Press, 1993), 109.

20. Jürgen Habermas, "Justice and Solidarity: On the Discussion Concerning 'Stage 6,'" *Philosophical Forum: A Quarterly* 21, nos. 1/2 (Fall–Winter 1989-90): 32–52.

Chapter 6

1. This chapter began as a manuscript with the title of "Philosophical Beasts." In the original draft, which I intended to send to *Radical Philosophy*, I focused on Mary Midgley and Donna Haraway, with side references to Agamben

and Derrida, and the philosophemes of the beast, animal, and the human. I am delighted that now we have a study of several women philosophers who have deeply influenced my thinking on the animal/human question. See Clare Mac Cumhaill and Rachael Wiseman, *Metaphysical Animals: How Four Women Brought Philosophy Back to Life* (New York: Doubleday, 2022).

2. Theodor W. Adorno, "The Idea of Natural History" *Telos* 60 (Summer 1984): 117.

3. C. S. Lewis, *The Abolition of Man* (San Francisco: Harper San Francisco, 2000).

4. Leon R. Kass, *The Beginning of Wisdom: Reading Genesis* (New York: Free Press, 2003). For a devastating and perspicacious review, see Phyllis Trible, "On Man's First Disobedience, and Soon," *New York Times Review of Books*, October 19, 2003, 28.

5. This work has been collected in Leon R. Kass, M.D., *Life, Liberty, and the Defense of Dignity: The Challenge for Bioethics* (San Francisco: Encounter Books, 2002).

6. For insightful criticisms of Kass see Gregory E. Pence, *Who's Afraid of Human Cloning?* (Lanham, MD: Rowman & Littlefield, 1997).

7. See the wonderful book by Jennifer Banks, *Natality: Toward a Philosophy of Birth* (New York: W. W. Norton & Company, 2023), and Anne O'Byrne, *Natality and Finitude* (Bloomington: Indiana University Press, 2010).

8. Erich Fromm, *Thou Shall Be As Gods: A Radical Interpretation of the Old Testament and Its Tradition* (New York: Fawcett Books, 1966), 57.

9. See Wolfhart Pannenberg, *Anthropology in Theological Perspective* (Philadelphia: Westminster Press, 1985), especially the part on "The Person in Nature."

10. For a discussion of negative and dialectical philosophical anthropology, see Stefan Breuer, "Adorno's Anthropology," *Telos* 64 (Summer 1985): 15–32.

11. Jürgen Habermas, *The Postnational Constellation: Political Essays* (Cambridge, MA: MIT Press, 2001), 163–72.

12. Jürgen Habermas, *The Future of Human Nature* (Oxford: Polity, 2003), 74.

13. I have offered a different analysis of this text in chapter 5 "Communicative Freedom and Genetic Engineering."

14. I have dealt with the political aspects of Habermas's formulation of an ethics of the species in chapter 4 above "Habermas on Human Cloning."

15. Arnold Gehlen, *Moral und Hypermoral: eine pluralistische Ethik* (Frankfurt am Main: Athenaeum Verlag, 1969), and *Man in the Age of Technology*, trans. Patricia Lipscomb (New York: Columbia University Press, 1980).

16. We now have translations of Plessner's most important works, which influenced Habermas: *Levels of Organic Life and the Human: An Introduction to Philosophical Anthropology*, trans. Millay Hyatt (New York: Fordham University Press, 2019), and *Political Anthropology* (Evanston, IL: Northwestern University Press, 2018).

17. See Arnold Gehlen, *Man: His Nature and Place in the World* (New York: Columbia University Press, 1988).

18. Hans Jonas wrote a fascinating paper that parallels very much Habermas's; see Hans Jonas, "Ontological Grounding of a Political Ethics: On the Metaphysics of Commitment to the Future of Man," in *The Public Realm: Essays on Discursive Types in Political Philosophy*, ed. Reiner Schürmann, 154–66 (Albany: State University of New York Press, 1988).

19. See Tom Rockmore, *Habermas on Historical Materialism* (Bloomington: Indiana University Press, 1989), especially chapters 2, 3, and 4.

20. Jürgen Habermas, *Knowledge and Human Interests* (Boston, Beacon: 1971), 312–13.

21. Ibid., 314.

22. Jürgen Habermas, "Arnold Gehlen: Imitation Substantiality," in *Philosophical-Political Profiles* (Cambridge, MA: MIT Press, 1983), 120, italics added.

23. A consideration of Derrida's negative philosophical anthropology would have to take into account his writing on Heidegger's *Geschlecht*, hands, and spirit, as well as his writing on the animal. The human being is poised dialectically between the animal and something that Heidegger called Dasein, but which certainly cannot escape the grip of history. In fact, a Derridian negative philosophical anthropology would have to be read in tandem with the whole notion of the prosthetic in his corpus. See David Wills, *Prosthesis* (Stanford, CA: Stanford University Press, 1995); see also Wills's essay presented at the colloquium on Derrida's *Politics of Friendship*, organized by the Humanities Institute of Stony Brook at Stony Brook Manhattan, fall of 2002. Major contribution to this type of research are H. Peter Steeves, ed., *Animal Others: On Ethics, Ontology, and Animal Life* (Albany: State University of New York Press, 1999), and Cary Wolfe, ed., *Zoontologies: The Question of the Animal* (Minneapolis: University of Minnesota Press, 2003).

24. Jacques Derrida, *Negotiations: Interventions and Interviews: 1971–2001* (Stanford, CA: Stanford University Press, 2002), 199–214.

25. Jacques Derrida, *Rogues: Two Essays on Reason*, trans. Pascale-Anne Brault and Michael Naas (Stanford, CA: Stanford University Press, 2005).

26. Derrida, *Negotiations*, 202.

27. This distinction merits a lengthy comparison with Heidegger's argumentative strategy in his classic "Letter on Humanism," which should be properly read as defending a form of negative philosophical anthropology. Peter Sloterdijk's comments would also fit in this tradition, see his *Regeln zur Menschenpark* (Frankfurt: Suhrkamp, 2001), now available at Peter Sloterdijk, "Rules for the Human Zoo: A Response to the Letter on Humanism," *Environment and Planning D: Society and Space* 27, no. 1 (2009): 12–28. See also my essay on Sloterdijk, "A Letter on *Überhumanismus*: Beyond Posthumanism and Transhumanism," in *Sloterdijk Today*, ed. Stuart Elden, 58–76 (Cambridge: Polity, 2012).

28. Habermas, *The Future of Human Nature*, 101–15.

29. I want to thank Martin Matustik for reminding me of this passage in Habermas's speech, which I had a chance to discuss with Habermas when he read an early version of the text during his visit to Stony Brook in the fall of 2001.

30. See Max Horkheimer and Theodor W. Adorno, *The Dialectic of Enlightenment: Philosophical Fragments* (Stanford, CA: Stanford University Press, 2002), especially "Odysseus or Myth and Enlightenment."

31. See Joseph Nigg, ed., *The Book of Fabulous Beasts: A Treasury of Writings from Ancient Times to the Present* (New York and Oxford: Oxford University Press, 1999), especially the introduction, "A History of Fabulous Beasts," 3–15.

32. See the excellent history of bestiaries in the appendix by T. H. White to his translation of *The Book of Beasts, being a translation from the a Latin Bestiary of the Twelfth Century made and edited T. H. White* (London: Jonathan Cape, 1954), 230–70, which is accompanied by an excellent bibliography. Note also the family tree that traces the genealogy of bestiaries on page 233. On page 263, White provides us with a fascinating map of the influences of bestiaries on literature in England and on the Continent.

33. See the preface and introduction to the English translation of *A Medieval Book of Beasts: Pierre de Beauvais's Bestiary*, trans. Guy R. Mermier (Lewiston, NY: Edwin Mellen Press, 1992), iii–xv.

34. See the discussion of the monstrous God in David D. Gilmore, *Monsters: Evil Beings, Mythical Beasts, and All Manner of Imaginary Terrors* (Philadelphia: University of Pennsylvania Press, 2003), chapter 4.

35. The notion of dialectical inversion and kratophany is discussed by Richard Kearney in *Strangers, Gods and Monsters* (London and New York: Routledge, 2003), 9–10.

36. The discourse of beast and barbarian overlap to produce genocidal ideologies. On the links, see Anthony Pagden, *The Fall of Natural Man: The American Indian and the Origins of Comparative Ethnology* (Cambridge: Cambridge University Press, 1982), 15–26.

37. See Kirkpatrick Sale, *The Conquest of Paradise: Christopher Columbus and the Columbian Legacy* (New York: Knopf, 1990).

38. Mary Midgley, *Beast and Man: The Roots of Human Nature* (Ithaca, NY: Cornell University Press, 1978). Henceforth, I will cite this edition in the body of the text.

39. See Mary Midgley, *Animals and Why They Matter* (Athens: University of Georgia Press, 1984), in which Midgley develops an ethical position on animals that argues for their moral considerability, but relatively. She calls this position "relative dismissal," and this involves the realization that "animals, since they are conscious, are entitled to *some* consideration, but must come at the end of a queue, after all human needs have been met" (13).

40. See the outstanding volume by Christa Davis Acampora and Ralph R. Acampora, eds., *A Nietzschean Bestiary: Becoming Animal beyond Docile and Brutal* (Lanham, MD: Rowman & Littlefield, 2004).

41. For a discussion of Derrida's contribution to the discourse on the "animal" see the useful essay "In the Shadow of Wittgenstein's Lion: Language, Ethics, and the Question of the Animal" by Cary Wolfe in his edited volume *Zoontologies: The Question of the Animal* (Minneapolis: University of Minnesota Press, 2003), 1–57, especially 19–34, where he addresses Derrida and Levinas.

42. Jacques Derrida, "The Animal That Therefore I Am (More to Follow)," *Critical Inquiry* 28 (Winter 2002): 369–418, quotation at 399. Henceforth, numbers in brackets refer to this essay.

43. For the use of this phrasing and its implications see Alan Bleakley, *The Animalizing Imagination: Totemism, Textuality, and Ecocritique* (New York: St. Martin's Press, 1999).

44. Another important point of reference for an proper study of Derrida's bestiary are his comments upon receiving the Adorno Prize in 2001, which he entitled "Fichus." See Jacques Derrida, *Paper Machine* (Stanford, CA: Stanford University Press, 2005), 164–81, especially 180–81.

45. See Jacques Derrida, *The Beast and the Sovereign*, Vol. 1, trans. Geoffrey Bennington (Chicago: University of Chicago Press, 2009), and *The Beast and the Sovereign*, Vol. 2, trans. Geoffrey Bennington (Chicago: University of Chicago Press, 2017).

46. Jacques Derrida, *Rogues: Two Essays on Reason*, trans. Pascale-Anne Brault and Michael Naas (Stanford, CA: Stanford University Press, 2005).

47. See Derrida, *Rogues*, 63–70, for the different etymologies of *voyous* (rogue).

48. See the discussion on translating this passage by the Pascale-Anne Brault and Michael Naas in the notes to the translation of *Rogues*, 161n1.

49. Matthias Fritsch "Derrida's Democracy to Come," *Constellations* 9, no. 4 (December 2002), 574–97.

50. Giorgio Agamben, *Homo Sacer: Sovereign Power and Bare Life* (Stanford, CA: Stanford University Press, 1998). Henceforth I will quote from this book in the body of the text. See also Giorgio Agamben, *The Omnibus Homo Sacer* (Stanford, CA: Stanford University Press, 2017), which gathers all the texts related to Agamben's investigations into *Homo sacer*.

51. Giorgio Agamben, *The State of Exception*, trans. Kevin Attell (Stanford, CA: Stanford University Press, 2005). Henceforth I will quote from this book in the body of the text.

52. Giorgio Agamben, *The Open: Man and Animal*, trans. Kevin Attell (Stanford, CA: Stanford University Press, 2004). Henceforth I will quote from this book in the body of the text.

53. Stuart Elden has written a lengthy, thoroughly detailed study of Heidegger's treatment of the problem of the animal. See Stuart Elden, "Heidegger's Animals," *Continental Philosophy Review* 39 (2006): 273–91.

54. This language comes from Donna Haraway's essay "Crittercam: Compounding Eyes in NatureCultures," in *Expanding Phenomenology: Companion to Ihde*, ed. Evan Selinger (Albany: State University of New York Press, 2006), 175.

55. Ibid., 177.

56. See for instance Donna Haraway, "Race: Universal Donors in a Vampire Culture: It's All in the Family: Biological Kinships Categories in the Twentieth-Century United States," in *The Haraway Reader*, 251–93 (New York and London: Routledge, 2003).

57. Haraway appropriates Whitehead's "concrescence" and gives it a geohistorical twist. See Donna Haraway, "Cyborgs to Companion Species: Reconfiguring Kinship in Technoscience," in *The Haraway Reader* (New York and London: Routledge, 2003), 297.

58. Donna Haraway, "The Promises of Monsters: A Regenerative Politics for Inappropriate/d Others," in *Cultural Studies*, ed. Lawrence Grossberg, Cary Nelson, and Paula Treichler, 295–337 (New York: Routledge, 1992). See also Haraway, *The Haraway Reader*, 63–124.

59. Bregje van Eekelen, Jennifer Gonzalez, Bettina Stötzer, and Anna Tsing, eds., *Shock and Awe: War on Words* (Santa Cruz, CA: New Pacific Press, 2004).

60. Haraway, "Cyborgs to Companion Species," 302.

61. Charis Thompson Cussins, "Ontological Choreography: Agency through Objectification in Infertility Clinics," *Social Studies of Science* 26 (1996): 575–610. See Haraway, "Cyborgs to Companion Species," 317.

62. Haraway, "Crittercam: Compounding Eyes in NatureCultures," 19.

63. Haraway, "Cyborgs to Companion Species," 300; see also Haraway, "Chicken," in *Shock and Awe*, 29.

64. Jacques Derrida, "And Say the Animal Responded?," in *Zoontologies: The Question of the Animal*, ed. Cary Wolfe (Minneapolis: University of Minnesota Press, 2003), 121–46.

Chapter 7

1. Steve Martin says in his acknowledgments to his wonderful book *Shopgirl* something to the effect that if writers write alone, why is it that their acknowledgments are so long? I agree with the sentiment. I certainly don't write alone: there are two dogs and two cats, running around, sitting on my writing table, warming my feet under it, nudging me when 6 o'clock (both a.m. and p.m., depending on the deadline) rolls around. There are two children, who come over and ask when they can borrow *my computer*, and when are we going sledding, to the library, or

to the beach. Sometimes, they just come over and hug me. But most importantly, and more to the point, I did not write this essay alone. First, I wrote an earlier version for a SPEP meeting, where I had some great questions. Later, I sent it Martin Woessner, who has read almost everything I have written, and always sends the best comments. But it was John Sanbonmatsu's improving questions, suggestions, and corrections that turned a conference paper into its present form.

2. Jacques Derrida, "Fichus," in *Paper Machine*, trans. Rachel Bowlby (Stanford, CA: Stanford University Press, 2005), 164–81, quote at 180.

3. Past recipients include Jürgen Habermas, Jean-Luc Godard, Pierre Boulez, Norbert Elias, Guenther Anders, Zygmut Bauman, the composer Giorgy Ligeti, Albrecht Wellmer, Alexander Kluge, Judith Butler, Georges Didi-Huberman, Margaret von Trotta, and Klaus Theweleit.

4. Derrida, "Fichus," 164–81.

5. Ibid., 177.

6. Ibid., 180.

7. Theodor W. Adorno, *Beethoven: The Philosophy of Music*, trans. Edmund Jephcott (Stanford:, CA Stanford University Press, 1998), 8, fragment 202. Italics added.

8. Derrida, "Fichus," 181; italics in the original.

9. Max Horkheimer and Theodor W. Adorno, *Dialectic of Enlightenment: Philosophical Fragments*, trans. Edmund Jephcott (Stanford, CA: Stanford University Press, 2002), 210.

10. Derrida, "Fichus," 180.

11. Giovanna Borradori, *Philosophy in a Time of Terror: Dialogues with Jürgen Habermas and Jacques Derrida* (Chicago: University of Chicago Press, 2003).

12. Jacques Derrida, "The Animal That Therefore I Am (More to Follow)," *Critical Inquiry* 28 (Winter 2002): 369–418. See also the extremely important discussion on animals and violence in Jacques Derrida and Elisabeth Roudinesco, *For What Tomorrow . . . a Dialogue*, trans. Jeff Fort (Stanford, CA: Stanford University Press, 2004), 62–76.

13. See Cary Wolfe, ed., *Zoontologies: The Question of the Animal* (Minneapolis: University of Minnesota Press, 2003), and David Wood, "Thinking with Cats," in *Animal Philosophy: Ethics and Identity*, ed. Peter Atterton and Matthew Calarco (London and New York: Continuum, 2004).

14. Martin Jay, *Adorno* (Cambridge, MA: Harvard University Press, 1984), 24.

15. See, Theodor W. Adorno, *History and Freedom: Lectures 1964–1965*, trans. Rodney Livingston (Cambridge: Polity Press, 2006), 299–300, note 5.

16. Quoted in Stefan Müller-Doohm, *Adorno: A Biography* (Cambridge: Polity, 2005), 240.

17. Detlev Claussen, *Adorno: Ein Letztes Genie* (Frankfurt am Main: S. Fischer, 2003), 301. See also the wonderful review essay by Robert Savage, "Adorno's Family and Other Animals," *Thesis Eleven*, no. 78 (August 2004): 102–12.

18. See Herbert Marcuse, *Eros and Civilization: A Philosophical Inquiry into Freud* (Boston: Beacon Press, 1966), chapter 8, 159–71.
19. Quoted in Claussen, *Adorno*, 305.
20. Ibid., 265.
21. Horkheimer and Adorno, *Dialectic of Enlightenment*, 43.
22. Ibid., 42–43.
23. Karl Marx, "Economic and Philosophic Manuscripts of 1844," in *Karl Marx and Frederick Engels, Collected Works*, Vol. 3 *Marx and Engels 1843–1844* (New York: International Publishers, 1975), 296. The passage I am paraphrasing is in the third manuscript, in the section where Marx discusses communism, and where he writes, and this merits lengthy citing: "*Communism* as the *positive* transcendence of *private property* as *human self-estrangement*, and therefore as the real *appropriation* of the *human* essence by and for man; communism therefore as the complete return of man to himself as *social* (i.e., human) being—a return accomplished consciously and embracing the entire wealth of previous development. This communism, as fully developed naturalism, equals humanism, and as fully developed humanism equals naturalism: it is the *genuine* resolution of the conflict between man and nature and between nature and man—the true resolution of the strife between existence and essence, between objectification and self-confirmation, between freedom and necessity, between the individual and the species."

This passage is remarkable because it announces the rejection of a humanism that is anti-nature while affirming a humanism that is a "fully developed naturalism." This humanism is not anthropocentric, but rather post-anthropocentric. It is one of my arguments in this chapter that Adorno stands within this tradition.

24. Theodor Adorno, *Minima Moralia: Reflections from Damaged Life* (London: Verso, 1978), 105.
25. T. W. Adorno, *Aesthetic Theory* (Minneapolis: Minnesota University Press, 1996), 113.
26. Ibid., 119.
27. Ibid., 78.
28. Thedor W. Adorno, *Negative Dialectics* (New York: Continuum, 1983), 365.
29. Ibid., 299. Translation amended.
30. Gerhard Schweppenhäuser, *Ethik nach Auschwitz: Adornos negative Moralphilosophie* (Hamburg: Argument-Verlag, 1993), 213.
31. Theodor W. Adorno, *Problems in Moral Philosophy*, trans. Rodney Livingston (Cambridge, UK: Polity Press, 2000).
32. Stefan Breuer, "Adorno's Anthropology," *Telos*, no. 64 (Summer 1985): 15–31.
33. Adorno, *Negative Dialectics*, 124.
34. Max Pensky, "Natural History: The Life and Afterlife of a Concept in Adorno," *Critical Horizon: Journal of Social and Critical Theory* 5 (2004): 227–58.
35. Bob Hullot-Kentor, "Introduction to Adorno's 'Idea of Natural-History,'" *Telos*, no. 60 (Summer 1984): 97–110.

36. T. W. Adorno, "The Idea of Natural History," *Telos* 60 (Summer of 1984): 111–24.

37. Adorno, *Negative Dialectics*, 358.

38. Derrida, "The Animal That Therefore I Am (More to Follow)." This is a translation of one of the longest parts of the lecture series.

39. Derrida and Roudinesco, *For What Tomorrow*, 65.

40. Ibid., 65. Evidently, Derrida's seeming rejection of the "rights discourse" here is in keeping with his overall rejection of the norm and the order of the law. Prior to the law there is a nonnormative affirmation and response to the ethical appellation of the other. Rights are posterior affirmation of our submission to a demand, the demand to respect the other in his/her/its otherness. Rights as such acknowledge a prior acknowledgment; they are responses that respond to a prior response.

41. There is now an outstanding treatment of this and related texts by Derrida; see Leonard Lawlor, *This Is Not Sufficient: An Essay on Animality and Human Nature in Derrida* (New York: Columbia University Press, 2007). See also Kelly Oliver's *Animal Lessons: How They Teach Us to Be Human* (New York: Columbia University Press, 2009).

42. Derrida, "The Animal That Therefore I Am (More to Follow)," 369.

43. Ibid., 393 ff.

44. Ibid., 397.

45. Quoted in Claussen, *Adorno*, 305.

46. Derrida, "The Animal That Therefore I Am (More to Follow)," 399.

47. Ibid., 397.

48. Adorno, *Negative Dialectics*, 15.

49. See my essay "Anthropodicies of Coloniality: Urbanocene, Plantationcene and Critical Theory," *Berlin Journal of Critical Theory* 7, no. 1 (January 2023), 103–30.

50. See Elizabeth Kolbert, "Enter the Anthropocene-Age of Man," *National Geographic*, March 2001, http://ngm.nationalgeographic.com/print/2011/03/age-of-man/kolbert-text. See also Elizabeth Kolbert, *Field Notes from a Catastrophe: Man, Nature, and Climate Change* (New York, London, New Delhi, Sydney: Bloomsbury, 2009), chapter 10: "Man in the Anthropocene," 183–89. See also her *The Sixth Extinction: An Unnatural History* (New York: Henry Holt and Company, 2014).

51. See Niles Eldredge, "The Sixth Extinction," http://www.actionbioscience.org/newfrontiers/eldredge2.html.

52. Edward O. Wilson, *The Future of Life* (New York: Vintage Books, 2002), 102.

53. David Quammen, "Planet of Weeds," in *The Best American Essays of 1999*, ed. Edward Hoagland (Boston and New York: Houghton Mifflin Company, 1999), 212–33. This essay first appeared in *Harper's Magazine*.

54. Leo Tolstoy in *The Kreutzer Sonata*, quoted by Peter Atterton, in "Ethical Cynicism," in *Animal Philosophy: Ethics and Philosophy*, 55.

Chapter 8

1. Eduardo Mendieta, "From Imperial to Dialogical Cosmopolitanism," in *Ethics & Global Politics* 2, no. 3 (2009): 241–58. See also Pauline Kleingeld, *Kant and Cosmopolitanism: The Philosophical Idea of World Citizenship* (Cambridge: Cambridge University Press, 2011), and Martha C. Nussbaum, *The Cosmopolitan Tradition: A Noble but Flawed Ideal* (Cambridge, MA; The Belknap Press of Harvard University Press, 2019), and the extensive and diverse handbook edited by Gerard Delanty, *The Routledge International Handbook of Cosmopolitanism Studies*, 2nd ed. (London and New York: Routledge, 2019).

2. Donna J. Haraway, *The Companion Species Manifesto: Dogs, People, and Significant Otherness* (Chicago: Prickly Paradigm Press, 2003). See also Donna J. Haraway, *Manifestly Haraway* (Minneapolis and London: University of Minnesota Press, 2016).

3. Stephen Toulmin, *Cosmopolis: The Hidden Agenda of Modernity* (Chicago: University of Chicago Press, 1990).

4. Donna J. Haraway, *When Species Meet* (Minneapolis and London: University of Minnesota Press, 2008), 38.

5. Haraway, *When Species Meet*, 19.

6. Kelly Oliver, *Animal Lessons: How They Teach Us to Be Human* (New York: Columbia University Press, 2009), 16–17.

7. Oliver, *Animal Lessons*, 21.

8. Haraway, *When Species Meet*, 36.

9. See Cary Wolfe, *Before the Law: Humans and Other Animals in a Biopolitical Frame* (Chicago: University of Chicago Press, 2013), Matthew Calarco, *Thinking through Animals: Identity, Difference, Indistinction* (Stanford, CA: Stanford University Press, 2015), Matthew Calarco, *Zoographies: The Question of the Animal from Heidegger to Derrida* (New York: Columbia University Press, 2008), and Martha C. Nussbaum, *Justice for Animals: Our Collective Responsibility* (New York: Simon & Schuster, 2022).

10. Joseph and Barrie Klaits, eds., *Animals and Man in Historical Perspective* (New York: Harper Torchbooks, 1974), 3.

11. Haraway, *When Species Meet*, 90.

12. Vinciane Despret, "The Body We Care For: Figures of Anthropo-zoogenesis," *Body and Society* 10, no. 2/3 (2004): 111–134, quote at 130.

13. Eduardo Mendieta, "The Bio-technological *Scala Naturae* and Interspecies Cosmopolitanism: Patricia Piccinini, Jane Alexander, and and Guillermo Gómez-Peña," in *Biopower: Foucault and Beyond*, ed. Vernon Cisney and Nicolae Morar (Chicago: University of Chicago Press 2015), 158–79.

14. Jacques Derrida, *The Animal That Therefore I Am* (New York: Fordham University Press, 2008), 136.

15. Haraway, *When Species Meet*, 12.

16. Donna J. Haraway, *Staying with the Trouble: Making Kin in the Chthulucene* (Durham, NC, and London: Duke University Press, 2016).

17. The following section uses parts of an earlier essay, Eduardo Mendieta, "Interspecies Cosmopolitanism: Towards a Discourse Ethics Grounding of Animal Rights," in *Recenterings of Continental Philosophy*, vol. 35, ed. Cynthia Willett and Leonard Lawlor, SPEP Supplement 2010 of *Philosophy Today*, vol. 54, 208-16.

18. Margaret Macdonald, "Natural Rights," in *Theories of Rights*, ed. Jeremy Waldron (Oxford: Oxford University Press, 2009), 26.

19. Jeremy Bentham *The Works of Jeremy Bentham* (Edinburgh and London: Simpkin, Marshall & Co, 1843), 500-501.

20. Jeremy Bentham, *An Introduction to the Principles of Morals and Legislation* (Mineola, NY: Dover Publications, 2007), 1-2. Italics in original.

21. Michel Foucault, *"Society Must Be Defended": Lectures at the Collège de France 1975-1976* (New York: Picador, 2003), 95.

22. See Jürgen Habermas, *Postmetaphysical Thinking* (Cambridge, MA: MIT Press, 1992), and Jürgen Habermas, *Postmetaphysical Thinking II* (Cambridge: Polity Press, 2016).

23. Judith Butler, "Is Judaism Zionism?," in *The Power of Religion in the Public Sphere*, ed. Eduardo Mendieta and J. VanAnterwen (New York: Columbia University Press, 2011), 76.

24. See Elizabeth Kolbert, "The Sixth Extinction? There Have Been Five Great Die-Offs in History, This Time the Cataclysm Is Us," *New Yorker*, May 2009, 53.

Elizabeth Kolbert, *The Sixth Extinction: An Unnatural History* (New York: Henry Holt and Company, 2014), 53; see also David Quammen, "Planet of Weeds," in *Natural Acts: A Sidelong View of Science and Nature* (New York and London: Norton, 2008), 161-88.

25. Ronald Dworkin, *Taking Rights Seriously* (Cambridge, MA: Harvard University Press, 1977), xi.

26. Jürgen Habermas, *Justification and Application: Remarks on Discourse Ethics* (Cambridge, MA: MIT Press, 1993). Henceforth I will quote from this text in the body of the chapter.

27. Jürgen Habermas, *Between Facts and Norms: Contributions to a Discourse Theory of Law and Democracy* (Cambridge, MA: MIT Press, 1996), 150.

28. Ibid., 150.

29. Ibid., 460.

30. Jürgen Habermas, "Human Dignity and the Realistic Utopia of Human Rights," *Metaphilosophy* 41, no. 4 (2010): 464-80, quote at 479.

31. Habermas, *Between Facts and Norms*, 150.

32. Svenja Ahlhaus and Peter Niesen, eds., *Animal Politics: A New Research Agenda. Forum I, Historical Social Research-Historische Sozialforschung* 40, no. 4 (2015): 7-31.

33. Sue Donaldson and Will Kymlicka, *Zoopolis: A Political Theory of Animal Rights* (Oxford: Oxford University Press, 2011).
34. Ivano Dionigi, "*Res publica naturalis*: animali politici," in *Animalia*, ed. Ivano Dionigi, 51–66 (Milano: BUR Saggi Iuglio, 2011).
35. Ahlhaus and Niesen, eds., *Animal Politics*, 10.
36. Quoted in Klaits, *Animals and Man in Historical Perspective*, 59.
37. Haraway, *When Species Meet*, 299.
38. Isabelle Stengers, *Cosmopolitics I* (Minneapolis and London: University of Minnesota Press, 2010), vii–viii.
39. Theodor W. Adorno, *Negative Dialectics* (London and New York: Routledge, 2004), 299.

Chapter 9

1. See Aristotle, *The Complete Works of Aristotle: The Revised Oxford Translation*, 2 vols., ed. Jonathan Barnes (Princeton, NJ: Princeton University Press, 1984).
2. See Aristotle, *Metaphysics* 986b14, 989b30, 990a3.
3. I want to thank my colleague Christopher Moore for the translation suggestion of "natural theorist" that I think captures best what Aristotle meant when he used the term φυσιόλογος to refer to the pre-Socratics.
4. Michael J. Curley, "Introduction," in *Physiologus: A Medieval Book of Nature Lore*, trans. Michael J. Curley (Chicago: University of Chicago Press, 2009), ix–xliii.
5. Ibid., xi.
6. Ibid., xv.
7. Isidore of Seville's (c. 560–636) etymology of *horse* is very telling. Here it is:

> Horses (equus) are so called because when they were yoked in a team of four they were balanced (aequare); those equal in size and alike in gait would be joined together. 42. The packhorse (caballus) was formerly called a cabo, because when walking it hollows (concavare) the ground with the imprint of its hoof, a property that the other animals do not have. Whence also the "charger" (sonipes) because it "clatters with its feet" (pedibus sonare). 43. Horses have a great deal of liveliness, for they revel in open country; they scent out war; they are roused to battle by the sound of the trumpet; when incited by a voice they are challenged to race, grieving when they are defeated, and exultant when they are victorious. Some recognize the enemy in war and seek to bite the foe. Some also respond to their own masters, and lose their tameness if their ownership changes. Some will allow

no one on their back except their master; many of them shed tears when their master dies or is killed, for only the horse weeps and feels grief over humans. Whence [also] in the Centaur the nature of horses and of humans is combined. 44. People who are about to engage in battle are accustomed to deduce what the outcome will be from the dejection or the eagerness of the horses.

In well-bred horses, so the ancients said, four things were considered: form, beauty, quality, and color. Form, that the body should be strong and solid, the height appropriate to the strength, the flank long, very lean, with well-rounded haunches, broad in the chest, the entire body knotted with dense musculature, the foot firm and solid with a concave hoof. 46. Beauty, that the head should be small and firm, the skin clinging close to the bones, the ears short and expressive, the eyes large, the nostrils flaring out, the neck upright, the mane and tail thick, the hooves of a firm roundness and solidity. 47. Quality, that it should be daring in spirit, swift of foot, with quivering limbs, which is a sign of strength, and easily roused from the deepest repose and controlled without difficulty when urged to speed. Indeed, the alertness of a horse is made known by its ears, and its valor by its quivering limbs.

Isidore of Seville, *Etymologies of Isidore of Seville*, trans. Stephen A. Barney, W. J. Lewis, J. A. Beach, and Oliver Berghof (Cambridge and New York: Cambridge University Press, 2006), 249–50.

 8. See Elizabeth Morrison, *Beasts: Factual and Fantastic* (Los Angeles: J. Paul Getty Museum; London: British Library, 2007), as well as her beautiful Elizabeth Morrison, ed., with the assistance of Larissa Grollemond, *Book of Beasts: The Bestiary in the Medieval World* (Los Angeles: J. Paul Getty Museum, 2019).

 9. See Sarah Kay, "The Textual Kaleidoscope of the Medieval Bestiary," in *Book of Beasts: The Bestiary in the Medieval World*, ed. Elizabeth Morrison, with the assistance of Larissa Grollemond (Los Angeles: J. Paul Getty Museum, 2019), 31–37.

 10. See my essay Eduardo Mendieta, "The Imperial Bestiary of the U.S.: Alien, Enemy Combatant, Terrorist," in *Radical Philosophy Today IV*, ed. Harry van der Linden and Tony Smith (Charlottesville, VA: Philosophy Documentation Center, 2006), 155–79, and chapter 2 in this book.

 11. Curley, "Introduction," in *Physiologus*, xxxii.

 12. To this category I would add the wonderful book by Alison Hawthorne Deming, *Zoologies: On Animals and the Human Spirit* (Minneapolis: Milkweed Editions, 2014).

 13. See my essay Eduardo Mendieta, "A Bestiary for the Anthropocene: The End of Nature and the Future of Animal Life on Planet Earth," in *The Human-An-*

imal Boundary: Exploring the Line in Philosophy and Fiction, ed. Nandita Batra and Mario Wenning (Lanham, MD: Lexington Books, 2019), 201–14.

14. Stephen M. Meyer, *The End of the Wild* (Cambridge, MA: MIT Press, 2006).

15. Dianne Ackerman, *The Human Age: The World Shaped by Us* (New York: W. W. Norton and Company, 2014), 154.

16. Meyer, *The End of the Wild*, 9.

17. See Elizabeth Kolbert, *The Sixth Extinction: An Unnatural History* (New York: Henry Holt and Company, 2014), and Richard Grusin, *After Extinction* (Minneapolis and London: University of Minnesota Press, 2018).

18. Ackerman, *The Human Age*, 12.

19. Meyer, *The End of the Wild*, 17.

20. See Eduardo Mendieta, "The Bio-technological *Scala Naturae* and Interspecies Cosmopolitanism: Patricia Piccinini, Jane Alexander, and Guillermo Gómez-Peña," in *Biopower: Foucault and Beyond,* ed. Vernon Cisney and Nicolae Morar (Chicago, IL: University of Chicago Press, 2015), 158–79.

21. Morrison, *Book of Beasts*, 11.

22. Morrison, *Book of Beasts*, 11.

23. See Wendy Williams, *The Horse: The Epic History of Our Noble Companion* (New York: Scientific American/Farrar, Strauss and Giroux 2015), 99–121, and Elaine Walker, *Horse* (London: Reaktion Books, 2008), 21–41.

24. Elwyn Hatley Edwards, *The Horse Encyclopedia* (New York: DK Publishing, 2016), 9.

25. Williams, *The Horse*, 147.

26. Christopher Lloyd, *The Story of the World in 100 Species* (London and New York: Bloomsbury, 2016), 243.

27. Pita Kelekna, *The Horse in Human History* (Cambridge: Cambridge University Press, 2009), 398.

28. Otto Brunner, Werner Conze, and Reinhart Koselleck, eds. *Geschichtliche Grundbegriffe: Historisches Lexikon zur Politisch-sozialen Sprache in Deutschland* (Stuttgart: Kleck-Cotta, 1972).

29. Reinhart Koselleck, "Der Aufbruch in die Moderne oder das Ende des Pferdezeitalters," in *Historikerpreis der Stadt Münster: Die Preisträger und Laudatoren von 1981–2003,* ed. Berthold Tillman (Münster: Lit Verlag. 2005), 159–74.

30. Ulrich Raulff, *Farewell to the Horse: The Final Century of our Relationship* trans. Ruth Ahmedzai Kemp (New York: Penguin Books, 2018), 109.

31. Koselleck, "Der Aufbruch in die Moderne oder das Ende des Pferdezeitalters," 161.

32. Ibid., 162.

33. Ibid., 164.

34. Ibid., 172.

35. There is also Ernst Jünger's *Das Antlitz des Weltkrieges: Fronterlebnisse deutscher Soldaten* [*The Face of the World War: The Front Experience of German Soldiers*] (Berlin: Neufeld und Henius, 1930). This is a book of mostly pictures of the battlefront, but also of veterans of the war. One thing that is certain is that the face of war is hideous, terrifying, and apocalyptic. There are three particular types of pictures that are deeply disturbing: soldiers with half of their face torn apart by bombs or a grenade, and of course, those without limbs; hundreds of dead horses in trenches, or the side of the road, and an eerie lunar landscaped made by nonstop bombing. It is astonishing that this incredible visual and visceral indictment of war was published less than a decade before Germany would launch another world war.

36. Koselleck, "Der Aufbruch in die Moderne oder das Ende des Pferdezeitalters," 172.

37. Raulff, *Farewell to the Horse*, 328.

38. Kelekna, *The Horse in Human History*, 398.

39. Raulff, *Farewell to the Horse*, 315.

40. Ibid., 316.

41. Charles Darwin, *From So Simple a Beginning: The Four Great Books of Charles Darwin*, ed. Edward O. Wilson (New York: W. W. Norton & Company, 2006), 452. My italics.

42. Darwin, *From So Simple a Beginning*, 746. My italics.

43. Kolbert, *The Sixth Extinction*, 54.

44. See Grusin, *After Extinction*.

45. See St. Augustine, *On the Free Choice of the Will, On Grace and Free Choice, and Other Writings*, ed. and trans. Peter King (Cambridge: Cambridge University Press, 2012), on Boethius see *The Consolation of Philosophy*, trans. P. G. Walsh (Oxford: Oxford University Press, 2008).

46. Susanna Forrest, *The Age of the Horse: An Equine Journey through Human History*. New York: Atlantic Monthly Press, 2017), 36.

47. Edwards in his *The Horse Encyclopedia*, section three, has nearly two hundred pages cataloging and showcasing the myriad of horse and pony breeds.

48. Raulff, *Farewell to the Horse*, 7.

49. Ibid., 9.

50. James Herriot, *It Shouldn't Happen to a Vet* (London: Pan Books, 2006 [1972]), 96.

Index

Page numbers with an *n* refer to an endnote.

A Bao A Qu, 13–14
abortions, 108
About Looking (Berger), 25
abstinence/self-limitation, Habermas, 118
Adorno, Theodor W.: about, 134; on animal rights, 171; fondness for animals, 162; on good animals, 48; Horkheimer's relationship with, 163–64; negative morality/negative anthropology, 168–69; on Odysseus, 16; photos of, 162; on role of philosophy, 172. *See also* Adorno's bestiary
Adorno, Theodor W., writing by: *Aesthetic Theory*, 12, 167; *Dialectic of Enlightenment*, 5, 15, 52, 165, 169; "Man and Beast," 160–61; *Minima Moralia*, 164, 166, 168; *Negative Dialectics*, 168, 169, 170; *Problems of Moral Philosophy*, 168
Adorno's bestiary: animal ethics, 162–70; Anthropocene (sixth extinction), 173–74; deconstructive zoontology, 159–62; natural history, 170–73
Aelian, 50
Aesthetic Theory (Adorno), 167

"The Aforementioned So-Called Human Genome" (Derrida), 138
Agamben, Giorgio: on beasts and animals, 153; *Homo Sacer: Sovereign Power and Bare Life*, 150, 151; *The Open: Man and Animal*, 152; *The State of Exception*, 151
The Age of Iron (Coetzee): animals in, 32–33; Mrs. Curren (character), 32–33; Vercueil (character), 32, 33
The Age of the Horse (Forrest), 209
agriculture, industrialization of, 116
Alexander, Jane, 12–13
Alien vs. Predator (film), 141–42
allegory: of the cave, 19, 53; of the philosophical dog, 53
animal companionship, 28
animal cruelty: in Coetzee's writing, 30–31; as precursor to human maltreatment, 28
animal ethics, 162–70
Animalia (Dionigi), 6
Animal Lessons: How They Teach Us to Be Human (Oliver), 176
animal philosophy, 13–21
animal politics, 190
animal rights: about, 10, 11; Derrida on, 170–71, 233n40; justification of,

241

animal rights *(continued)*
    189–90; Lacan on, 170–71; Levinas on, 170–71
animals: about, 73; in *The Age of Iron* (Coetzee), 32–33; Aristotle's work on, 56–57; awareness of impending death, 31; communication of, 80; cows, 202–3; Derrida on, 161; duties to, 184, 186–88; exceptionalism, 177–80; human coexistence with, 9–10; humans as, 178; human separation from, 152; kinship with, 176, 178; medieval imagery, 195; perishing, 32; silence of, 79–80; suffering of, 188; traits of, 64; understanding of death, 32; virtue of, 61–62; virtues of, 141. *See also* beasts; dogs; horses
"The Animal That Therefore I Am" (Derrida), 2, 171–72
Anthropocene (sixth extinction): about, 173–74; industrialization, 197; pollution, 197; species survival/loss, 185, 198–99
anthropocentrism, 177
Anthropocentrism and Its Discontents (Steiner), 17
anthropological-cognitive grounding of knowledge, Habermas, 96
anthropological machine, retooling, 140–42
Antipater, 58
ants, Aristotle on, 57
Apel, Karl-Otto, 11
Appiah, Kwame Anthony, 184
Arendt, Hannah, 105, 124, 133, 134
Argos (dog), 17
Aristotle: about, 50; *Generation of Animals*, 194; *History of Animals*, 194–95; *Metaphysics*, 195; *Movement of Animals*, 194; *Parts of Animals*, 194; *Plants* and *Clouds*, 194; *Politics*, 140; *Progression of Animals*, 194; role in positive philosophical anthropology tradition, 134; work of, 194–95
Aristotle's zoology, 56–62
artwork, expression in, 166–68
Attridge, Derek, 26
Augustine, 134, 208
Auschwitz, 168
authors, influences on, 42, 230n1
autonomy, Habermas on, 99

bare existence, 150–51
Beast and Man: The Roots of Human Nature (Midgley), 144–45
beasts: about, 143; *The Book of Beasts*, 50; *Book of Beasts: The Bestiary of the Medieval World* (Morrison), 199; in the continuum, 141–42; Hobbesian Leviathan, 145; human entwinement with, 144–45; internal, 145–46; killing, 70; myths about, 146; noble, 144; roguish, 144–47; violence of, 66, 145, 152
Beckett, Samuel, 26
becoming-with-companions, politics of, 175–76, 177
bees: Aristotle on, 57; Kant on, 65
The Beginning of Wisdom: Reading Genesis (Kass), 131–32
Being and Time (Heidegger), 71–72, 83
Being and Truth (*Sein und Wahrheit*), 72
Being of the German people, 76–77
Benjamin, Walter, 159–60
Bentham, Jeremy: critique of *Declaration of the Rights of Man and of the Citizen*, 182; *Introduction to the Principles of Morals and Legislation*, 182–83; on the origin of the commonwealth, 183
Berger, John: *About Looking*, 25; "Why Look at Animals," 29

Berlin zoo, animals as food, 4
Bespaloff, Rachel: *On the Iliad*, 17–18
bestialization machines, 70–71
bestiaries: about, 6, 69–71, 193–94; Adorno, 161 (*see also* Adorno's bestiary); and bestialization, 70; as Christian version of Greek *Physiologus*, 69; of colonizing powers, 197; Derridian, 148, 153, 161; diversity of, 196–97; of extermination, 89, 197–99; of extinction, 12; Flower of Virtue, 197; Harawayan, 153, 154; horses (*see* horses); imperial, 70; moral lessons from, 69, 142–43; Nietzschean, 153; paradisaic, 148; pedagogy of, 142–44; philosophical, 147–48; *Physiologia* as predecessors to, 194; questions raised by, 142; role of, 143; traces of violence, 64; typology of, 69–70; as works of art paid for by wealthy patrons, 196; zoos as counterparts, 4. *See also* beasts
bestiaries, Christian, 56, 62–63
bestiaries, genocidal, 87–89
bestiaries, Heidegger's: about, 68–69; Derrida on, 67; Heidegger's Animals, 71–87
bestiaries, political: about, 49–50; Aristotle's zoology, 56–62; good animals vs. demonic beasts, 62; Homer's beasts, 50–52; Plato's bestiary, 52–56; sovereign beasts, 65–66
Between Facts and Norms (Habermas), 188
biodiversity depletion, 185
biological determinism, 104–5
Biophilia: The Human Bond with Other Species (Wilson), 3

biotech revolution, industrialization of, 115–16
Bloch, Ernst, 134
The Book of Beasts, 50
Book of Beasts: The Bestiary of the Medieval World (Morrison), 199
The Book of Imaginary Beings (Borges), 13–14, 20–21
Borges, Jorge Luis: author influences, 42; *The Book of Imaginary Beings*, 13–14, 20–21
Borradori, Giovanna: *Philosophy in a Time of Terror*, 161
Bovey, Alixe, 64
Boyhood: Scenes from Provincial Life (Coetzee), 30–31
Broch, Hermann, 17–18
Burger's Daughter (Gordimer): Rosa Burger (character), 27, 39
Butler, Judith, 184

Cacciari, Massimo, 6
Calarco, Matthew: and Heidegger, 7; *Zoographies: The Question of the Animal from Heidegger to Derrida*, 3–4
Canguilhem, Georges, 100
Cassirer, Ernst, 73
caste system, 110
Cato, 58–59
censorship in South Africa, 26
Cerise-La-Salle conference, 4
Cerisy-la-Salle conference, 170
characters as representing/philosophical ideas, 29–30
"Chicken" (Haraway), 154
Chicken Little, end of the world announcement, 155
Christianity, emergence of, 133
Christian theologians, 10
Christian theology, ancient knowledge assimilated into, 196

Christian-Wolff Lecture, Habermas, 118
Circe (character), 60–61, 140, 141
civic activism, 112
Claussen, Detlev, 163–64
Coetzee, J. M.: about, 5; on animals as "fellow" companions, 29; bio, 36–37; breadth of writing, 42–43; David Lurie (character) (*see* David Lurie); Elizabeth Costello (character), 36, 37, 40; fiction by, 26–27; Nobel Prize, 26, 41, 42; novels of, 26–27, 29, 30; philosophical depth, 42; self-reflexivity of, 26; on suffering, 25; Tanner Lectures, 26, 36–37
Coetzee, J. M., writing by: about (listing of), 214n3; *The Age of Iron*, 32; *Boyhood: Scenes from Provincial Life*, 30–31; *Diary of a Bad Year*, 43; *Disgrace* (see *Disgrace*); *Dusklands*, 31–32; *Elizabeth Costello* (book), 5, 37; Elizabeth Costello (character), 36, 37, 40; "He and His Man," 41–42; *The Lives of Animals*, 2, 35; *The Master of Petersburg*, 33–34; "Meat Country," 41; "The Narrative of Jacobus Coetzee," 31–32; *Waiting for the Barbarians*, 32
colonialism, genetic, 113–14
colonization, use of horses in, 205
Columbus, Christopher, 144
Commoner, Barry, 104
commonwealth: contract for, 181–82; origin of, 183
companion species, 17, 155, 175, 190–91
concentration camps: Auschwitz, 168; deaths in, 89; *Homo sacer* of, 152; indifference to, 39–40; Levi & Kogon on, 70; responsibility for, 48; slaughterhouses as parallel, 35, 37–38, 39
"Contemporary Philosophy of Mind" (Rorty), 1
contingency, 180
Copernicus, Nicolaus, on earth decentering, 179–80
corporeal compassion, 5
cosmopolitanism: about, 175–77; animal rights, 10; companion species, 190–91; contradictions in, 181; dialogical, 128; exceptional animals, 177–80; Habermas on, 184; on peaceful kingdoms, 181–86; and postmetaphysics, 183–84, 186–90
cows, 202–3
creatures of God, humans as, 178
Crime and Punishment (Dostoevsky), 27
Critical Theory, 161
crop diversity, decrease in, 113
cultural conventions, disease and health as functions of, 100
Curley, Michael J., translation by, 195–96
Cyclops (character), 14–15, 50–52, 140–41

Darwin, Charles: *On the Origin of Species*, 207; theory of evolution, 180, 207–8
Dasein (existence), 7, 71–72, 75, 77, 79–80
David Lurie (character): euthanasia at animal shelter, 35–36, 48; Lucy (daughter), 47–48; Melanie (character), 46–47; Melanie's boyfriend (character), 46; plot, 45–47; prostitute, relationship, 45
death, Heidegger on, 89
de Buffon, Comte: *Histoire naturelle*, 190

Declaration of the Rights of Man and of the Citizen, critique of, 182
Defoe, Daniel: *Robinson Crusoe*, 41
de Fontenay, Elisabeth: on rights, 11; *Without Offending Humans: A Critique of Animal Rights*, 13
deliberative democracy, Habermas on, 118
DeLillo, Don, 30
Derrida, Jacques: about, 7; on animal rights, 170–71, 233n40; on beasts and animals, 153; on cloning, 135, 138, 139; on divinimality, 155–56; Habermas collaboration with, 161; historical traumas defined by, 179; on limitrophy, 173; philosophical bestiary of, 147–48; on reason, 149; on role of philosophy, 172; Theodor W. Adorno Prize, 159, 229n44; *Voyous*, 138
Derrida, Jacques, writing by: "The Aforementioned So-Called Human Genome," 138; *The Animal That Therefore I Am*, 2, 4, 67, 171–72; "Rogue States," 138; *Rogues: Two Essays on Reason*, 148, 149; "The World of the Enlightenment to Come," 138
Descartes, René, 170–71
Despret, Vinciane, 179
Dialectic of Enlightenment (Adorno & Horkheimer), 5, 15, 52, 165, 169
Dialectic of the Enlightenment, 160–61
Diamond, Cora, 5
Diary of a Bad Year (Coetzee), 43
Diderot, Denis, 30
difference principle, Rawls on, 110
Dionigi, Ivano: *Animalia*, 6; on animal politics, 190
discourse ethics, 102, 103
Disgrace (Coetzee): Bev Shaw (character), 35, 48; Lucy (David Lurie's daughter), 47; meaning of, 44; plot, 45–47; plot of, 35–36; Soraya (character), 45; types of disgrace, 36; Willett on, 43. See also David Lurie
disgrace, types of, 44, 47
divinimality, 156
dogs: Argos (Odysseus's dog), 17; comparisons, 54–55; philosophical, 53, 62–63; priests compared with, 63; relationship to priests, 64; traits of, 56; virtues of, 62–63; wolves vs., 54
Dolly the sheep, 94
Donaldson, Sue, 11, 190
Dostoevsky, Fyodor: *Crime and Punishment*, 27; fictionalization of, 33; techniques and insights, 26
dragons, 64
Dr. Margrit-Egnér Prize, Habermas, 118
Dusklands (Coetzee): as early writing, 26; "The Narrative of Jacobus Coetzee," 31–32

Eckhart, Meister, 134
ecological crisis, 184–85
Economic and Philosophic Manuscripts (Marx), 166
Elden, Stuart, 7, 71
elephants: Antiochus' use of, 58–59; Christ personified by, 58; as nemesis of dragons, 64; Pliny the Elder on, 58–59; relationship to Jesus, 64; as representation of Adam and Eve, 63–64; virtues of, 63–64
Elizabeth Costello (book), 5, 37
Elizabeth Costello (character), 36, 37, 40
encyclopedias, Pliny the Elder's role in, 58

Engels, Friedrich, 105
ethics: Coetzee on, 28; of cohabitation, 180; Habermas, 118–19; Haraway on, 176; of human exceptionalism, 177
"Ethics of the Dog-Man" (Willett), 43
eugenics: about, 93; selectivity in, 117; US/German differences on, 111. *See also* liberal eugenics
Eurocentrism, 128
Euthyphro, 53, 54
exception: embodiments of, 152; paradox of, 151
exceptionalism: of animals, 177–80; of humans, 177, 178, 179
extinctions: 5th, 203; 6th (*see* Anthropocene); of early horses, 203–4; evolutionary role of, 207

The Fable of the Bees (Mandeville), 65
Farewell to the Horse (Raulff), 206
Fascism, Derrida on, 160
fiction, readers as active participants in, 42
finitude, 180
Forrest, Susanna: *The Age of the Horse*, 209
Foucault, Michel, 38, 183
Frankfurt School Critical Theory, 11, 159, 171, 185
freedom: assumptions/arguments on, 119–20; assumptions/arguments on, 136; socialization and, 124
Freud, Sigmund, 180
friendship, Socrates on, 54
Frodo (character), 52–53
Fromm, Erich, 133–34
The Fundamental Concepts of Metaphysics, 72–73
future generations: genetic engineering impact on, 97–98, 99–100, 122–23; and genetic intervention, 136; moral identity of, 124; species extermination impact on, 185
The Future of Human Nature (*Die Zukunft der menschlichen Natur*) (Habermas): about, 94–95, 103, 111, 117–18, 135, 137, 220n4; components of, 117–18; as political text, 95; US/German differences on, 111
The Future of Human Nature: On the Way to a Liberal Eugenics? (Habermas), 103
The Future of Life (Wilson), 173–74

Garcia Marquez, Gabriel: *Memories of my Melancholy Whores* (*Memorias de mis Putas Tristes*), 45
GATT (General Agreement on Tariffs and Trade), 113
Gattaca (film) (Niccol), 106–7
Gehlen, Arnold: Habermas on, 138; *Man in the Age of Technology*, 137; *Moral und Hypermoral*, 137; philosophical anthropology of, 137
General Agreement on Tariffs and Trade (GATT), 113
generational asymmetry, 110
generational continuity, 120
Generation of Animals (Aristotle), 194
Genesis, 131–33, 140
genetically modified organisms: intellectual property rights, 113; natural history and, 174
genetic colonialism, 113–14
genetic determinism, 103–4, 106, 123
genetic engineering: assumptions/arguments on, 119; biotech century and political modernity, 115–19; corporeal integrity/moral identity, 119–21; Greenspan on, 224n10; Habermas on, 136; irreversibility, 122; Kass on, 223n4; legality of, 7; Mendieta on, 121–22; moral burden

for, 125; natality/futurity, 121–26; outcome of, 126; political response to, 127–28; postmetaphysical thinking, 126–27
genetic intervention: assumptions/arguments, 120–21; and future generations, 120, 136; Habermas on, 107; impact of, 94, 95
genetic optimization: arguments against, 106; embracing, 111; impact of, 124
genetics: debate/decisions on, 96; ethical/moral implications in, 97
genetic screening, 117, 136
genetic therapy, legality of, 7
genomics: about, 101; political tools for, 128; social problems resolved with, 93; study of, 221n17
German Ideology (Marx), 170
germ-line gene therapy, 126
Gesamtausgabe (Heidegger), 75–76
Gestell, Heidegger on, 131–32
ghost species, 198–99
global warming, 184–85
God, man vs., 73
Gomez-Peña, Guillermo, 12–13
good animals vs. demonic beasts, 62–65
Good/Evil confrontation, 64
Gordimer, Nadine: *Burger's Daughter*, 27, 39
Gordon, Lewis: "Tragic Revolutionary Violence," 47
Greek terminology for life, 150
green revolution, 116
Greenspan, P.S., 224n10
Gretel (Adorno's wife), 162
"Ground Zero for a Postmoral Ethics in J. M. Coetzee's Disgrace and Julia Kristeva's Melancholic" (Willett), 43
Gryllus (character), 60–61, 140, 141
Grzimek, Bernhard, 162

Habermas, Jürgen: about, 7; author as student of, 11; on cloning, 135; on cosmopolitanism, 184; Derrida collaboration with, 161; German Booksellers Association, Peace Prize, 94, 117, 140; Goethe University inaugural lecture, 7–8; Jonas as influence, 137; on law, 10; on law and democracy, 11; and philosophical anthropology, 7, 8; on physical vulnerability of animals, 187–88; postmetaphysics of, 185; Sonning Prize, 125. *See also* human cloning
Habermas, Jürgen, writing by: *Between Facts and Norms*, 188; *The Future of Human Nature* (*Die Zukunft der menschlichen Natur*), 94–95, 103, 111, 117–18, 135, 137, 220n4; "Human Dignity and the Realistic Utopia of Human Rights," 188–89; *Knowledge and Human Interests*, 137; *Knowledge and Human Interests* lecture, 7–8; "On the Way to a Liberal Eugenics?," 135; *The Postnational Constellation*, 135; "Remarks on Discourse Ethics," 186, 221n11; *Theory of Communicative Action*, 7
Hacking, Ian, 11
Haraway, Donna: on animal companionship, 28; bestiary of, 154; "Chicken," 154–55; on companion species, 9, 175; on cosmopolitanism, 191; embodiments of, 154; "four-part" composition, 155; on genomics, 8; on NatureCultures, 153; on nonanthropomorphic sensibility, 179; "The Promises of Monsters," 154; "Species Matters, Humane Advocacy," 9
Hawke, Ethan, 106

"He and His Man" (Coetzee), 41–42
Hebrew Bible images, 152–53
Hegel, Georg Wilhelm Friedrich, 127, 134
Heidegger, Martin: Agamben vs., 152; on animal rights, 170–71; on Coetzee's work, 33; on death and dying, 32; *Gelassenheit*, 33; *Kehre*, 68; work of, 7; *zu-handen/vor-handen*, 33. *See also* bestiaries, Heidegger's
Heidegger, Martin, writing by: *Being and Time*, 71–72; *Being and Truth* (*Sein und Wahrheit*), 72; *The Fundamental Concepts of Metaphysics*, 72–73; "Letter on Humanism," 227n27; *Logic as the Question Concerning the Essence of Language*, 73
Herf, Jeffrey: *The Jewish Enemy*, 70
Herodotus: about, 50; *Histories*, 70
Hesiod: Plato modeled on, 18; *Theogony*, 6; *Works and Days*, 6
Histoire naturelle (de Buffon), 190
Historia Animalium (Aristotle), 56–57
Historical Basic Concepts (Koselleck), 204
historical greatness, Heidegger on, 76
Histories (Herodotus), 70
history: Heidegger on, 84, 85f; pre-horse/horse/post-horse ages, 12, 204; role of horses in, 206–7
History of Animals (Aristotle), 194–95
history/temporality, Heidegger on, 83
Hobbes, Thomas: about, 134; *Leviathan*, 65, 181, 183; Schmitt on, 218n38; on state as artificial creation, 182
Hobbes-Bentham problem, 183
Hobbesian Leviathan, 145
Holocaust. *See* Treblinka

Homer: about, 6, 17–18, 50; *Iliad*, 16–17; Plato modeled on, 18. *See also* Odysseus; *Odyssey*
Homer's beasts, 50–52
hominids, appearance of, 204
Homo Sacer: Sovereign Power and Bare Life (Agamben), 150, 151
Homo sapiens: evolution of, 172, 204; *Homo martialis*, 156; nature/culture product, 105
Horkheimer, Max: Adorno's relationship with, 163–64; *Dialectic of Enlightenment*, 5, 15, 52, 165, 169; *Minima Moralia* dedicated to, 168; on Odysseus, 16
horses: about, 12, 202; in bestiaries, 203; breeds of, 209; Equidae since Eocene, 203; Forrest on, 209; human use of, 204–5; Isidore of Seville on, 236n7; migration to Europe and Asia, 204; Raulff on, 206–7; recent replacements for, 206; use in warfare, 204–5, 206, 239n35
horses, writing on: *Farewell to the Horse*, 206; *On Horsemanship*, 207
The House on Eccles Street (hypothetical novel), 40
human, meaning of, 68
human cloning: ban on, 137; legality of, 7; moralizing, 112; and philosophical anthropology, 135–40; shortcomings of, 111–14; species ethics, self-understanding, 95–102; species ethics, slippery slope, 103–11; technological advances, 93–95
human dignity, Habermas on, 98
"Human Dignity and the Realistic Utopia of Human Rights" (Habermas), 188–89
human essence, questions, 116
human existence, insight into, 132

human genotype alteration, Mendieta on, 122
humanism, staunched, 10
humanity: about, 1–2; Derrida on, 147; ferocity of, 146; in jeopardy, 134; moral identity, 125; theses, 137; transformation of, 172
humanization, Marx on, 166
human reproduction, 131–33
human rights: animal rights predicated on, 171; Derrida on, 233n40; Habermas on, 188–89
humans: about, 1–2; animalization of, 70–71; as animals, 178; animal separation from, 152; beast entwinement with, 144–45; beasts in the continuum, 142; as creatures of God, 178; death, 203; differentiation from animals, 140; dual citizenship, 181; dying, 32; essence/unity of, 138–39; evolution of, 178–79, 180; exceptionalism, 152, 176, 177, 178, 179; futurity of, 134, 136; history/temporality, 83; horse domestication, 204; interspecies relationship, 176; as likeness of God (see *imago Dei* doctrine); moral responsibility for nonhuman environment, 186; natural history and, 208; as political animals, 6, 175; population growth, 173–74; unprecedented transformation of, 172; violence of, 146–47; war impact on, 165
Hyland, Ann, 206
hypermodernity/hypermorality, 95

idealism, Derrida on, 160
Iliad, 16–17
imago Dei doctrine: Arendt on, 222n23; Derrida on, 140; humans as image of God, 105–6, 177; philosophical anthropology, 131–35
income gap, 124, 125–26, 185
information, commodification of, 116
intellectual property rights, 113
interspecies cosmopolitanism: about, 10, 175–77, 191; as autremondialisation, 177. *See also* cosmopolitanism
Introduction to the Principles of Morals and Legislation (Bentham), 182–83
Irigaray, Luce, 18–19
Isidore of Seville, 196, 197, 236n7

Jay, Martin, 162
The Jewish Enemy (Herf), 70
Jonas, Hans, 123, 128–29, 131–32, 137, 220n4
Joyce, James: *Ulysses*, 40
Judeo-Christian monotheism, 178
Judeo-Christian tradition, 177, 178
Justification and Application: Remarks on Discourse Ethics, 186

Kafka, Franz: about, 26, 30; on dignity, 160; "A Report to an Academy," 37; "The Silence of the Sirens," 20
Kant, Immanuel: about, 134; on animal cruelty as precursor to human mistreatment, 28; on animal rights, 170–71; on bees, 65; on contradiction of cosmopolitanism, 181; duties to animals, 184; *Lectures on Ethics*, 28; moral philosophy of, 185; philosophical anthropology, 181; on role of philosophy, 184
Kass, Leon R.: about, 134; *The Beginning of Wisdom: Reading Genesis*, 132; on genetic

Kass, Leon R. *(continued)*
  engineering, 223n4; on human
  reproduction, 131–32
Kelekna, Pita, 204, 206
Klaits, Joseph and Barrie, 178–79
Klostermann, Vittorio, 85
knowledge, Habermas on, 8
Knowledge and Human Interests
  (Habermas), 137
Kogon, Eugene, 70
Kolbert, Elizabeth, 208
Körper, Leib vs., 136, 137, 224n6
Korpersein/Korperhaben, 101
Koselleck, Reinhart: *Historical Basic Concepts*, 204; historical periods defined by horses, 12, 204, 205; Münster historians prize, 204
Kristeva, Julia, 43, 44
Kymlicka, Will, 11, 190

Lacan, Jacques, 170–71
la Fontaine, Jean de: "The Wolf and the Lamb," 149
Land and Sea (Schmitt), 65–66
Lander, Eric, 126
language: Habermas on, 137–38; Heidegger on, 77–78, 79, 86, 88–89; Odysseus use of, 140–41
law: and ethics, 10–11; Habermas on, 10, 188–89; legitimacy of, 182
lawless cruelty, 145, 148
Laws (Plato), 53
Le Bras-Chopard, Armelle: *The Zoo of the Philosophers*, 3, 4
Lectures on Ethics (Kant), 28
Leib, Körper vs., 136, 137, 224n6
Leibniz, Gottfried Wilhelm, 208
Levi, Primo, 70
Leviathan (Hobbes), 65, 183
Levinas, Emmanuel, 170–71
Lewis, C.S.: about, 132; Christian bestiaries as influence, 69; Coetzee within the tradition of, 30

Lewontin, Richard, 103
liberal eugenics, 95, 96–97, 99, 107–8, 118, 135–36. *See also* eugenics
likeness of God. See *imago Dei* doctrine
limitrophy, 173
literary contract, 42
The Lives of Animals (Coetzee): empathy in, 41; lectures, 2, 37; slaughterhouses/concentration camps comparison, 35
Lloyd, Christopher: *The Story of the World in 100 Species*, 209
Locke, John, 134, 182
logic, Heidegger on, 80–81, 82, 86
Logic as the Question about the Essence of Language, 80
Logic as the Question Concerning the Essence of Language, 73
The Lord of Rings (Tolkien), 52–53
Lucretius, 181
Lucy (David Lurie's daughter), 47–48
Lysis, 53, 54

Macdonald, Margaret, 181–82
man: God vs., 73; as world-forming, 74
"Man and Beast" (Adorno), 160–61
Mandeville, Bernard: *The Fable of the Bees*, 65
Man in the Age of Technology (Gehlen), 137
Mann, Thomas, 26, 30
Marcus Aurelius, 181
Marcuse, Herbert, 164
Marion Bloom (character), 40
Marx, Karl: about, 127, 134; on communism, 232n23; *Economic and Philosophic Manuscripts*, 166; *German Ideology*, 170; shortcomings of, 11
The Master of Petersburg (Coetzee): dog in, 33–34; Ivanov (character), 33–34

McNeill, William, 7
"Meat Country" (Coetzee), 41
medicine: advances in, 117; socialization of, 116
medieval manuscripts, defacement in, 64–65
Memories of my Melancholy Whores (Memorias de mis Putas Tristes) (Garcia Marquez), 45
metaphysical anthropocentrism, 140
Metaphysics (Aristotle), 195
Meyer, Stephen M., 197–98
Midgley, Mary: *Beast and Man: The Roots of Human Nature*, 144–45; on beasts and animals, 153; on lawless cruelty, 148, 152
Mignolo, Walter, 128, 184
Mill, John Stuart, 134
Minima Moralia (Adorno), 164, 166, 168
ministers of purification, sophists vs., 54
modernism, 26
monotheism, 208
Montaigne, Michel de, 30
moral autonomy, 103
Moralia (Plutarch), 58–59, 140
moral identities, 120, 125
morality, 53, 168–69
moral norms/rules, Habermas on, 99, 102
moral philosophy, 176–77, 185
Moral und Hypermoral (Gehlen), 137
moral vacuum, Habermas on, 136
Morpurgo, Michael: *War Horse*, 206
Morrison, Elizabeth: *Book of Beasts: The Bestiary of the Medieval World*, 199
Movement of Animals (Aristotle), 194
Müller-Doohm, Stefan, 162
Musil, Robert, 26, 31

"The Narrative of Jacobus Coetzee" (Coetzee), 31–32

natality, Arendt on, 133
natural history: about, 170–73; Adorno on, 169; genetically modified organisms in, 174; Habermas on, 8; Heidegger on, 83–84; humans and, 208
Natural History (Pliny the Elder), 58
natural rights, Bentham on, 182
natural selection, 207
nature, domesticating, 105
NatureCultures, 153
Nazi concentration camps. *See* concentration camps
Nazism, Heidegger on, 75
negative anthropology, 168–69
Negative Dialectics (Adorno), 168, 170
negative duties: Habermas on, 108–9; Rawls on, 111
negative morality, 168–69
negative rights, Habermas on, 128
neomodernism, 26
Niccol, Andrew: *Gattaca* (film), 106–7
Nietzsche, Friedrich, 68, 147
Nobel Prize, 26, 41, 42
noble savage, 144
novels: of Coetzee, 26–27, 29, 30; philosophical, 29
Nuremberg Race Laws, 83
Nussbaum, Martha, 184

O'Connor, David K., 18, 19
Odysseus (character): dialogue of, 60–61, 140–41; plot, 14–16, 50–52; as prototype of bourgeois subjectivity, 165–66; Sisyphus as father of, 141
Odyssey: dialogue, 60–61, 140; Horkheimer and Adorno on, 169; plot, 14–16, 50–52
Oliver, Kelly: *Animal Lessons: How They Teach Us to Be Human*, 176; on exceptionalism, 178
On Horsemanship (Xenophon), 207

On the Iliad (Bespaloff), 17–18
On the Origin of Species (Darwin), 207
"On the Way to a Liberal Eugenics?" (Habermas), 135–36
The Open: Man and Animal (Agamben), 152
Orwell, 30

paradisaic zoospheres, 147–50
Parts of Animals (Aristotle), 194
Patzig, Günther, 186–87
Pence, Gregory, 110–11
Pensky, Max, 169
people (Volk), Heidegger on, 82–83, 86
PGD. *See* preimplantation genetic diagnosis
Phaedrus, 53
philosophical anthropology: about, 137–38; and cloning, 135–40; Hobbes-Bentham on, 183; *imago Dei* doctrine, 131–35; Kant on, 181; negative and positive, 7, 8, 134, 138, 139–40, 227n23, 227n27
philosophical bestiary, 147–48
philosophical biology, 137
philosophical novels, types of, 29–30
philosophy: about, 3–4, 10, 36–37; Heidegger on, 77; Pre-Socratic, 195; role of, 20, 172; sophistry vs., 53
Philosophy in a Time of Terror (Borradori), 161
Physiologia: about, 195–96; as Christian texts, 195; Latin translations, 195; as predecessors to bestiaries, 194, 195
physiologus, 56, 143
Physiologus: about, 50; bestiaries as Christian version of, 69
Physiologus of Theobaldus, 197
Piccinini, Patricia, 12–13

Pick, Anat, 2
Pico della Mirandola, Giovanni, 68, 105
piety, 54
Plants and *Clouds* (Aristotle), 194
Plato: about, 17–18, 50; Homer and Hesiod as models for, 18; *Protagoras*, 6; *The Republic*, 6, 18, 52, 53, 54–55, 145–46; *Sophist*, 6
Plato's bestiary, 52–56
Plessner, Helmut, 137
Pliny, 50
Pliny the Elder: on elephants, 58–59; *Natural History*, 58
Plotinus, 134
Plutarch: about, 50; on animals in the Homeric corpus, 141; Coetzee within the tradition of, 30; on metaphysical anthropocentrism, 140; *Moralia*, 59–60, 140; role in preservation and transmission of Aristotle's work, 57–58
poetic species: about, 1–13; animal philosophy, 13–21
poetry: sympathetic imagination in, 40; virtues of, 36–37
political liberalism, 102
political modernity, 115, 117, 127
political ontology as genocidal bestiary, 87–89
politics, 6–7, 175–76, 182
Politics (Aristotle), 140
Polyphemus (character), 14–16, 19, 50–52
population growth, 173–74
postcolonialism, Coetzee's writing as, 26, 47–48
posthumanism, 10
postmetaphysical law, 186–90
The Postnational Constellation (Habermas), 135
preimplantation genetic diagnosis (PGD): assumptions/arguments

for/against, 106, 119; children and future generations borne from, 97–98, 99–100; debate/decisions on, 96; embracing, 111; genetic engineering impact on, 123; Habermas's interest in, 95; legal and moral implications of, 97; Mendieta on, 121–22; political response to, 127–28
Pre-Socratic philosophers, 195
preventive principle, 108, 109–10
priests as watchdogs, 63
Problems of Moral Philosophy (Adorno), 168
proceduralist reason, 127
processed foods, engineered ingredients in, 113
Progression of Animals (Aristotle), 194
"The Promises of Monsters" (Haraway), 154
Protagoras (Plato), 6

Quammen, David, 174
Quin Shi Huang, Terracotta Army of, 205

Raulff, Ulrich: *Farewell to the Horse*, 206
Rawls, John, 110–11
reason: Habermas on, 8; in Homer's texts, 16–17; reasoning with, 149, 150; topography of, 18–19
Red Peter (educated ape), 37
relational symmetry, Habermas on, 98
relic species, 198
"Remarks on Discourse Ethics" (Habermas), 186, 221n11
reproductive technologies, Kass on, 132
The Republic (Plato), 6, 18, 52, 53, 54–55, 145–46
Rifkin, Jeremy, 112

rights: de Fontenay on, 11; Habermas on, 11, 188–89
right to life, 128–29
ring of Gyges, 52–53
Robinson Crusoe (Defoe), 41–42
"Rogue States" (Derrida), 138
Rogues: Two Essays on Reason (Derrida), 148, 149
Rorty, Richard: "Contemporary Philosophy of Mind," 1; on literature vs. philosophy, 12; on poetic species, 3, 4
Rosa Burger (character), as Coetzee's alter ego, 27–28
Roudinesco, Elisabeth, 170–71
Rousseau, Jean-Jacques, 181, 189

Sartre, Jean-Paul, 30
Satyrs (character), 19–20
Scheler, Max, 137
Schmitt, Carl: on defeat of Nazi Germany, 66; on Hobbes, 218n38; on human prowess, 218n37; *Land and Sea*, 65–66; on life (bios), 150
Schweppenhäuser, Gerhard, 168
seeds, monopolies, 113
self-limitation/abstinence, Habermas, 118
self-reflexivity, 26
Shock and Awe: War on Words, 154–55
silence, Heidegger on, 78–80
"The Silence of the Sirens" (Kafka), 20
Singer, Peter, 11, 108, 109–10
Sirens (character), 14, 16, 19, 20
Sisyphus (father of Odysseus), 141
slaughterhouses: chickens in, 155; concentration camps as parallel, 35, 37–38, 39; death in the air, 32; and zoos, 7
Sloterdijk, Peter, 68, 94–95
Slow Man (Coetzee), 26

socialization, Habermas on, 99
social justice, genomics as solution, 93
Socrates: on friendship, 54; Plato's hagiography of, 53–54; plot of, 19–20
Solinus, 50
somatic sociability, 9
Sophist (Plato), 6, 53
sophistry, philosophy vs., 56
sophists, 54
South African colonial history, 47
speaking, Heidegger on, 78
species: commitments to the preservation of, 101; ethics of, 103–11, 121, 136–37; extermination of, 208; genetic intervention impact, 94, 95; self-understanding of, 94, 95–102
"Species Matters, Humane Advocacy" (Haraway), 9
Spielberg, Steven: *War Horse* (film), 206
Springborg, Patricia, 65
state (government), Heidegger on, 86–87
The State of Exception (Agamben), 151
Steiner, Gary: *Anthropocentrism and Its Discontents*, 17
stem cell research, 95
Stengers, Isabelle, 191
St. Michael killing a dragon, 64
Stoic intuition, 185
The Story of the World in 100 Species (Lloyd), 209
Strauss, 134
suffering: of animals, 188; Coetzee on, 25–26, 27–28; of women, 43–44
surveillance technology, 112
symmetrical relationality, autonomy as outcome, 102

symmetrical relationality, Habermas on, 99
sympathetic imagination, 37, 40

Tanner Lectures, 26, 36–37
Terracotta Army, 205
Theodor W. Adorno Prize: Derrida as recipient, 159, 229n44; other recipients, 231n3
Theogony (Hesiod), 6
Theory of Communicative Action (Habermas), 7
Thomas of Aquinas, 134
Thomas of Cobham, 50
Thomists, 10
Tiberius Psalter, 64
Tolkien, J. R. R., 52–53, 69
Tolstoy, Leo, 174
"Tragic Revolutionary Violence" (Gordon), 47
transgressions, past/future generations, 107
Treblinka, 38–39
triple helix, 103
truth, Heidegger on, 77–78, 79, 80
Tsing, Anna, 176

Uexküll, Jakob Johann von, 137
Ulysses (Joyce), 40

verminization, 71
violence: of beasts, 64, 66, 145–46; genocidal, 146; of human established order, 146. *See also* warfare
Voltaire, M. de, 30
von Wilamowitz-Moellendorff, Ulrich, 15
Voyous (Derrida), 138

Waiting for the Barbarians (Coetzee), 32

warfare: as depicted in the *Iliad*, 16–17; horses used in, 204–5, 206, 239n35; human impact, 165. *See also* violence
War Horse (film; Spielberg), 206
War Horse (Morpurgo), 206
war without hatred, 165
weedy species, 198
Western political order, 150
White, T.H., 50, 62, 217n26
"Why Look at Animals" (Berger), 29
Will, David, 171
Willett, Cynthia: "Ground Zero for a Postmoral Ethics in J. M. Coetzee's *Disgrace* and Julia Kristeva's *Melancholic*," 43–44
Wilson, Edward O.: *Biophilia: The Human Bond with Other Species*, 3; *The Future of Life*, 173–74
Without Offending Humans: A Critique of Animal Rights (de Fontenay), 13
Woessner, Martin, 41
"The Wolf and the Lamb" (la Fontaine), 149
Wolfe, Cary, 161
wolves: about, 62; dogs vs., 54; as false prophet, 64; flayed alive, 145; as representation of the devil, 64; sophists compared to, 53–54; traits of, 56; tyrants vs., 55–56
women, suffering, 43–44
Wood, David, 161
Works and Days (Hesiod), 6
world, animal/human role in, 73–74
world agriculture, advances in, 113
worldhood, Heidegger on, 75
"The 'World' of the Enlightenment to Come" (Derrida), 138
World Trade Organization (WTO), 113
World War I, 81–82

Xenophon: *On Horsemanship*, 207

Zeus, 51, 52
zoe/bios, Greek, 150
Zoographies: The Question of the Animal from Heidegger to Derrida (Calarco), 3–4
zoological compendium, Pliny the Elder's role in, 58
zoomorphism, 178
The Zoo of the Philosophers (Le Bras-Chopard), 3, 4
Zoopoetics, 40–41
zoopolitics, 190
zoos, 4, 7
zoospheres, paradisaic, 147–50
zu-handen/vor-handen, 33

www.ingramcontent.com/pod-product-compliance
Lightning Source LLC
Chambersburg PA
CBHW030535230426
43665CB00010B/900